Small Christian Communities:
A Vision of Hope

THOMAS A. KLEISSLER
MARGO A. LEBERT
MARY C. MCGUINNESS

PAULIST PRESS
New York/Mahwah

This material has been reviewed by a theological commission appointed by Archbishop Theodore E. McCarrick, Archbishop of Newark, under whose auspices the International Office of RENEW ministers. It has been found to be sound in doctrine and pastorally well-balanced.

Library of Congress Cataloging-in-Publication Data

Kleissler, Thomas A., 1931–
    Small Christian communities: a vision of hope/Thomas A. Kleissler, Margo A. LeBert, Mary C. McGuinness.
        p.   cm.
    Includes bibliographical references and index.
    ISBN 0-8091-3217-6
    1. Christian communities—Catholic Church.   2. Prayer groups—Catholic Church.   3. Laity—Catholic Church.   4. Catholic Church—Adult education.   5. Church group work.   6. United States—Religion—1960–   I. LeBert, Margo A., 1947–   . II. McGuinness, Mary C., 1933–   . III. Title.
    BX2347.7.K44   1991
    250—dc20   90-28188
                                                                          CIP

Published by Paulist Press
997 Macarthur Boulevard
Mahwah, New Jersey 07430

Printed and bound in the United States of America

Contents

With gratitude to Gary Garofalo,
Dolores Duggan and all others
who have pioneered Christian communities

Acknowledgements

We wish to acknowledge the thousands of small Christian community members whose experience over the years has contributed to this work. Because of their faith, insights, stories, and struggles our lives have been enriched.

We also wish to express special gratitude to all those who served in the Small Christian Communities Department of the Archdiocese of Newark and the past and present members of the International RENEW staff whose individual and cumulative efforts have contributed greatly to this work. This book was enlivened through their prayer, ideas, reflections, critiques, support, and diligent work for the renewal of our church.

We acknowledge with gratitude those whose direct feedback and guidance have helped and sustained our efforts, particularly Suzanne Golas, C.S.J.P., Peg Bisgrove, Ron and Dawn Green, Monica Garofalo, Mary Jo Pedersen, Charlie and Peggy Lockwood, and Reverend Raymond F. Collins.

We especially thank Father John Russell, O. Carm., whose wisdom, patience and loving care have guided us in so many ways.

In addition we offer gratitude to our typists, Peg Harahan and Sandra Spina, whose graciousness and hard work saw us through many revisions.

We also wish to thank Robert Hamma, our editor from Paulist Press, who has been consistently supportive and helpful throughout this project.

Finally we are grateful to all who read this book, share its vision, and strive to enliven the church and transform the world through small communities.

Foreword

When Nelson Mandela visited New York in 1990, here was a figure in the mold of Moses. Here was a man inexorably committed to the journey of his people to freedom. That journey of the whole people, that goal of a new land of non-racial unity, remained his sole concern. Reporters continually asked him about his own future leadership role. Without hesitation, never dallying to garner personal acclaim, he inevitably turned the question away from himself, allowed no self-identity other than as a representative of his people, and pointed to others back home or traveling with him who, like Aaron, might more likely bring the people into the promised land of non-racialist society.

This figure reminded me of our Christian tradition, namely that it is the Lord who prepares the kingdom and we must go forward to find it. We do not possess the kingdom, we the church, we the ministers of the church. If the blind see and the lame walk, the kingdom is at hand, God's reclaiming of creation has begun, God's power is present. It is the task of those in ministry to encourage people to go forward. It is the task of the leaders, whether these are the parents of families, the pastors of parishes, or the bishops of local churches, to help their people find the path into the kingdom, to come to their defense when they seem to falter, and to plead on their behalf with God that he will offer us the nourishment and light that will strengthen and guide our steps.

It is my opinion that in the church's present wandering through a desert of discontent—the kind of discontent that eats away at the soul of our society and the spirit of the church—the leadership, whether this will come from among the people of the church or from those who occupy offices of ministry in the church, must in some concerted fashion fix on those matters of church community and mission that most need attention and that must shape the ministerial energies of the church. At present, we seem preoccupied on the one hand with preserving the institution's humanly defined resources—the ministerial personnel, the funds, and the store of authentic teaching—which are perceived as endangered. This threatens to leave the church in the

vii

condition of an overly cautious talent steward who simply buried what
had been entrusted to him.

On the other hand, individuals seem jealously protective of their
independence, that form of individualism that resists peer obligations
and that afflicts every level of the church. This individualist independence, the very contrary of the collegial spirit the council has urged,
prevents us from committing ourselves to a sufficiently specific common mission that can make claims on us and require us to collaborate
with others. It can infect those in church offices as much as the ordinary Catholic; it can be as true of members of religious communities as
of single lay persons.

The desperate need in our time for a truly evangelizing community—both self-evangelizing and extending the gift of the gospel to a
world needing hope—can be sorely neglected when community gets
lost between overly institutional and overly individualist preoccupa-
tions. It seems to me that all church leaders must now commit themselves to forging a new, deeply personal community of faith in and
through which Christians can acquire the confidence, clarity, and mutual support necessary to act out the gospel in public. This community
of faith is a community that is personal without being merely private,
moving beyond the "circle of intimacy" of family and friends and
entering into the "company of strangers" whom the Lord has made our
brothers and sisters. It is a community where commitment is not re-
duced to mere compliance, where the fact of communion created by
the Lord becomes an obligation for mutual respect and interdependence, a task of freeing the expression of each one's gifts for the good of
all and the mission of all. It is a communion that enables each member
to move beyond "self-development" and "growth," for its own sake, as
if this could be a purely individual matter, to the use of one's abilities
for the good of others.

In recent times there seems to emerge an unfortunate and mis-
placed competition in the implicit either/or framing of church concerns between some who seem more concerned to parse the letter of the
council in formulations that seem restrictive and overly authoritarian
and others who focus on the openness available in the spirit of the
council. There is in this competition the veiled suggestions that we
must either foreclose all nuance and development in the name of orthodoxy and identity, or be prepared to remain adrift in a sea of plural-
ism in order to preserve the pastoral character of a council that resisted
definitions. In fact, neither is true. We need the kind of authentic and
consensual formulations of faith that enable us to be faithful, dialogic,
and cooperative, but we also need to remain open to still emergent

expressions of the new ecclesiology the council simply inaugurated. We need to be accountable to the common truth of the church's faith while respectful of the ultimate individuality of belief and conscience.

Perhaps nowhere more than in the emergence of "small groups" in the church has the challenge of balancing these evangelical imperatives been evident. The debates over base communities in Latin America especially, their popularism and politics, have been paralleled by disputes in this country regarding the orthodoxy and respect for authentic teaching to be found in some small group expressions. Sometimes it can even be made to seem that orthodoxy and magisterium, on the one hand, and popular participation and personal sharing of faith, on the other, are antithetical to each other. From this perspective, concern for orthodoxy requires tight control over the popular gatherings and expressions of faith while concern for popular participation entails rejection of hierarchy. In fact, however, there is evidence that the full development of each requires respect for the other. In a time when authority in general and the teaching authority of the church in particular are contested, people are much more disposed to hear and accept the teaching of the church the more their own views and participation are respected. This is more than a political statement; it is an ecclesiological statement that the fullness of the church's wisdom is distributed throughout the body of the church. Nonetheless, it is also true that the more efforts are made to include the people in decision-making and ministry, the more they will invest their time and money in the institutional works of evangelization. On the other hand, the more people can be open to the unifying power of a common truth, to the power of a living tradition and to the special responsibility of the custodians of that tradition, the more their popular, participative efforts will not degenerate into a lowest-common-denominator, essentially individualist, populism.

In this context, the RENEW program, the parish renewal program that originated in the archdiocese of Newark and has now spread throughout the world, has played a unique role in the post-conciliar church. While, prior to the council, pastoral movements such as the Christian Family Movement (and its lesser known partner, Young Christian Students), the Legion of Mary, the St. Vincent de Paul Society, and various other groups such as Holy Name Societies, Sodalities, and Altar Rosary Societies, fostered a sense of action-oriented community within the context of parish life, after the council most of these groups atrophied and new groups such as Marriage Encounter and the Charismatic Renewal arose, often existing apart from parish life. RENEW was aimed directly at the parish and, as the heart of its approach to renewal, fostered the development of small groups ("communities") within the framework of parish life. From the start, therefore, it combined the personal and the institutional, the self-selecting small community with the more heterogeneous community of the neighborhood eucharist. Undoubtedly, no post-conciliar program has brought more people together in the context of parish life for personal sharing of faith and its consequences than has RENEW. Furthermore, RENEW's small groups were directed not only toward each individual's relationship with God but also toward the works of justice and evangelization in the world.

The present book is written within three contexts. It evidences the RENEW leaders' conviction that building more deeply personal communities of faith is one of the major pastoral needs of the church in the United States today. It expresses their concern that these personal, more intimate, and thereby more homogeneous communities should be part of the universal, inclusive, and heterogeneous solidarity represented by the parish structure of church life. And it reflects from RENEW's experience of building more such small communities in today's parishes than any other organization. The authors, including the founder of RENEW, Monsignor Thomas Kleissler, and his associates, make a strong statement of the need for such community building, acknowledge three of the many possible basic forms of small groups, and provide very practical help for organizing and sustaining these small groups in parishes. It is clear from everything they write that they regard this pastoral movement as essential to the future of the church. It is also clear that they are trying to allow for enormous differences among pastors and parishioners regarding their disposition to enter into small "faith-sharing" communities. It is patently clear that the authors speak from extensive experience regarding what it takes to foster small group development in parishes. Finally, there is no doubt about their balancing of the many factors we have discussed that are required to make small groups both authentic and engaging expressions of conciliar ecclesiology.

RENEW has had a major impact on parish life in the United States, now that over one hundred American dioceses (and eighty-five international ones) have already availed themselves of the program in one form or another. This book represents a possible second-stage of impact on church life. Its publication could be the occasion for bishops and pastors to decide clearly that some form of small community development is no longer optional, that pastoral leadership must give priority to this small group development within parish life if we will take on wholeheartedly the 1990s as a decade of evangelization. If this pastoral strategy does become a priority, then this book's presentation of the vision and experience of the RENEW program will be invaluable. It will help to ensure that the small groups or communities will be linked to the larger assembly of the eucharist, that development of one's personal relationship with God will be linked to stronger relationships with others who recognize the same parentage, and that the growth in private charity will engender courage for public justice.

Philip J. Murnion

Introduction

Small Christian communities are a source of great hope in the church today. The revised Code of Canon Law acknowledges how essential the notion of community is in understanding the mystery of God's presence in our church by speaking of the Christian faithful as "constituted as the people of God" (Canon 204).[1] Within the context of a more complete understanding of church, this book, *Small Christian Communities: A Vision of Hope,* will focus on this particular aspect of church. Specifically, parish-based small communities will be explored as a means by which the gospel values of Jesus may be lived and proclaimed effectively.

Small Christian Communities: A Vision of Hope is essentially a pastoral work intending to offer enough concrete "how to's" to facilitate healthy small community development. It is offered for all who are interested in exploring the possibilities of small communities within parish life. Basic theological, ecclesiological, scriptural, and sacramental concepts are drawn upon to the extent that they will be helpful and even necessary for sound and healthy growth.

In 1986 the Vatican Secretariat for Promoting Christian Unity published a document, *Sects or New Religious Movements in the World,* which addressed a serious concern expressed by episcopal conferences around the world. The document delineates the reasons for the spread of sects and new religious movements: the quest for belonging or the sense of community, the search for answers, for cultural identity, for wholeness, for transcendence, and the need for spiritual guidance, vision, participation, and involvement. The Vatican Secretariat cites the breakdown of traditional values, feelings of frustration, rootlessness, and disillusionment apparent in our world today that cause people to look for fulfillment and belonging.

This document summarized information gleaned from a questionnaire sent to episcopal conferences around the world. In response to the question of how to address the challenges of this situation, almost all of the responses suggested the following:

a rethinking . . . of the traditional *parish community system;* a search
for community patterns which will be more fraternal, more adapted
to people's life situation; more *basic ecclesial communities:* caring
communities of lively faith, love (warmth, acceptance, understanding, reconciliation, fellowship), and hope; celebrating communities;
praying communities; missionary communities: outgoing and witnessing; communities open to and supporting people who have special problems: the divorced and remarried, the marginalized.[2]

There is, in fact, a growing need and desire in people to have these
concrete experiences of community. The fact that two million people
have participated in RENEW small groups over the past decade speaks
to this interest. Many dioceses have reported that as a diocesan average
thirty percent to as high as forty-seven percent of active Catholics have
participated in these groups. The time has come to acknowledge the
spiritual potential of small communities.

Cardinal Bernardin's suggestion that the parish be a "community
made up of many small communities"[3] can be seen as a natural follow-
through to the days of Catholic Action. It is time to fully explore the
possibilities that a much higher percentage of parishioners are ready to
be involved conscientiously in the work of evangelization, of integrating the gospel into all areas of their life, and bringing Christian values
to impact upon our world. Where Catholic Action groups may have
once served as a peripheral parish activity, small Christian communities might well be an integral part of parish life today.

However, the mention of small communities is capable of eliciting
varied images. To some, small communities have proven to be a very
satisfying and exhilarating experience. To others they are seen as a
dangerous phenomenon where people might become insulated and
complacent, and their faith privatized.

It is important, therefore, right from the beginning to state clearly
what *Small Christian Communities: A Vision of Hope* wishes to convey. This book is intended to offer guidance to pastors and parish
leaders in the development of parish-based small groups and communities. Many people who have been in RENEW small groups continue to
meet on a regular basis. Through their desire to grow spiritually and
the commitments they make to one another, they might rightfully become small Christian communities. We who have been involved in
this experience feel a sense of responsibility to aid the ongoing journey
through offering sound suggestions and direction. It seems appropriate
to collate and share what has been learned through the history of RE-
NEW not only for the benefit of those following through from this

experience, but also for the benefit of all interested in small communities.

Essentially we are motivated by the remarkable growth of small groups and communities in our time and by the highly positive diocesan evaluations of RENEW small groups in terms of the spiritual growth of parishioners. We desire to encourage and expand this type of vibrant faith experience.

And what is *Small Christian Communities: A Vision of Hope* not intending to do? This is not an attempt to form an ecclesiology of small communities. Small communities are not seen here as a church of themselves, but as part of the larger parish, indeed of the whole Catholic Church, the people of God, its tradition, teaching, leadership, and guidance. This book does not address free-floating communities but rather parish-based communities that play an important role in parish life and exist in relationship to the authority of the local pastor and bishop. These small communities benefit from their role in the larger Catholic Church in living the life of the Spirit. Offering guidance for small communities as a regular and valued part of the institutional church is one of the major aims of this work.

Just as we, the authors, want the content of this work to be understood within the context of the larger church, so we also want its emphasis on small communities to be understood within the reality of parish life. While highlighting the value of many small communities in the parish, this work in no way wishes to imply that everyone needs to be in a small community to be a good parishioner. While speaking to a value, we do not intend to make that value exclusive or to devaluate other experiences. However, if an imbalance exists today, it is probably that small Christian communities receive too little attention from parish leadership. In view of the potential spirituality they offer, a suggestion of ten to twenty percent of time and energy from parish leadership in assisting small communities would hardly be neglectful of the overall parish, but rather a pastoral effort appropriate for our time.

Small Christian Communities: A Vision of Hope speaks to the value of small communities and envisions the dynamic possibilities of a parish that places a pastoral emphasis on their development. It also offers various approaches to small community development along with many suggested "how to" steps. The role of the pastor and parish staff in relationship to small communities is explored. Finally, it looks at the relationship of small communities to many other important aspects of parish life today.

An accompanying book, *Resources for Small Christian Communities: A Vision of Hope,* provides specific sessions and processes for small group leaders, parish pastoral councils, parishioners, small communities and core communities. In addition, a companion volume, *Called To Lead: Leadership Development in a Small Community Context,* by Suzanne Golas, C.S.J.P., is a program designed specifically for developing small Christian community leaders. It provides both theological content and practical skills for the development of good pastoral leadership. The introduction to *Called To Lead* explains in detail the intent and methodology of the program.

We acknowledge that no dynamic of itself can renew the church. Ultimately, it is the Spirit of God who renews the church. Small Christian communities are promoted here primarily because they have shown themselves to be an effective instrument for experiencing the power of the Holy Spirit. It is precisely that power that will renew not only the church but the face of the earth.

CHAPTER 1

Small Christian Communities: A Source of Parish Renewal

We live in the rarest of moments. Not only a century but the second millennium of history since the birth of Christ is drawing to a close. As we approach the twenty-first century we are called to analyze what has taken place in the course of history and to project possibilities to shape the future. Tumultuous events and frequent change have been the hallmarks of our time. Yet a continuing and ever-constant element in our lives has been the enduring love that God has for us.

Over the course of the church's history small communities have played a significant role in proclaiming and developing that love. Small communities have enabled believers to develop a more profound union with God and one another. They have also been a means for renewing and expanding the church. As we approach the next millennium, small communities offer greater hope than ever that Christians will deepen their love for God, for one another, and for all of creation, and in this process renew the face of the earth.

We believe that the recent increase of small communities is one of the more significant events of our age for the renewal of the church and the transformation of the world. Thus we will explore throughout this work how they can best be utilized in the average Catholic parish.

Certainly community, which provides a general experience of belonging and commitment, is an essential element of any understanding of church. People frequently evaluate parish life on the quality of community. Judging whether the parish is "alive" or "dead" is often merely a reflection on whether or not people discover community there. Through small groups and small communities many people are discovering the value of community. Today as many varieties of small communities develop around the world they offer the promise of new vitality for the church and give added impulse for people to live gospel values.

5

HISTORICAL OVERVIEW

We will begin by reviewing the value of small groups and communities through an historical approach. This overview will be a confirmation to those who are already convinced of their value and a consideration for reflection for those who may be wondering whether the time has come for small communities to become a mainstream part of parish life. We will then explore some of the sociological factors which shape our contemporary society as well as the challenges which these factors present for our church in the post-modern world.[1]

Small Communities in the Early Christian Tradition

As we look at the experience of the early church we see that Jesus invited his disciples into a community where they were formed in the ways of discipleship of Jesus Christ. After the Pentecost experience the community of disciples shared the good news as they traveled, preaching, baptizing, and gathering people together in small communities which met in homes. There they retold and reflected on the meaning of the life, death, and resurrection of Jesus. It was the household church which provided the basic structure of early Christian communities.

These Christians prayed together, broke bread as they were taught by the Lord, and shared their lives and sustenance. As they grew in understanding the personal and social implications of their faith in Jesus, they supported one another by faithfully living the values of Jesus in the midst of a pagan environment. Without doubt it was the communitarian character of the early church "that determined the extraordinary expansion of Christianity into the socially fragmented Greco-Roman world."[2]

With the conversion of Constantine in the fourth century, Christianity was officially recognized and became the preferred religion. Huge pagan temples were turned into churches. Following the example of Constantine, masses of people embraced Christianity and filled the new church buildings. The small communities came out of their house churches and joined the large masses of people to worship. The persecutions were over. It was no longer dangerous to be a Christian; it was now easier and even fashionable to profess the Christian faith. Yet even after the peace of Constantine the church did not abruptly change from small communities to large congregations. In some places the small group experience continued to be an integral part of the life of the church.

To name just one example, episcopal households of the fourth century drew their inspiration from the idea of the communal life portrayed in the Acts of the Apostles (2:42) and the ascetic ideal of the desert fathers. In many of the households of bishops people gathered as small communities for liturgical prayer and works of charity.[3]

Max Delespesse speaks of the formation of communities alongside the ordinary church. Through the Edict of Milan in 312, Christianity became the accepted religion of the Roman empire. Two or three decades before the edict and especially after it, some Christians, wanting to rediscover the "apostolic life" and the primitive community, formed into groups. These cenobites or monks, "not finding their place any longer in a departmentalized and in a certain way secularized Church, went out into the desert to form communities there."[4] The monastic experience, which received the approval of the bishops and the faithful, integrated community support with prayer and mission. Monasticism in the east and the west proved to be a source of vitality for the church even though it gave rise to the idea that spirituality could not easily be lived in ordinary "secular" life.

Small Communities in the Middle Ages

Small communities of lay women who lived an austere lifestyle developed in the Low Countries during the twelfth and thirteenth centuries. These women, called Beguines, took no vows and had no common rule or general religious superior, but gave themselves to works of charity, to prayer, and to devotional exercises. Some reported mystical experiences. Although most of them lived together, they were free to retain private property and were able to leave at any time. The Beghards, associations of lay men, lived similar lifestyles. Unlike the Beguines they held no property in common, but relied upon the common purse.[5]

History bears witness to a wide variety of religious communities, orders, and congregations founded by charismatic leaders. These leaders attracted others because of both the spirituality they professed and the apostolic works in which they were involved. Members of these groups lived in solitude or in small communities. They cared for the sick and the poor, educated youth, and committed themselves to a wide variety of social services. Some of these congregations remained local communities; others reached out in missionary zeal to people in distant lands.

Differing from religious communities yet having a communal dimension were guilds and sodalities. During the middle ages guilds flourished to support merchants and craftspeople. By applying Christian principles to the life of laborers and artisans these guilds helped to transform a whole society. In addition to settling matters of employment, the guilds took care of workers when ill, attended funerals of deceased members, and helped support widows and orphans. Although not pious confraternities which were subject to the assent of the local bishop, guilds were definitely Catholic in character and received their inspiration from the church.[6]

Religious guilds, too, were organized for the promotion of social work, collective almsgiving, and instruction.[7] These guilds, made up of all classes of people, were forerunners of groups later organized for Catholic Action, and were, indeed, foundational to the small Christian communities which would follow.

Sodalities

Various kinds of sodalities were established throughout the centuries under church authority for the promotion of some work of devotion, charity, public worship, or outreach. Usually these sodalities were associations of lay people who met to perform pious exercises, followed a set of principles or rules, and submitted to the spiritual direction of a leader.

Sodalities of Our Lady established in Rome in 1563 proposed a Christian way of life through a particular program of spiritual formation. The Sodality "tried to unify the sacramental nature of the Christian at prayer and the Christian in action. Its characteristic mark has been service of the church under the patronage of our Lady and the direction of the hierarchy."[8]

Sodalities, throughout the years they flourished, brought together people involved in the same occupations, (e.g. small groups of sailors, fishermen, teachers, doctors, business people, lawyers) who met to apply their sodality principles and way of life to their particular social and professional circumstances. Young adult sodalities were formed in high schools and colleges. Their members channeled their apostolic endeavors into areas of local need.

After the Second Vatican Council the National Federation of Sodalities, founded in the U.S. in 1957, sought to guide sodalities in the mature Christian thought and action enjoined on them by the council. The *Notre Dame Study of Catholic Parish Life* reports that devotions to the Blessed Virgin Mary, altar societies and sodalities are especially important sources of vitality for some parishes even today.[9]

Catholic Action Groups

In the twentieth century under the broad heading of Catholic Action several movements developed with a strong community base. Prominent among these were the Young Christian Workers (YCW), Young Christian Students (YCS), and the Christian Family Movement (CFM).

Founded by Cardinal Joseph Cardign in Belgium in 1925, the YCW served to enable young workers to re-Christianize their own lives, their working and social environments and those with whom they worked. This movement took root in the United States as Young Christian Students (YCS) which aimed to Christianize the school environment and to enlist Catholic students in apostolic action.[10]

The Christian Family Movement (CFM), founded in 1947, sought to restore family life to Christ and create small communities which would influence their parishes and the wider society.[11] Today the expressed vision of CFM is to improve the quality of family life by reaching out to others.[12]

Each of the above mentioned groups adopted the inquiry approach with the observe, judge, and act methodology which St. Thomas Aquinas used for arriving at prudent action.[13] These Catholic Action groups and similar groups developed lay leadership and helped to transform our church and our society. They were, and wherever they flourish today are, in fact, small Christian communities.

In the past, Catholic Action was sometimes seen as an expression of the apostolate in which the laity extended the work of the hierarchy. Small Christian communities which are emerging today, however (including those previously mentioned, e.g. CFM groups), are an expression of the church in which the laity assume their rightful role in the mission of Jesus.

Contemporary Society

In the last several decades more than one hundred thousand small Christian communities in various parts of the world have come into being.[14] In the United States these small Christian communities have

taken the form of scripture study groups, support groups, prayer
groups, ministerial communities, and other ongoing Christian
communities.

In their book *Dangerous Memories,* theologian Bernard Lee and
social scientist Michael Cowan examine the movement of small communities of faith emerging throughout the world, but especially in the
United States.[15] They also provide an excellent overview of how intentional Christian communities have developed in different cultural settings. In Latin America where the basic Christian communities exist
principally among the poor and the oppressed members of the Catholic
population there is a strong concern for social justice. These basic
church communities which are supported by the Latin American bishops received great confirmation at the Medellin (1968) and Puebla
conferences (1979) held in Colombia and Mexico, respectively.
Africa's small Christian communities, initiated by the hierarchy,
"correspond with the growing need being experienced by African
Christians to express their own values of community, harmony, and
solidarity in the context of their Christian faith."[16]

These small communities have their own characteristics and expressions based upon the various histories, cultures, and church traditions in their countries or areas of origin. Similarly these groups are
called by a variety of names. For example, in Africa the terms "small
Christian communities" (SCC), "living ecclesial communities," or
"neighborhood gospel groups" are used. In Latin America groups are
called "base ecclesial communities" (BEC) or "communidades ecclesial de base."

Most sociologists and pastoral leaders agree that the Latin American form of small Christian communities cannot be transferred to the
American scene. Small communities developing in the United States
are taking on their own unique characteristics. One sociologist, Joseph
F. Fichter, S.J., recalls that the parish was once both a means for preserving the faith and a means for Americanizing the immigrants. He
suggests that the parish be a resource for mission and ministry to the
world and a vital center for celebrating the gift of faith.[17] Small communities are quite suited to be instruments for personal and social/com-
munal regeneration as well as centers of evangelization.

In summary, we can state with Raymond Collins "that small
groups served the continuity of the church in the midst of affliction,
the vitality of the church in times of complacency, the renewal of the
church in moments of infidelity and the growth of the church in changing historical and cultural circumstances."[18]

Sociological Overview

Sociologists acknowledge that we live in an age of unprecedented change. As long-range social forces converge, people's ways of feeling, thinking, and acting all change. In reality a cultural shift occurs. Bernard Longeran says that "Social and cultural changes are, at root, changes in meanings that are grasped and accepted." He goes on to say that "changes in the control of meaning mark off the great epochs of human history."[19] As we study the history of society over the centuries, it becomes even more evident that these changes in meanings shake the very ground of society's value system. Cultural historians have noted that the period of the 1960s with its intense, rapid ferment began a time of such cultural transformation. A new era dawned with changing values, meanings, and symbols.

Sociological Factors Shape Our Society

This age has brought with it an explosion of knowledge, systems of mass communication which instantly bring us in contact with almost any part of the planet, advancement in all forms of technology, a growth in materialism and consumerism, the quest for freedom from oppressive governments, dislocations of people from many countries, social instability, and countless other sweeping changes. In addition, questions affecting our ecological systems, economy, health, peace, the family, and so on continue to confront us.

Today many forces which influence our ways of thinking, feeling, and acting are far from being supportive of Christian values. The pressures of consumerism, militarism, and privatism that affect families, neighborhoods, and parishes attract people toward a lifestyle that reflects little of the gospel message. One need only listen to the prevailing voices of materialism and consumerism to assess some of the forces at work in shaping our ways of feeling, thinking, and acting.

Since these forces are frequently not supportive of Christian life, the situation of a Christian in today's society in some ways parallels the situation of Christians prior to the official acceptance of Christianity which occurred at the time of Constantine. The early Christians had to reject the values of their society and often suffered ridicule, persecution, and even death as they remained faithful to the way of Jesus. In certain parts of our world it is becoming increasingly clear that to live as Jesus did, to help the poor, the alienated, those treated unjustly and to question why people are poor, is often to invoke the wrath of the powerful. Those who truly try to live the Christian life put themselves in the position of being persecuted today as in the early church.

Observers of our times try to analyze what is happening as a result of high technology and a host of dehumanizing factors. The Secretariat for Promoting Christian Unity recently noted that "A breakdown of traditional social structures, cultural patterns, and traditional sets of values, caused by industrialization, urbanization, migration, rapid development of communication systems, all-rational technocratic systems, etc., leave many individuals confused, uprooted, insecure, and therefore vulnerable."[20]

An analysis of the responses to a questionnaire distributed by this Secretariat reveals further symptoms of society's problems. Although not all symptoms can be listed here, the following offers a sampling:

Many people feel anxious about themselves and the future. They suffer a loss of direction, lack of participation in decision-making, lack of real answers to their real questions. They experience fear because of various forms of violence, conflict, hostility, concern about ecological disaster, war, and nuclear holocaust.

Many feel frustrated, rootless, homeless, lonely, lost in anonymity, alienated. They are disillusioned with technological society, the military, church laws and practices, and government politics.

In summary all these symptoms represent many forms of alienation. And the needs and aspirations experienced are so many forms of a search for a more conscious presence to oneself, to others, to God.[21]

Small Groups Respond to Needs

Because of this need, fifteen million adults in the United States come together in some form of small groups.[22] They may be neighborhood associations, Alcoholics Anonymous groups, or religious meetings. The identity of the groups varies, but for many of them the need to belong in a more intimate way is constant. The need to know and to be known and the need to care and to be cared for are essential to human life.

A sense of belonging is often achieved in parochial life through involvement in parish worship, ministries, and activities. This sense of belonging is sustained over longer periods of time through small Christian communities. Personal experience and recent studies bear witness to the fact that when these needs for belonging, recognition, and care are not met in our parishes, parishioners seek to fulfill these needs elsewhere. Some join small fundamentalist communities, evangelical communities or sects where they experience this sense of belonging, support, and basic security. Once they have made friends and have people who care about them, spend time with them, and miss them when they are absent, then they have that sense of belonging. The need to belong, to relate, and to care applies to parish life as much as to any other segment of society.

Besides offering the richness of sacramental life and of Catholic tradition, parish life has the additional capacity to respond to these needs through the development of small Christian communities where a greater sense of belonging can be felt, where people who know one another better can care for one another. In addition those who are searching for a fuller faith life and a greater sense of God, find support, insight, and encouragement in these small group relationships.

Positive trends in the religious life of the American Catholic today that have been outlined by George Gallup can be very encouraging for the parish. These are (1) "A renewed search for depth in our spiritual lives, arising out of disenchantment with materialism as well as concern for the many problems affecting our society"; (2) "a renewed search for deeper relationships arising out of loneliness and a feeling of isolation. This search is seen in the growth of self-help groups and in the uptrend in Bible study and prayer fellowship groups. People are increasingly making the discovery that faith grows best in the presence of faith."[23]

PARISH POTENTIAL FOR SMALL COMMUNITIES

Many pastoral leaders have testified to the fact that an increased percentage of people are seeking to be part of small communities.[24] And since the American parish already has many small groups or communities as part of its structure in the form of support groups, ministry groups, etc., the underpinnings for developing small Christian communities are already present.

Fichter points to this reality as he describes the small community in the American urban parish today.

> The basic Christian community is not a small close-knit church group nor does it focus exclusively on the personal salvation of its members. It begins in a number of small prayer and discussion groups within the large parish area, but it develops into an influential secondary association. It has a ministerial purpose, a goal of service which makes it an instrument for the contemporary church

which emphasizes evangelization with a concern for social justice. The basic Christian community, in the form of a modern urban American parish, is not traditionalist, nor covenantal, nor underground. The organizational pattern is easily adjustable to the large urban parish which contains within itself numerous necessary subsidiary functional groups.[25]

The potential for small Christian communities already exists in our parishes. The potential needs only to be activated by greater awareness and dedicated leadership.

Although the preceding socio-historical overview has admittedly been brief and far from comprehensive, it nevertheless gives evidence that small communities which have always been a part of the church have surely exerted their influence in the church. It also points to the value that parish-based small communities can have for our present and future church. This value will continue to be developed as we turn in Chapter 2 to some theological and pastoral principles which support the development of small communities.

CHAPTER 2

Implementing the Vision of Vatican II

As we approach the third millennium, it is amazing to realize how small Christian communities are developing all over the world. One of the prime reasons for this growth is the increasing recognition and acceptance by Christian laity of their vocation and mission in the world today.

Contrast contemporary experience with an incident which took place in the last century. The story has been told that in 1867, Msgr. George Talbot, an advisor to Pius IX, wrote to Henry Manning, archbishop of Westminster. In that letter Talbot both asked an important question and gave a provocative response, "What is the province of the laity? To hunt, to shoot, to entertain. These matters they understand, but to meddle with ecclesiastical affairs they have no right at all."[1]

No doubt this incident is not representative of the total thinking of the time; nevertheless it gives some insight into the thought of one prominent nineteenth century church leader. Talbot's reply is a far cry from the way the Second Vatican Council has described the role of the laity as participating in the priestly, prophetic, and kingly mission of Jesus (LG 34, 35, 36).

> It is clear that the participation by the lay faithful in this threefold mission of Christ derives from their being members of the church, which is his body. In other words, it derives *from the communion of the church.* Therefore, this mission must be lived, and realized *in communion* and *for the increase of communion itself.*[2]

Small communities are a means for Christians to live the mission more fully through communion with other Christians. Support for the value of small Christian communities is found in three principles which were highlighted during the Second Vatican Council. They are (1) the communitarian nature of the church, (2) renewed focus on the

15

word of God, and (3) a greater understanding of the social mission of the church. Each of these principles will be briefly explored in relationship to small communities together with some pastoral challenges and approaches for implementing these communities.

THE COMMUNITARIAN NATURE OF THE CHURCH

Contemporary society places great stress on individualism. Scientific and technological advancements have isolated both families and individuals. In this individualistic culture the concept of community may be a very welcome one indeed.

We are called to community in various aspects of our lives—for example, family, the community in which we worship, the community in which we live, the global community, the communion of saints. Recently our consciousness has been awakened to the community of nature as a primordial community. As we increasingly recognize the fragility of the eco-systems of the earth, we are called to realize more profoundly our relationship and bondedness with all living beings, the earth, and the universe. As we come to these new awarenesses about community, we are prompted to reflect more earnestly on the communitarian nature of the church.

A basic theme of the Second Vatican Council was the church as communion or people of God. The church, bound together by the indwelling of the Holy Spirit, strives to live the prayer of Jesus "that all may be one . . . as we are one" (Jn 17:21–22). For God dwells in community. The three persons of the Blessed Trinity love and share to such a degree that they are one God. Jesus implied a similarity between the union of the three divine persons and the union of God's children when he prayed that prayer of unity.

This likeness to God reveals that human beings cannot find themselves fully except through a sincere gift of themselves. It is through self-giving, therefore, that communion with God and others is established. Sacred scripture teaches that the love of God cannot be separated from the love of neighbor (GS 24).

The Second Vatican Council repeatedly emphasized this communitarian character of the church in its many dimensions. The various relationships of ecclesial communion include the following:

- individual members to God,
- the whole ecclesial community to God,

- each member to every other member,
- each particular church to the universal church,
- pastors and communities to their local bishops,
- the bishops with the successor of Peter,
- the universal church to the whole human race.

Because the communitarian character of the church is partially immersed in mystery, it is impossible to grasp fully the significance of the concept of "communion." Yet the call to live in communion is integral to human beings and to the church itself.

The community of the Trinity is not only the model of community but the source of grace, strength, faith, hope, and love which sustains and nurtures Christians in community. John Paul II in his address to the U.S. bishops (9/17/87) declared that the notion of communion was "at the heart of the church's self-understanding." This communion is "primarily a sharing through grace in the life of the Father given us through Christ and in the Holy Spirit." The church as a communion "is realized through the sacramental union with Christ and through organic participation in all that constitutes the divine and human reality of the church, the body of Christ which spans the centuries and is sent into the world to embrace all people without distinction."[3]

Community Expressed in Worship

The Christian community expresses its communitarian nature in diverse ways, but particularly through its worship. As the sacramental rites of the church were studied and reformulated following Vatican II, the communal nature of virtually every sacrament was stressed. The catechumenate was restored through the Rite of Christian Initiation of Adults (RCIA). This rite heralds a process for the spiritual journey of those inquiring into the faith, while also providing a paradigm of on-going conversion for those already baptized. The RCIA itself presupposes the presence of a vibrant faith community. The rite challenges the local parish to be witness to Christian community not only to those inquiring but also to those embracing the Catholic faith.

The small community is the ideal life-giving environment for the process of Christian initiation. Inquirers and those seeking entrance into our faith can do so, not in isolation, but within a community of believers. Some parishes have small Christian communities which welcome into their midst those inquiring about the faith. As part of their ministry they are prepared to respond to inquirers and encourage them in their faith journey. Many times they accompany them with community support through the various steps and stages of the RCIA. They thus enable the realization of the major aims of the RCIA: evangelization, catechesis, spiritual enlightenment, initiation, deepening of the neophyte's sacramental life, and continuing conversion. In turn they impact on the larger parish community.

Community Concretely Expressed

The emphasis on community which emanated from Vatican II and the power of the Holy Spirit working in the church encourage Catholics to live that gift of community more concretely within their families and in the variety of small faith communities which are emerging. In small communities people can feel they belong. They come to know each other, to support and care for one another, and to experience increasing bonds of unity with one another, with God, with the wider church, and with their sisters and brothers throughout the world. Through shared prayer they realize more profoundly the unifying power of the Spirit which bonds them.

It is in small Christian communities, therefore, that our approach to the mystery of God tends to unite the love of God and love of our neighbor. In small Christian communities people can experience and share these experiences of receiving grace, strength, faith, hope, and love from God who dwells in community.

Leaders Speak to Community

Various theologians and pastoral leaders have noted how Christians are coming to a new awareness of the communitarian nature of the church and are seeking to express this more concretely in family life and small communities. Theologian Sandra Schneiders, I.H.M. describes this reality.

> Christians in every walk of life today are coming to a renewed (or new) realization of the essentially communitarian nature of Christianity and seeking ways to make this important dimension of their Christian vocation concrete for themselves. The experiments have ranged from full-scale covenant communities sharing residence and economic resources to subgroups in parishes or on university cam-

puses meeting periodically for a sharing of faith, prayer, and mutual support.[4]

The American bishops in their document *Called and Gifted: The American Catholic Laity* (1980) observed how today's Christians seek to make the communitarian nature real for themselves in Christian communities:

Because lay women and men do experience intimacy, support, acceptance, and availability in family life, they seek the same in their Christian communities. This is leading to a review of parish size, organization, priorities, and identity. It has already led to intentional communities, basic Christian communities, and some revitalized parish communities.[5]

In 1984 the American bishops in their pastoral letter on Hispanic ministry called for the parish to be a community of communities. They stated that "The small community has appeared on the scene as a ray of hope in dealing with dehumanizing situations that can destroy people and weaken faith."[6]

The Vatican Secretariat for Christian Unity, in naming a host of depersonalizing structures, forms of alienation prevalent today, and people's needs and aspirations which are seemingly not being met in the mainline churches, gives some indication as to why some people are joining sects and religious movements. The Secretariat suggests positive pastoral approaches for spiritual and ecclesial renewal. First and foremost is a developing sense of community. Thereafter is listed a wide variety of small communities that could be part of the parish community system: caring communities of lively faith, hope and love where people feel warmth, acceptance, understanding, reconciliation, fellowship; celebrating and praying communities; missionary communities which are outgoing and witnessing, supportive communities for those who have special problems.[7]

When bishops and pastors and other pastoral leaders urge the development of parish-based small Christian communities, they recognize the value that small communities have in building up the parish, the larger church, and the wider society. When small communities are connected to the parish with the guidance of the pastors and bishops they have the capacity to enliven the church in its worship and in its mission of proclaiming the reign of God.

RENEWED FOCUS ON THE WORD OF GOD

Too often in the past "Catholicism tended to become the church of law and sacraments rather than the church of the gospel and the word. Catholics too often neglected the spiritual riches contained in the Bible. Emphasizing the precepts of the church they allowed the proclamation of the good news to fall into some neglect."[8]

The impact of the Second Vatican Council together with the scriptural studies encouraged by Pius XII focused renewed attention on the word of God. In 1943 Pope Pius XII encouraged the church to promote biblical study and renewal in his document, *Divino Afflante Spiritu*. The Vatican II document *The Dogmatic Constitution on Divine Revelation* (Dei Verbum) also strongly recommended the use of scripture by all Catholics. "Easy access to sacred scripture," it stated, "should be provided for all the Christian faithful" (DV 22). It also clearly asserted that the magisterium, the living and teaching office of the church, has the task of giving an authentic interpretation of the word of God, whether in its written form of scripture or in the form of tradition (DV 10).

In addition the council urged frequent reading of the scriptures accompanied by prayer (DV 25). "Just as the life of the church grows through persistent participation in the eucharistic mystery, so we may hope for a new surge of spiritual vitality from intensified veneration for God's word, which lasts forever" (DV 26). Praying or studying the scriptures can help Christians come to new realizations about their own lives in light of the word of God. Doing all of this in a community of believers can enliven faith as Christians discover together the truth which God chooses to reveal.

The Dogmatic Constitution on the Church (Lumen Gentium) spoke of the church as a people made one with the unity of the Creator, the Son, and the Holy Spirit and used predominantly scriptural images in describing this reality (temple, body, people). As the faithful began to be in touch with their Christian roots through scripture study and sharing, they discovered, many for the first time, a fresh view of church as the early Christians experienced it.

In addition many came to realize through their reading of scripture, the social teachings of the church, and the signs of the times that the church's mission was not exclusively a "religious one, aimed at preparing individuals through faith, worship and right behavior to attain eternal life."[9] It sought as well right relationships, justice, and human liberation through the Spirit of Jesus.

Paul VI expanded this understanding of salvation in *On Evangelization in the Modern World* (Evangelii Nuntiandi) to include the intra-historical liberation of all people, on personal, interpersonal, and social levels.

Scriptures Form and Motivate

The document on *Sects or New Religious Movements* speaks of the need of a vision and involvement in that vision. "Many seekers not only feel the need of a vision in the present world society and toward the future; they also want to participate in decision-making, in planning, in realizing."[10] When the centrality of the scriptures is emphasized in the ongoing formation of small communities a gospel vision emerges and becomes the motivating life force for small community members.

An example of how the centrality of the scriptures helps to form people is revealed in Monique's story. A member of the San Egidio community in Rome for more than ten years, Monique commented on the value of the community for her. "Before I became a member of this community," she said, "I never knew the gospels, I never knew I could help the poor. Since I became a member I learned to love the gospels, to know and love Jesus, and how to help the poor." Monique works part-time as a researcher and spends several hours each day teaching Gypsy children. The gospels became the motivating life force for Monique and many others in her community.

Small communities, then, offer the possibility with the guidance of the pastor and other pastoral leaders to be attentive to the word of God and to apply gospel values in creating a better society. Thus when small community members participate in the liberation of people whether that be on a personal, interpersonal, or social level, they become active witnesses to the word of God. They participate in the evangelizing mission of the church; in truth, they participate in evangelizing the culture itself.

Let us look more closely at some aspects of the social mission of the church and how small communities can support parishioners as they become aware of and respond to the social mission of the church today.

The Social Mission of the Church

The last one hundred years have been one of the richest centuries in highlighting the social mission of the church beginning with the encyclicals of Pope Leo XIII and Pope Pius XI. Increasingly these messages are reaching people and beginning to affect their attitudes and behavior. The fact that the U.S. bishops made statements in sensitive areas, including nuclear disarmament, the economy, and racism, indicates the church's belief that the gospel message must be connected to real issues.

Let us simply highlight some of the statements relating to the social mission of the church since Vatican II and then show how the parish can help people connect these statements to the real issues of life through small communities.

John XXIII and Vatican II stated that the work of peace and justice is a requirement of the church's mission to carry on the ministry of Jesus. Both saw the social mission of the church as an implementation of the gospel.

The Pastoral Constitution on the Church in the Modern World (Gaudium et Spes) developed Catholic social teaching begun by Leo XIII and Pius XI. This work considered extraordinarily broad spheres of interest: the dignity of human persons, the proper development of culture, socio-economic life, the life of the political community, the fostering of peace, and the promotion of a community of nations.

Paul VI gave added impetus to the social ministry of the church in his encyclical *On the Development of Peoples* (1967). A few years later the bishops of the church in the synod document on *Justice in the World* (1971) boldly asserted that the struggle for social justice and the transformation of society were constitutive elements of preaching the gospel.

Sensitive to the council's mandate to discern the signs of the times in light of the gospel (GS 4) the popes and episcopal conferences have increasingly spoken on matters of public policy. Furthermore "the preferential option for the poor" which was first expressed by the Latin American bishops has become a part of the consciousness of many other Christians around the world.

Pope John Paul II in his encyclical letter *On Social Concern* (Sollicitudo Rei Socialis) calls not only Catholic Christians but all women and men and especially leaders to a profound transformation in their accustomed ways of thinking and acting.

> Thus one would hope that all those who, to some degree or other, are responsible for ensuring a "more human life" for their fellow human

beings, whether or not they are inspired by religious faith, will become fully aware of the urgent need to *change* the *spiritual attitudes*
that define each individual's relationship with self, with neighbor,
with even the remotest human communities and with nature itself;
and all of this in view of higher values such as the *common good* or,
to quote the felicitous expression of the encyclical *Populorum Pro-
gressio,* the full development "of the whole individual and of all
people."[11]

Small Communities Highlight Social Mission

Since the full acceptance of the social implications of Christianity
will require faith and personal conversion, opportunities which help
people to deepen faith and be open to conversion are necessary.

The parish needs to provide an environment for ongoing conversion to this "constitutive element" of the gospel spoken of by the
bishops:

> Actions on behalf of justice and participation in the transformation
> of the world fully appear to us as a constitutive dimension of the
> preaching of the gospel, or, in other words, of the church's mission
> for the redemption of the human race and its liberation from every
> oppressive situation.[12]

Parishioners need to continually study the social teachings of the
church so that they may be challenged by their message. In this way
they can encourage one another to look at the hard questions of their
lives and lifestyles in light of the church's social teachings and the
gospel.

One of the most acceptable and effective ways of taking people
where they are and helping them to grow is to provide parish-based,
supportive small communities. It is here that people can study social
issues and the social teachings of the church, where they can speak
honestly to one another, and where they can pray over these social
concerns issues.

Believers in the gospel message are called to be counter-cultural in
many ways. By being authentic and truthful they can call others to be
counter-cultural. Where bonds of caring and trust are established
among people in small communities it is much easier to be honest
about one's life and lifestyles and to speak freely about unjust systems
and structures.

Small Christian communities can provide opportunities for parishioners to be open to conversion and to reflect upon how their life-

style may impact upon others. Through study, reflection, and discussion on the social teachings of the church, small community participants can apply the message and meaning of these teachings to their lives and society. Through mutual support and sensitive challenging they can be encouraged to act on this message. The small community setting then offers a place for them to come back to in order to reflect upon their action. In summary, small Christian communities can support and empower parishioners as they become aware of and respond to the challenging social mission of the church today.

Indeed the social teachings of the church and renewed attention to the word of God have broadened our understanding of the mission of Jesus and, therefore, of the church. That mission is proclaiming in word and deed, the reign of God, that is, God's redeeming and liberating action, reconciling and freeing humankind through the presence of the Spirit of Jesus.

RENEW PROMPTS GROWTH OF SMALL GROUPS

Many creative pastoral approaches have been developed since Vatican II to bring life to the mission of Jesus. Notable among these is RENEW, a process designed to deepen the spirituality of the entire parish. One vital component of the RENEW process is small-group faith sharing in parish life. Rev. Philip J. Murnion, director of the Parish Project of the National Conference of Catholic Bishops, while acknowledging the many contributions of RENEW to the parish and diocesan church, highlights the small group experience. He states:

> The value of RENEW seems to be that it touches on critical issues (personal faith, family, liturgy, social justice), provides for both parish-wide focus and small group reflection, offers training for everyone taking any leadership position and provides helpful material with many options. The small group experience has been the strongest feature, attracting about 40,000 people in Newark's parishes, some few thousand of whom had been uninvolved in church life. Imagine 40,000 people discussing justice!

> The participating parish is left at the end of the three-year program with newly trained leaders, new structures (small groups) and a renewed sense among the people of being a community of faith and church.[13]

This Newark experience of RENEW has been repeated in more than one hundred dioceses in the United States and Canada. In addi-

tion, great numbers of dioceses are already becoming involved world-
wide. The experience of these dioceses participating in RENEW
reveals common interest in small groups. Diocesan and parish evaluations consistently register highest satisfaction and success with the parish small-group experience. More than two million people in ten thousand parishes have already participated in small groups. It is
significant for today's church that so many people are opting for this
experience. These evaluations reveal emerging pastoral approaches
which are meaningful for our church today. The knowledge gained
from this widespread experience of renewal in many countries moves
us to speak of the value of small communities. It also impels us to
greater pastoral responsibility in fostering a responsible course of action for the continued development of small faith communities as a
regular ongoing part of parish life.

SUMMARY

Thus far, we have looked at some of the socio-historical aspects of
the growth of small communities in Chapter 1 and some of the theological and pastoral challenges which have occurred since Vatican II in
this present chapter. Viewed together, these aspects and challenges
offer many insights for the renewal of our church today.

We have seen that the increased development of small Christian
communities can be a valuable, effective response to the needs of our
day. Catholic Christians need one another to bond together in mutual
love and support of gospel living. The Spirit of God is bringing about
just such connections all over the world; small groups of people are
coming together to share faith and life in small communities. These
experiences allow individuals to come to know and love God more
deeply and know one another's struggles and joys as they share and
pray together. They find it easier to cope with an often confusing existence when their questions, anxieties, and burdens of life are shared
with other believers. Scripture comes alive as the word speaks to their
lives. In small communities people are free to speak about Jesus and
about their faith. They gain courage to share their faith stories and
witness to what the Spirit has done in their lives. Thus they are evangelized. In reaching out to serve a needy world they themselves become
evangelizers proclaiming the good news to others. Through this cycli-
cal process they learn more about the faith they profess. For "social
action . . . cannot be completed without evangelization. Evangeliza-

tion conversely will always have a certain impact upon social structures."[14]

When small community members participate in Sunday eucharist they bring with them the richness of their faith lives which they have expressed in action. Nourished by the word and eucharist, they hear the commission again to live and proclaim the gospel to others.

The emergence of small Christian communities affirms clearly the vitality of the Catholic Church to adapt and to renew itself. Experience bears witness to the fact that in and through small communities people grow in living authentic Christian lives. In order to demonstrate the value of small communities one story has been chosen. This true story illustrates how participation in a small faith community changed the life of one couple and how that couple has changed the lives of many others and helped to transform one segment of society.

Mary and John's Story

Mary and John have been in small communities for most of their married life. In the early 1970s they were leader couple for CFM in their parish in Chicago and then later in Ridgewood, an affluent suburb of northern New Jersey. They were also leaders in charismatic renewal groups. Mary and John were faithful Catholics, but they knew they were called to more. As parents of five children, they reached a point where four of their five children were independent—the fifth was a senior in college.

Mary and John had a history of involvement in social concerns. For example, while living in the south they tutored in a literacy program for adults. In their parish they had active leadership positions on the social concerns committee, and participated in Bread for the World and other activities. Motivated by these activities and especially sparked by their small group experience in RENEW, they realized they were called to live their faith by making a fuller commitment to the values of the gospel.

John, managing a sales firm of five hundred, had highly developed organizational skills. He requested a part-time sabbatical from his company so that he could devote more time to his justice involvements. A particular attraction was the diocesan office which concentrated on developing parish social concerns efforts. John had previously done some volunteer work with this office and realized his skills could be used in the efforts of the office to build a network of people throughout the diocese who would facilitate parish social concerns committees. John volunteered his two-day-a-week sabbatical to this work. Mary became a volunteer facilitator. All of this was done in a communal style, that is, the department staff which supported John and Mary and also the volunteer facilitators and parishioners with whom they worked all prayed together, shared scripture, mutually supported one another, and learned together in small groups. Commitment and conviction grew. Eventually Mary and John arrived at a monumental decision. They were ready to scale down their lifestyle and deepen their social involvement. John went to work for the social concerns office with a drastic cut in salary. They moved out of their lovely split level home and into an integrated urban neighborhood.

For the next four years John and Mary worked on helping urban and suburban parishes reflect on the scriptures and social justice, educated them on issues and organization, and empowered them to address social needs and injustices. Their efforts and lives were sustained by the small communities, which enabled them to do all of this.

John's contacts made him increasingly aware of the disastrous effects of unemployment among the urban poor. Again, John recognized how he could utilize his skills. Through Mary's support and ongoing reflection, prayer, and assessment with others, John opened an employment agency in Newark, one of the poorest cities in the nation. Today, six years later, John and Mary continue to offer hope through their own dedication as they help thousands of urban job seekers find employment each year.

John and Mary's story and the preceding cursory examination of the socio-historical, theological, and pastoral aspects of small communities reveal many values which small communities help to develop. The common thread woven throughout these values is spirituality. In pastoral terms the greatest value of small Christian communities is the spiritual growth which takes place in them. In today's society small communities present a wonderful opportunity to address the spiritual hunger of the people of God. It is particularly because of this value that we encourage and promote small Christian communities with such vigor. The following chapter will further explore in realistic pastoral terms that aspect of spiritual growth that is occurring in small Christian communities.

CHAPTER 3

Spirituality: The Foundation of Small Christian Communities

There is little doubt that throughout the world today there is great interest in small communities. That is not to say that the enthusiasm for small communities means they will come about easily. Marriage is an age-old institution, quite universally accepted, and yet happy marriages are achieved only with great effort. Like marriage, small communities involve the inter-relationship of people. We have strong human desires for unity and love. On the other hand we have the human foibles of jealousy, competition, and insecurity that tend to make real community something for which we must strive.

St. Paul recognized our human nature in many of his letters.

Put on then, as God's chosen ones, holy and beloved, heartfelt compassion, kindness, humility, gentleness and patience, bearing with one another and forgiving one another, if one has a grievance against another; as the Lord has forgiven you, so must you also do. And over all these put on love, that is the bond of perfection. And let the peace of Christ control your hearts, the peace into which you were also called into one body (Col 3:12–15).

The Christian is called to be a person of great hope. We believe that by God's gracious action in our lives we are able to overcome our human weaknesses to the point of strong relational bonds and real community. Therefore in our quest to develop small Christian communities we wish to acknowledge a dependency on God's grace and the primacy of spiritual development to achieve this desired goal. Precisely for this reason, this chapter considers basic spiritual realities upon which our small community efforts will be founded.

An interesting juxtaposition is seen in that good spirituality is necessary to achieve community, while efforts to build small communities result in good spirituality. A strong emphasis of the spiritual and a quest for holiness are necessary to arrive at true Christian community. At the same time, efforts made in developing small Christian communities offer a unique opportunity for the church in helping many more people to grow spiritually and achieve holiness.

Our focus on spirituality will keep in mind these dual aims: the development of solidly based small communities and small communities as a means of great spiritual enrichment for the body of the church.

HOLINESS

What does it mean to be holy?

> We are accustomed to apply the word "holy" to men and women who have striven to live wholly for God. Yet no human efforts are sufficient to make a person *holy*. Only because God takes a person . . . into his own holiness does he belong to God and become holy. No one, on the other hand, becomes holy without willing it. This is the meaning of this sentence of the Old Testament: "It is I, Yahweh, who am your God. . . . You must therefore be holy because I am holy" (cf. Lev 11:44–45).[1]

To be holy is to be like God, to live in conformity to God's life and will, to have heart and mind and will in harmony with God. "The call of every Christian to a life of holiness is a call to live one's life, in whatever situation one finds oneself, according to the spirit of Christ."[2]

Paul's second letter to Timothy reveals God's intention in this call. God "saved us and called us to a holy life, not according to our works, but according to his own design and the grace bestowed on us in Christ Jesus before time began, but now made manifest through the appearance of our savior Christ Jesus" (2 Tim 1:9–10).

All Are Called to Holiness

Vatican Council II issued a strong call to holiness for all the baptized: "All the faithful of Christ of whatever rank or status are called to the fullness of Christian life and to the perfection of charity" (LG 40). The vocation to holiness then is the vocation to perfection in love. Jesus himself has told us we must be made perfect as God is perfect (Mt

5:48). "All who follow Christ are invited and bound to pursue holiness and the perfect fulfillment of their proper state" (LG 42).

Our call to holiness is not only an individual call, but also a collective call, to be part of the Christian community. All that is said, therefore, with regard to living out this call applies both to individuals in their own personal lives and to their participation in the various communities to which they belong.

Practically speaking, how is this universal call to holiness conveyed? How do large numbers of people experience that they are personally called to be holy? How is this call to holiness effectively translated to the lives of "grassroots" parishioners? Many are finding that this happens best in smaller, more personal settings where people can reflect on the life of faith together. Small Christian communities can provide an effective way for inviting large numbers of parishioners to understand and to concretize the grace of holiness in their own lives. In this way they better enable the church to realize more fully a universal call to holiness.

Spirituality: A Way of Seeking Holiness

Spirituality is a way of seeking God and serving the call to holiness of life. Spirituality is a stance out of which a person lives and acts and prays. It is a way of expressing one's relationship to God, to others, to the whole of creation, including one's relationship to oneself. Spirituality can be defined as the efforts of a person to recognize, acknowledge, and respond to God's loving action in one's life.

Christian spirituality encompasses each aspect mentioned above but stresses a relationship with the three persons of the Trinity and embodies all that Christianity teaches. God then is the central focus of a spiritual life. For Christians the spiritual life focuses on God as revealed in the person of Jesus Christ. The lives of the saints in our tradition indicate clearly to us that developing an intimate personal relationship with Jesus is the heart of Christian spirituality. Developing this relationship includes living out the paschal mystery. Because Jesus became incarnate, the inherent basis of Christian spirituality is an entering into his life, death, and resurrection. In baptism we die with Christ and rise again to newness of life in him. We are called to live and love as Jesus did and to incarnate the Spirit of Jesus in our lives.

The Paschal Mystery

The essence of Christian spirituality, then, is living out the paschal mystery—the life, death, and resurrection of Jesus. Through his sufferings and death Christ saved us from sin and set us free (Col 1:14). Through his total self-giving, Christ invites us to repentance and resurrection—to be freed from the slavery of personal and social sin and to rise to new life with him. Christ challenges us to enter completely into his life, suffering, death, and resurrection so that we may experience the power flowing from his resurrection.

Paul's response to this invitation reveals his own understanding of the paschal mystery:

> . . . to know him
> and the power of his resurrection,
> and [the] sharing of his sufferings
> by being conformed to his death,
> if somehow I may attain
> the resurrection from the dead (Phil 3:10–11).

Entering into the paschal mystery calls us to a special intimacy with Jesus and invites us to share that same marvelous intimacy which he shares with the Father (Jn 14:23). One condition for sharing that intimacy and demonstrating our love is obeying the commandments (Jn 14:15). On the one hand we cannot keep the commandments and moral teachings of Jesus as spelled out and applied over time by the church except through the saving power of God. On the other hand we cannot fully experience the saving power of God without really living the moral life to which God calls us. Recognizing this paradox is critical for understanding Christian spirituality.

Through the saving action of Jesus' death and resurrection and the coming of the Holy Spirit we are empowered to live a new life consonant with the moral teachings and the mission of Jesus.

Jesus changed the whole course of human history. He freed us from enslavement to sin; he taught us the paradox of gaining life through death. "Unless a grain of wheat falls to the ground and dies it remains just a grain of wheat" (Jn 12:24). But if it seemingly dies, it bears new life and much fruit. The surrendering of ourselves to Jesus is absolutely essential if our lives are to bear fruit.

Small Communities and the Paschal Mystery

Small communities are uniquely suited to help people reflect on the paschal mystery and to incorporate aspects of this mystery into their lives. The sharing in Jesus' life, suffering, death, and resurrection can take many forms. Let us consider several of these in relationship to small communities.

In small communities people are able to look at their lives as in a mirror. They can speak of their values and their approaches to life in light of the gospel with other people of good will who are seeking to live Christian lives. Frequently in these circumstances people are reached more profoundly than through either a teaching or a homily because they come to a self awareness of the discrepancies between their own lives and what the gospel calls for. This need not only apply to inconsistencies in areas of personal morality, but also in areas of social morality, e.g. issues of racism or prejudice. Perhaps only in the gentle but conscientious approach used in a small-group setting will people allow themselves to be confronted with such issues.

The small Christian community is admirably designed to help people reflect on the mysteries of Jesus' life. When people reflect on Jesus' suffering and death as a positive act of love, they gain insight into a corresponding positive response of loving action. As people reflect, share, make application to their own lives, and believe deeply in what Jesus did in his life, they come to a richer appreciation and realization of the power of the cross and the meaning of his mission.

Small communities ideally help people to live in the power of the Spirit by choosing freedom and liberation from sin. As they die to their sinfulness and live in ever greater fidelity to the commandments and moral teachings, they come nearer to experiencing the fullness of the power of the Spirit.

Jesus' total self-giving is not a point simply to be taught. It must become a part of our lived experience. The gospel message and our shared response to the gospel in small communities challenge us likewise to die to ourselves, to give completely, and to commit ourselves without reservation to Jesus and his way of life. This commitment affects every aspect of our lives and calls us to greater responsibility in the works of charity and justice.

It is this total commitment which opens us to the power and gifts of the Holy Spirit. The small community gives us the courage and the support we need to make this total commitment. Our sharing in community encourages our receptivity to the movement of the Spirit and enables us to discern the application of the gifts of the Holy Spirit in our lives. We learn how our gifts are to be used in meeting the needs of society. The mission of Jesus thus finds concrete fulfillment in our actions.

SPIRITUALITIES: A MEANS TO HOLINESS

Throughout the ages individuals and communities developed specific types of spiritualities to attain holiness. These spiritualities reflected responses to the needs of the time as well as cultural expression. Different social and historical situations helped create varying spiritualities. Throughout the centuries the gospel has invited people to specific lifestyles and activities that witnessed to Jesus in their particular cultural setting. However, the constant human quest for ultimate meaning and transcendence, for personal identity and God is seen in every age.

Therefore a diversity of styles appears in the history of Christian spirituality. Specific spiritualities have developed throughout the ages: the monastic spirituality found in the Benedictine and Cistercian tradition is well known; mendicant spiritualities arose with the Franciscans, Dominicans, and the other great mendicant orders; more apostolically centered communities arose in time such as the Jesuits and the Vincentians. Women and men religious have always attempted an intense response to the gospel. Eastern forms of spirituality have provided further expressions of faith response within the church.

Vision and Technique of Spirituality

In their book *The Desert and the City,* Jesuits Thomas M. Gannon and George W. Traub claim that in the final analysis "spirituality consists in the style of a person's response to the grace of Christ before the challenge of everyday life in a given historical and cultural environment."[3] They remind us that each spirituality has a vision and a technique. The vision of spirituality is a framework that gives us direction and enables us to experience a breakthrough in our search for God.

The techniques of spirituality are practical approaches used to achieve its end. They are determined by the vision which is more general and by the needs of a given age.

We propose that a vision of spirituality of small Christian communities may be based on church teachings from Vatican II and post-Vatican II documents. The technique of this spirituality would be the small community dynamic itself. This vision and technique will be amplified as we explore holistic spirituality.

Integrated Spirituality

While it may be difficult to adequately describe a spirituality for today, there is movement toward a type of integrated or holistic Christian spirituality. This spirituality draws from the past and the present. It is based on the life of God who dwells in community as well as in each individual. Because we are created in the image of God who is creator, redeemer, sanctifier, we tend to God's creation through human ingenuity—healing and reconciling, in a word, as persons who strive to be holy and help others to achieve holiness in a world that needs healing.

It appears that this kind of integrated spirituality is what the prophet Micah spoke about when he told us to act justly, love tenderly and walk humbly with God (Mic 6:8). Jesus built on Micah's teaching and called us to embody the good news in all dimensions of our lives when he gave us the beatitudes as a way of life and urged us to love the least of our sisters and brothers.

Through baptism the individual is incorporated into the community of the church and therefore is involved in a communal spirituality which embraces the whole tradition of the church and is especially nurtured through the sacramental life of the church. This Christian spirituality is always marked by a sense of the mission of Jesus. This missionary dimension of spirituality embraces the areas of family, work, the economic and political order, ecumenism, and the ecological and social dimensions of our lives. Vatican II helps to broaden the understanding of Jesus' mission of proclaiming God's reign. Given the council's emphasis on scriptural foundations and on God's revelation in "the signs of the times" Catholics are encouraged to relate their faith to the events and realities of life in an ever more integrated way.

Small communities tend to develop integrated spirituality. Recent church documentation supports the vision of spirituality found in small communities. *The Dogmatic Constitution on the Church* encourages all the people of God working in harmonious community. *The Pastoral Constitution on the Church in the Modern World* is very possibly the church's clearest teaching on the integration of all life and holistic spiritual responsibility. The post-conciliar document on the Rite of Christian Initiation of Adults challenges all Christians to see life as a continuing journey and conversion as a lifelong challenge. All of these documents find rich expression in the life and activities of small communities. Thus the spiritual vision of small communities can be said to be based on the teaching documents of the church while the very dynamics of the small community provide the technique.

Approaches to an Integrated Spirituality

Keeping in mind the interplay between well-formed small communities and the development of a healthy spirituality within the larger church through small communities, let us further explore some approaches to integrated spirituality. For this consideration we shall reflect on moving away from the privatization of spirituality and a concern over dualism, the healthy effects on a parish of a dynamic spiritual life cycle, the interconnectedness of conversion and the reign of God, and storytelling in relation to small communities. We will conclude with an example of how small communities can help people achieve the integrated experience of God that they seek.

From Privatization of Spirituality to Mission

Spirituality calls us to a mission that is broader than simply ministry or service within the parish. Joe Holland, a contemporary thinker who specializes in the relationship between theology and social theory, says that the Catholic laity are presently being formed by a privatized spirituality which does not allow them to connect their creative spiritual energy with public life.

> Privatization of spirituality means that spiritual consciousness is confined to the sphere of intimacy—self, family, friends, parish. It does not extend to the sphere of non-intimacy, that is to the public and technologically institutional structures of culture, politics, and economics. This is a typically American phenomenon, inevitably found in the American Catholic experience.[4]

Other observers of contemporary society corroborate this fact.[5] In essence they acknowledge that public life is one area where the Catholic laity find it most difficult both to relate their spiritual life and to draw nourishment for their spiritual life. Although the desire to reach out to secular society is present, Catholic laity frequently lack certainty about what this means or how they are to accomplish it.

Jesuit theologian Avery Dulles states that U.S. Catholic lay people still have an "immense" way to go to make their mark on society. In addition, he says, once-thriving Catholic apostolic groups seem to have been replaced since the 1960s by "more inward-looking organizations."[6]

John Paul II's *Apostolic Exhortation on the Laity* speaks of the need to address the continuing lack of impact on society from the Christian message. He seems hopeful when he speaks of "a new era of group endeavors of the lay faithful." Although these lay groups are very diverse from one another in various aspects,

> they all come together in an all-inclusive and profound convergence when viewed from the perspective of their common purpose, that is, the responsible participation of all of them in the church's mission of carrying forth the Gospel of Christ, the source of hope for humanity and the renewal of society.[7]

He elaborates how those who participate in movements, small groups, or communities can have a great impact on the transformation of society.

Catholic spirituality cannot be a flight from the world nor simply interior renewal. It must move beyond merely interior attitudes in order to break out of the prison of privatization.

Dualism and Spirituality

The privatization of spirituality has been partially caused by the concept of dualism which has shaped some of our thinking and action. Perhaps at this juncture a brief consideration of the role of dualism in our past history will shed more light upon our consideration of spirituality.

To some extent, our concept of church, and consequently our concept of spirituality, has been influenced by the ancient dichotomy drawn between spirit and matter. Hellenistic thinking of the third and fourth centuries, which embraced a philosophy of Neo-Platonism, adopted a two-world view of life. Body and soul were seen in great tension and basically at war with each other. The soul struggled throughout life to break through, to soar to the heavens, to live the superior life of the spirit. The spirituality arising from this basic dualism of body and spirit is characterized by flight from the body and the world. This dualism is also reflected in the categories of "sacred" and "secular." Frequently people have had the notion that the sacred belongs to those in the clerical state, the secular to the laity. This spirituality suggested "that those who are 'holy' or 'spiritual' are not deeply involved in earthly affairs, and especially not in political matters."[8]

A dualistic approach to spirituality can be seen in the person who believes she is spiritual because she is a weekly communicant yet whose business practices are questionable. When confronted about a particular unjust practice she may simply respond, "That's the way business is!" She fails to connect spirituality to daily events of life.

Today there is much movement away from this dualistic approach espoused for centuries toward a one-world view of reality.

> In modern thought, there has been a shift towards a one-world view. There are two ways to get a one-world view. The first is to deny everything that used to be denominated as supernatural; then only one kind of reality is left. The second approach to a one-world view is think of God and history as naturally related, naturally interconnected, mutually involved, and of temporal reality and human history as theater for the drama of redemption.[9]

The document on the *Church in the Modern World* fosters this one-world view when it speaks of church and the world as mutually related (GS 40). Yet because we have been conditioned through the years—through our culture, thinking, literature and language—it is not always easy to move away from dualistic concepts.

A Dynamic Life Cycle

How can the one-world view of the *Church in the Modern World* be effectively experienced in parish life? How can community be part of a dynamic life cycle for parishioners that will provide opportunities for spiritual growth? How does the weekly cycle affect the way people live? We propose a three-phase cycle. Let us name the three phases first and then comment.

A. Parishioners live their lives throughout the whole week, not just on Sundays. They strive to live by Christian principles and values.

B. Parishioners gather weekly in their respective small Christian communities. There they have the opportunity to reflect on that life, to break open the word of God, and connect the word with life. As people think through the implications of the word and are strengthened by the community and the scriptures, they come to new insight and resolutions about their lives.

C. Those in small communities then take all of the aspects of life that have been reflected on in their small community and bring it to the parish eucharistic celebration. As they unite the sacrifice of their lives to the sacrifice of Jesus they are nourished at the banquet. This nourishment sends them forth into everyday life with new strength and vitality—to be truly apostolic, with the knowledge that God is with them.

Growth in appreciation of the scriptures in small communities during the week prepares the members to be more attentive and receptive to the word as it is proclaimed at the Sunday liturgy. This preparation helps parishioners to listen more attentively to the homily which is intended to make the word of God meaningful in our time.

At the celebration of the eucharist small-community participants are reminded that they are part of a universal church community where they intercede for one another. As they offer their lives at the sacrifice of the mass they enter into union with the Lord who is made present in the eucharistic banquet. They are strengthened for mission and are sent forth to live that mission wherever they are called—in their family, their community, the larger church, the workplace, and the social arena.

The third part of the cycle, the eucharistic celebration, is essential because "The liturgy is the summit toward which the activity of the Church is directed; at the same time it is the fountain from which all its power flows" (SC 10).

Small-community members grow in holiness through living out this weekly cycle of reflecting on their experience in the light of God's word and bringing all of this to the eucharistic assembly. The renewed faith and the sense of mission which they have found through their small community experience enrich the larger community. The joy of the gospel finds its highest expression in the eucharist. It is there that we celebrate what God has done for us in Christ Jesus.

All of us can help to enliven worship with the richness of our faith which has been strengthened in our small communities. We are both nourished and sent forth to nourish others through the celebration of the eucharist. The eucharistic celebration truly has the capacity to shape and transform the entire community in all its beliefs and endeavors. It goes without saying then that the eucharist also helps to shape and transform small Christian communities. Hence, the Sunday parish celebration of the eucharist is the most significant gathering place for small Christian communities!

When this dynamic life cycle becomes part of people's lives the potential for spiritual growth increases. The liturgical renewal in our century, which has made all liturgical rites more expressive, finds a rich pastoral complement in the reflection on the mysteries in small communities.

The small community members strengthen the larger gathering by their developing sense of commitment and mission. Their reflection on events of Jesus' death and resurrection enables them to enter more fully into the rites. Through both reflection in small communities and participation in liturgical celebrations then, participants are drawn more closely into union with Christ and share more fully in the reality of the salvation offered through him. In turn, the rites speak more clearly to them and enable them to enter into the mysteries with deeper faith and to celebrate more wholeheartedly. An ongoing cycle occurs where faith is strengthened, lived out, and celebrated! Lent, Easter, Pentecost come alive!

THE REIGN OF GOD AND CONVERSION

Throughout his life Jesus proclaimed the reign of God, described its characteristics in the parables he told, and gave witness to the inbreaking of God's reign through his miracles. The relational aspects of the reign of God are more easily recognized in people's lives through the sharing in small communities.

Through his life, death, resurrection, and sending of the Spirit Jesus showed us that a radically new relationship is possible between God and humans and among human beings. It is a relationship of integrity, wholeness, and freedom from fear and anxiety. It is a relationship of justice and peace. It is the coming of the reign of God.

Following Jesus in the power of the Spirit requires a conversion according to the scriptural word. Our attitudes, our values, our commitments need to be in accord with the call and the teaching of Jesus Christ. Strength is provided us through prayer, the sacramental life, and our commitment to community life. The reign of God touches all of life itself.

The ever present reality of human sinfulness will demand ongoing conversion of each person and prevent a full acceptance of the reign of God until the end of time. Yet as persons who are empowered by the Spirit struggle for integrity, compassion and reconciliation, the reign of God will increasingly be experienced here and now in the personal lives of people, in community, and in the wider society.

Acceptance of and commitment to Jesus Christ then are at the heart of Christian spirituality. Being open to God's grace, being in dialogue and communion with God through Jesus, and responding to God's grace and word through the action of our lives are all part of a Christian spirituality.

STORYTELLING

Embracing the reign of God, facing the challenge of conversion, and launching out on our spiritual journeys are frequently made possible through the storytelling which small communities so beautifully foster.

Healthy persons share their stories with others, and a healthy parish respects and values its individual members and their stories. In the large parish there is often nowhere to tell the story of our faith journey. It is taken for granted. Yet contemporary awareness has rediscovered the value and power of telling our stories and listening to others to interpret the meaning of our lives.

As we look at the concept of story in relationship to small Christian communities, we note certain elements:

- The gospels are narratives, the actual stories of Jesus as remembered by members of the early Christian communities. Every time small communities read the gospel they are reviewing the story of Jesus.
- When we tell our faith stories we are telling how God is acting in our lives. In the telling we may *hear,* perhaps for the first time, how God is moving in our lives. It is often in the telling itself that we experience the Spirit's presence. This helps others see and believe in the God who is really at work in us.
- As we hear others talk about their lives we realize how God is present and acting in their lives.
- Not only do we hear the narrative of Jesus' life but we start to apply the word to our lives today.
- As we listen to one another we have a sense of the Spirit acting in the community.

In all of these aspects we are trusting in Jesus' words, "Where two or three are gathered together in my name, there am I in the midst of them" (Mt 18:20). We trust that Jesus is present and his story is being retold and applied to our lives. We might call this an immanent experience of God. Yet in the sharing of scripture and life there is also a profound search for God—for the answer to the question, "Who is God?" This search for God is truly a transcendental experience of God who dwells in mystery.

A favorite scripture story for small-community members is the Emmaus story (Lk 24:13–25). Briefly told, two disciples walking along the road to Emmaus sharing a life experience (storytelling) were joined by a "stranger." The stranger chides them, "What little sense you have," and starts to unfold the meaning of the scriptures beginning with Moses and the prophets. In the telling the disciples are captivated by this stranger and invite him to share a meal. As they eat supper they recognize Jesus in the breaking of bread. But he vanishes. They remember! They recall: "Didn't our hearts burn within us on the road while we were dialoguing, didn't we feel a change in our hearts?" They get up immediately and return to Jerusalem to tell the good news—a new story of God with them. They go back to the larger community to share the marvelous events that had happened to them that day!

Parallel dynamics occur in small communities. In sharing a life experience, in telling our stories, we are joined by Jesus present in the community and in the word. The meaning of our faith lives unfolds as we break open the scriptures with others in small community. These events are then celebrated when we gather with the larger community at Sunday eucharist.

We recognize the presence of God in our midst. We dialogue and pray and our hearts are changed—never to be the same again. And because we cannot contain the new story of God acting in our lives— we reach out and give witness to our families and the wider community. We have a sense of being on mission! The God story seeks release and must be told in and through us!

A Life Example

Many people are searching for meaning in their lives. They seek God and desire to be holy. They desire an integration of faith in their daily lives.

Consider the following story which illustrates this point: One of our priest staff members was working with RENEW in New Zealand. In flying from one island to another he was expectantly awaiting the beautiful view of Mount Cook. A flight attendant began to speak with him and in the course of conversation said, "I used to be an R.C. myself—now I belong to a fundamentalist faith." He then related how his seven sisters and brothers who had all gone to Catholic schools, had also left the church. The inquisitive young man asked the reason for the priest's travels. Realizing time was of the essence, the priest outlined five key aspects of the RENEW work he was engaged in. He shared that through the small communities which RENEW promoted, people came to know Jesus personally. They reflected upon scripture and came to a deeper appreciation of the word of God. They were finding it easier to pray and to share prayer with others. Through small communities people felt a sense of belonging and mutual support and, finally, in these communities they were able to connect their faith to their daily life.

When the flight attendant heard this he exclaimed, "It's too bad we didn't have this a long time ago. I'd still be a Roman Catholic myself."

The flight attendant's response is all too typical. People are looking for more than intellectual understanding of their faith. They are looking for the place where they can best experience God. The Catholic Church offers a rich means for spiritual growth and of experiencing God through the sacraments, especially the eucharist, and through teaching and guidance in the tradition of our Catholic heritage. Complementing these can be the ways of experiencing God that so attracted the young flight attendant: strong emphasis on scripture, personal relationship with Jesus, deeper prayer life, connecting faith to life, and a more intimate sense of community. Small Christian communities wonderfully promote and bolster these practices.

No matter how many times the flight attendant's story is told, people nod in agreement. The experience of countless families seems to verify the reality of this story. These five aspects contained in RENEW, mentioned above, resonate with their deepest heart wishes. Perhaps the small communities forming all over the world are the Spirit's way of showing us how to help people experience God more fully, and how to be holy.

In our existential society parish life can be strengthened by offering a strong experience of God through small Christian communities. Integrating the richness of the Catholic tradition with small Christian communities offers a long-term path to spiritual growth for parishioners. It is precisely because God's presence and power can be dynamically experienced in small communities that we promote these communities with such enthusiasm in this book.

CONTEMPORARY EXPRESSIONS OF SPIRITUALITY

Because different social and historical situations call for different spiritualities or different expressions of spirituality, new forms of spirituality are being articulated today. In small communities participants have the opportunity to study and reflect upon these. In so doing some of their own understandings may be challenged and broadened.

Expressions of spirituality today reflect needs of people as well as developing levels of awareness. Included among these expressions would be the following:

1. recognition of the connections between a person's relationship with God, with one another, with the whole living community;
2. creation as revealing the divine;
3. greater sensitivity to women and to the feminine dimension of God and life.

Among writers who have developed a spirituality that includes ecological sensitivity is Father Thomas Berry, C.P. He claims that it is now time for the most significant change that Christian spirituality has yet experienced. This change is part of a much more comprehensive change in human consciousness brought about by the discovery of the evolutionary story of the universe. In speaking about a new cosmology he reminds us that we are the earth come to consciousness and, therefore, we are connected to the whole living community—that is, all people, animals, plants and the living organism of planet earth itself. He calls us to realize that the earth is a primary revelation of the divine.[10] If we become more conscious of this realization, we would reverence and better care for the earth, respect the dignity of all our sisters and brothers, and be moved to wonder and contemplation of God revealed through all of creation.

With this new awareness we might choose a simpler lifestyle. We might have a better sense of collective responsibility to the planet and the human community.

Perhaps seeing with new eyes and reverencing the earth as a revelation of the divine is part of John Paul II's hope that we will change our "spiritual attitudes that define each individual's relationship with self, with neighbor, with even the remotest human communities and with nature itself."[11]

As in every age the church strives to bring together its rich tradition of our Catholic heritage with contemporary society and our expressions of spirituality. The task is demanding. It requires great prayer, study, analysis, dialogue, and action.

We attempt to cooperate with God's creative providence and action in our world as we understand that response through ecological, social, and ecclesial concerns. The more we strive to cooperate with God, the less danger there will be to a privatization of spirituality. To the extent that this is not achieved, our church, our earth, our society will be impoverished. It appears that the task of pastoral leaders is to help parishioners to discover the revelation of God in family, work, leisure, in the earth itself. The family is the fundamental structure of society, and it is within the family and within our work and leisure that we both discover God and express our creativity with God. (An extended treatment of the family and small communities is found in Chapter 16.)

BEYOND A PRIVATIZED SPIRITUALITY

The type of holistic spirituality that small Christian communities are capable of nurturing has a clear ecclesial dimension. It is integrally connected to all facets of life from the domestic church to the larger church, from the marketplace to the broader society.

Because community intrinsically includes mission, small communities move beyond a self-nurturing social type of group. Mission is never an addendum but is well integrated into the life of the community members.

Through involvement in small Christian communities people have the experience of a healing, reconciling, challenging community and thus are helped to envision the potential for such a communal dynamic in the wider society. Moved by the Spirit, small Christian communities reflect on the scriptures and come to understand the breadth of the applications of God's word. When people authentically share the scriptures, they see the implications not only for their personal lives but for the wider society as well. Therefore, they are led out of a privatized spirituality into a spirituality which embraces all of creation.

At the National Forum for Small Christian Communities held in Parma, Ohio in October 1988, participants crystallized the concept of small communities moving them beyond a privatized spirituality. Among the comments were the following:

> Small Christian communities are a way to be church on a personal level for people, where they experience Christ's unconditional love which empowers them to serve in the mission of church for their brothers and sisters.
>
> Jane Bensman
> Archdiocese of Cincinnati, Ohio

Small Christian community enables people to own their faith by helping them articulate how that faith has and does sustain them in their every day life, finding the presence of the sacred in the ordinary, as well as extraordinary life experiences.

Dawn Green
Diocese of Omaha, Nebraska

Small Christian community—a personal experience of love, support and care (I've had many, this is the *most* profound) that gives impetus to live out the Gospel.

Jean Eakins
Archdiocese of Seattle, Washington

Through small communities parishioners can challenge each other to die to self and be co-creators with God as they struggle to build economic, political, social systems that uphold the dignity of all human beings. They can express their creativity as they become more in touch with the evolutionary study of our universe, particularly our earth, and work to make it ecologically safe for ourselves and our children. They can be reconcilers and healers in bringing the wisdom, justice, and love of God into play in every area of their lives. In all of this they can discover and experience God in their relationships, in their worship and work, in all of creation!

PASTORAL QUESTIONS

A significant question arises. Is this not the Catholic moment for the church to actively promote small communities within the context of church life? This deserves consideration given the points of value for small Christian communities from historical, sociological, theological and pastoral considerations (mentioned in the previous chapters) and from the fact that people around the world are turning to small communities.

Cannot the church seize this moment and offer leadership and motivation for parishioners to gather in small Christian communities, thus meeting many of their spiritual and human needs? By promoting small communities the church has a tremendous opportunity of offering the fullness of the spiritual life to its people who in turn can offer that life to the whole living community.

Knowing how powerfully God moves in small communities we boldly ask: Cannot those in small communities gather precisely to be in communion with God and one another for the sake of Jesus' mission? Can they not be the shapers and designers of a holistic spirituality as they embody the good news of God's justice and love in all dimensions of their lives?

We therefore encourage small communities as a means of spiritual renewal. This goal must always be kept primary if they are to achieve their full potential. Moreover small communities are promoted in this book as part of the very mainstream of the Catholic Church. We propose that small communities be at the heart of church life, that they become an integral ongoing part of parish life. With the renewal of the church as a pastoral priority, the healthy development of parish-based small communities is suggested as a means of that renewal.

Therefore in the following chapter we will look more closely at the parish and at the implications for the parish if small communities are implemented in a full and realistic way. We call this chapter, "Proposing a Pastoral Direction."

CHAPTER 4

Proposing a Pastoral Direction

The value of small Christian communities is being recognized from a variety of perspectives. The world Synod of Bishops (1987), whose theme was the "Vocation and Mission of the Laity in the Church and in the World Twenty Years after the Second Vatican Council," noted "with great satisfaction that the parish is becoming a dynamic community of communities, a center where movements, basic ecclesial communities and other apostolic groups energize it and are in turn nourished."[1] Among the propositions which the synod sent to Pope John Paul II was one which stated that basic Christian communities, with local pastors, are true examples of church unity and evangelization.

John Paul II, in his *Apostolic Exhortation on the Laity,* recalled that the synod fathers had given much attention to the present state of many parishes and have called for a greater effort in their renewal. He incorporates their own words in describing how many parishes cannot do their work effectively because they lack priests or material resources or are too large geographically, or because of the particular circumstances of some Christians (e.g. exiles and migrants).

> So that all parishes of this kind may be truly communities of Christians, local ecclesial authorities ought to foster the following: a) adaptation of parish structures according to the full flexibility granted by canon law, especially in promoting participation by the lay faithful in pastoral responsibilities; b) small, basic or so-called "living" communities where the faithful can communicate the word of God and express it in service and love to one another; these communities are true expressions of ecclesial communion and centers of evangelization in communion with their pastors.[2]

Is it possible that what was said at the Synod of the Laity and again by John Paul II is a vision of the future parish? A theme has been touched here that will revitalize not only evangelization but all aspects of parish life. The recurring theme of the parish "becoming a dynamic community of communities" has been highlighted by the Synod of the Laity, the U.S. Catholic bishops, and many others. This concept of the parish as a community of communities may well provide us with a pastoral direction for parish life today and in the years to come—a direction which can strengthen our faith as we live in a secular society and call us forth from the climate of privatized religion.

Cardinal Joseph Bernardin of Chicago, in looking at parishes in the United States, proposes such a direction so that evangelization may more effectively take place in our age and time.

> In the U.S., many of our parishes are quite large and, consequently, may exhibit anonymity more than community. In such settings, it is often difficult for effective evangelization to take place. A possible solution is to re-structure the parish as a community of communities. In such a vision and structure, Catholics gather in small groups determined by neighborhood, family, needs, interests, or a common ministry in order to pray, read Scripture and share.
> Authentic community is vital to effective evangelization. It nurtures believers. If Catholics experience community on a smaller scale, they may form and experience more of a community when they gather for parish liturgies on the weekend.[3]

What Cardinal Bernardin says about the importance of small communities for evangelization also applies to other aspects of parish life. Restructuring the parish as a community of communities will develop authentic community and nurture believers, thus infusing all of parish life with new vitality.

PASTORAL DIRECTION: AN IDEAL TO MOVE TOWARD

Before proceeding further let us first consider the nature of a pastoral direction. Any pastoral direction flows from a long-term, ideal vision which inspires and motivates people to strive for its realization. A pastoral direction clarifies the vision by giving a sense of direction and energizes those carrying it out by giving a sense of purpose. It does not define the total picture but gives a desired goal toward which to move. The pastoral direction must be suitable for those for whom it is intended and ideally come into being through a collaborative process.

In the pages which follow we apply this term "pastoral direction" to the implementation of the vision of the parish as a community of many small communities. The proposed pastoral direction is a long-term line of action, an ideal to move toward. Years of working at it will bring us closer to the goal. It has the capacity to energize, to give life to parishioners and staff alike, and to give an added sense of purpose to the parish. When a parish chooses this pastoral direction, it does not realistically expect that every parishioner will be involved in a small community. Historically, pastoral directions or invitations were never stated or acted upon with the intention of making "others" feel excluded. For example, in parishes where every woman is invited to be part of the Altar and Rosary Society it is never realistically expected, in fact, that all will be members.

While not every parishioner will participate in a small community, the pastoral direction will serve everyone. Ultimately the richness of faith lived in the small community setting will spread to every aspect of parish life and beyond.

While we do not expect to see the complete fulfillment of the vision, the ideal gives great energy and hope as we strive for it. Hopefully, when this pastoral direction is adopted in parishes and dioceses, it will come into being through a collaborative process and express mutuality in relationships.

In exploring this pastoral direction two main points will be examined: first, the significant components of this pastoral direction and, second, the implications of the pastoral direction for the parish.

THE SIGNIFICANT COMPONENTS OF THIS PASTORAL DIRECTION

"The Parish"

The U.S. bishops have said that "the parish is for most Catholics the single most important part of the church. This is where for them the mission of Christ continues. This is where they publicly express faith, joining with others to give proof of their communion with God and with one another."[4]

The parish, then, is the focus of this pastoral direction. The parish, the community of believers who gather to celebrate their faith, can be spiritually renewed in faith through the experience of small communities. It is through such renewal that the mission of Christ can be fostered and sustained with a deepening sense of commitment and indeed enthusiasm.

"The Parish as a Community"

Vatican II clearly states that "efforts . . . must be made to encourage a sense of community within the parish" (SC 42). In describing the role of the pastor in forming a genuine Christian community, the council also speaks of the community spirit embracing "not only the local church but the universal church." "The local community should not only promote the care of its own faithful, but, filled with the missionary zeal, it should also prepare the way to Christ for all" (PO 6).

Vatican II also notes that "no Christian community . . . can be built up unless it has its basis and center in the celebration of the most holy eucharist" (OT 6). The pastoral direction of the parish as a community of communities supports the centrality of the eucharist which builds up the larger community. Small communities in the parish provide people the opportunity to deepen faith, thus enriching the Sunday liturgy. Small communities create a balance of word and worship and through both lead people to works of charity, mutual help, missionary activity and different forms of Christian witness.

"Made Up of Many Small Communities"

There will be no renewal of the church without parish renewal. Too often people look beyond the parish for spiritual nourishment. The parish itself can be a powerhouse of spiritual renewal as small communities become rooted in the parish. Small faith-sharing communities are a great means of ongoing spiritual formation and growth. Not only will small communities help parishioners but they will also be at the service of the parish helping the entire parish to experience renewal.

The proposed pastoral direction fosters a style of parish life with a great variety of small communities. Therefore, we shall not attempt to state one concrete definition of small communities. We are not referring to covenanted communities nor to in-depth communities where people live under one dwelling. We shall speak only to parish-based communities of mobile people. Some of the small gatherings manifest deepening bonds of faith and mutual support, affirmation and strength. Probably small parish associations range from groups together for a specific purpose only to communities reflecting a broader concern for shared faith life through prayer, dialogue, mutual support, and community action. What we have found is a general movement toward community.

The pastoral direction does not imply that everything in the parish changes. Nor does it imply a pastoral burden of totally rearranging the parish into newly created communities. Many small groups and small communities are already in place. The modification of their style toward community will be enriching for all involved in these groups.

Those adopting the pastoral direction would encourage all parish small groups, committees, ministries, societies and organizations to adopt a more communal approach in their meetings. By incorporating the following elements of community building into their gatherings they begin to move from group to community: prayer, mutual support, sharing, mission and learning. (These elements are described in greater depth in Chapter 7.)

Groups becoming more communal and, in some instances, truly becoming communities will become a part of the ongoing lifestyle and structure of the parish. They will contribute to a more spiritually alive church and help parishioners to think and act more readily out of gospel values. Since small communities have the capacity to form and empower Christians for mission in a world crying out for the good news, can we not echo and heed Cardinal Bernardin's words?

> Let us create faith communities in the Catholic tradition where the active, the inactive, the unchurched, the young, the middle-aged, and the old will find life-transforming experiences of Jesus, prayer, Scripture, and community.[5]

It is just such small faith communities that are the heart of the proposed pastoral direction!

IMPLICATIONS OF THE PASTORAL DIRECTION FOR THE PARISH

In the remainder of this chapter we will highlight some of the implications of the parish as a community of small communities.[6] We will further sketch how the small basic communities urged by the 1987 synod and John Paul II, as well as other pastoral leaders, will influence the parish and why they ought to receive serious consideration as a pastoral approach for parishes.

Evangelization

> Embracing all the activity of the parish is a basic vocation and commitment to evangelization. This means not only calling active be-

lievers to ever deeper faith, but also bringing the message of Christ
to alienated Catholics, inviting people to join in the church's belief
and worship, and making the Gospel real by applying it to the issues
and conditions of our lives. The witness to the Gospel of Jesus ac-
quires power from the continual reflection on faith and its demands
to which parishioners devote themselves. Although the parish un-
dertakes special efforts to bring the Gospel of Christ to those not
active in the church community, it realizes that the most effective
instrument of evangelization is the parish's visible hospitality, its
vitality, and its own faithfulness to Christ.[7]

We believe that this call to evangelization can best be responded
to through small Christian communities. If parishes were a community
of communities they would be structured to do the work of evangelization. Parishes would not need an evangelization committee, a passing
event such as a rally, or a periodic evangelization program. Instead
they would constantly have people in small communities sharing faith,
speaking about gospel values, and gaining courage from small-community members to share with others such as the alienated or the
unchurched.

Christian hospitality, too, can be developed effectively in small
communities, providing a means for all parishioners, including newcomers and inquirers, to experience a friendly and gracious environment to support them in their faith life. Thus small communities
would become places of warm welcome.

In effect, if all small communities understood that evangelization
was intrinsic to their being Catholic Christians, then we would have
parishes that were well on their way to being evangelizing parishes.
Small communities would be a training place for that evangelization
process. No matter what their main focus (liturgy preparation, social
concerns, etc.) each would be about the work of evangelization. Christian community calls each person to the basic responsibility of evangelization. Leaders of small communities can be prepared to see that this
call is constantly being issued.

Let us now take a brief look at how the four aspects of evangelization as articulated by the U.S. bishops can be lived out through small
communities.

1. Calling Active Believers to Ever Deeper Faith

In small communities active believers challenge one another to
deeper faith through sharing prayer and their own faith stories in light
of the scriptures. Members of small communities have a unique capac-

ity to call forth the goodness and faith of one another at appropriate "teachable" or "transformable" moments. This is part of the process of being evangelized.

2. Bringing the Message of Christ to Alienated Catholics

Once people come to a deeper faith they usually want to share this with others. It is often easier for small-community members to invite an alienated Catholic to their small group than to any other place. The small community has been a stepping-stone for many to come back to the church.

3. Inviting People To Join in the Church's Belief and Worship

Once the alienated or even the unchurched have been a part of a small community for a period of time, they may seek to join in the church's belief and worship. If they do not do this on their own, small-community members can invite them to join, letting them know how welcome they would be, yet avoiding any pressure. If a person chooses to join the church, the small community can be a support as the person goes through the stages of the Rite of Christian Initiation of Adults.

4. Making the Gospel Real by Applying It to the Issues and Conditions of Our Lives

Small communities prepare people to share the gospel message and apply it to the real issues and conditions of their lives. In small communities people gain strength and courage to proclaim in word and deed their gospel values. This renewing action takes place not only within small communities but as members of these communities impact on the family, the marketplace and the world. In small communities people can trust others enough to think through the implications of the gospel and apply these to their world. Consider the following story.

Joe, a rising New York executive, was a member of a small community. Holding a position of responsibility in his corporation, he was influential with other corporate managers. For a long time he was a rather quiet member of his CFM group. Finally, after two years of praying and sharing with his small community, he gained the courage to go into work and challenge an unjust corporate policy. Joe could not have risked his career without the loving support of his community. No matter what the outcome at work, Joe knew he had his community to return to for love, support, and encouragement to live the gospel values he believed in.

It may be asked why the small community is an effective way of impacting on the world. What is the dynamic that takes place?

As the Christian community is always open, never closed-in upon itself, so small Christian communities are never closed-in but are always in the stance of being evangelized. Like the larger church, these communities, by being open, retain their freshness, vigor, and strength in order to proclaim the gospel. Small communities, therefore, both nourish the faith we have received and help us to be always open to the newness of God's word, the newness of God's revelation through creation and through our sisters and brothers.

The pastoral direction of a community of communities provides a means by which evangelization can be part of the fabric of parish life through ongoing action of more permanent small communities. As these communities grow in number, the parish will arrive at a most practical, concrete way to engage the average parishioner in the work of evangelization. (Chapter 14 will treat the topic of evangelization and small Christian communities in greater detail.)

Rite of Christian Initiation of Adults

One of the formal ways the church evangelizes is through the Rite of Christian Initiation of Adults. Small communities are an effective pastoral complement to the RCIA and its ecclesiology for parish life. The small community concept is integral to the process of Christian initiation so that inquirers and those seeking entrance into the faith do so, not in isolation but within a communion of believers. Small communities, therefore, provide an ideal setting for the pre-catechumenate or evangelization period and can easily be related to the other periods of the RCIA journey: catechumenate, purification and enlightenment, and mystagogy or post-baptismal catechesis. Small communities, as indicated earlier, create a welcoming environment for alienated and/or inactive Catholics by enabling them to discover within small groups the support needed to pray, to dialogue, to question, and to be strengthened for their journey of faith.

In this regard some parishes have in place a number of small communities which are prepared to receive and support those who are inquiring about the faith. In addition some parishes have begun a process called "Re-Membering Church" for those who have been alienated or felt alienated while remaining a part of the church. This process, too, uses the structure of small communities to create a welcoming, hospitable environment where hurts and feelings of alienation can be aired, where reconciliation becomes a possibility. (See Chapter 15 for additional information on Re-Membering Church.)

Consider the potential of a parish where there were many small communities, all of whose members had the mindset of outreach and welcome. Through these small communities we could easily experience the greatest instrument of evangelization our Catholic faith has yet utilized. (Chapter 15 addresses the RCIA and small communities more completely.)

Spiritual Growth

Although the concept of spiritual growth in small communities was explored in Chapter 3 we consider it here to reinforce its importance as an implication of the pastoral direction.

The most compelling reason for parish-based small communities is the spiritual growth that takes place in the lives of so many parishioners. Small Christian communities set a climate that is very favorable and helpful to individuals and to the parish community in experiencing spiritual renewal and a deeper relationship with God. Through the small community it appears that the grace of God touches lives in authentic and life-forming ways. Through the small-community process people are drawn to Christ and to Christian living in vibrant ways.

If small Christian communities challenge people in a gentle way to grow spiritually, then why should we not multiply that opportunity for as many as possible by adopting the pastoral direction of the parish as a community of small communities? Today there is a greater degree of readiness on the part of parishioners to become members of small communities than ever before. Therefore, the potential for a larger number of parishioners to be involved in a process of spiritual growth is greater than ever before. As small communities invite people to pray, to read and reflect upon the scriptures together, and to apply the word of God to daily life, they also call people to take ownership of their Christian faith in a more participatory way. A great synergistic flow of good will is created which can have a very positive impact upon the life of the parish, its ministries, its outreach, its worship, and the world in which we live.

Ministry

Today many people are involved in ministry without a good support base. Some experience a sense of burnout because they are constantly giving of themselves without receiving support in their spiritual life or ministry.

In a parish that adopts this pastoral direction, all those involved in ministries would be urged to incorporate the elements of community building previously mentioned—sharing, mutual support, prayer, learning and mission—into their ministry meetings. As small ministering communities develop, many diverse needs can be addressed. Peer ministry can take place within small communities. Individual members or the small ministering community itself can reach out to others in loving service. And because Christians are not called simply to be involved in church ministries, small communities offer special support for people to live their family and life commitments and to be about their work in the world. In our society a structure is needed in order to help people to remain faithful and to be quickened to action.

While individual ministries can certainly adopt the small community model, it makes better sense for the parish to adopt this pastoral direction, thus creating a climate in which all ministries are encouraged to consider their spiritual formation. When the parish leadership promotes this richer pastoral approach, those engaged in ministry will more easily and surely move to accept and adopt it. (Further implications of how the pastoral direction can enliven ministries will be explored in Chapter 7.)

Existing Structures

Existing structures in the parish, such as councils, ministries, or organizations, are supported and strengthened by a communal style of meeting. In addition new structures can be created by inviting parishioners to be part of newly formed small groups or small communities. This pastoral direction is certainly not a whole new way of being parish. It reminds us how the early church formed itself into small communities. It emphasizes a prayerful, communal style of being church for the whole parish.

Small Christian communities unify the spirit of the parish. This one common thread of small communities, woven throughout the parish in all its varied activities, has the potential to give marvelous new life and creative energy to every ministry and every aspect of parish life.

Mission

The pastoral direction of the parish as a community made up of many small communities is not only well-suited for life in our "secular" society but is essential to support people in their faith journey and missionary work.

The Decree on Church's Missionary Activity (Ad Gentes), which calls the work of evangelization the fundamental task of the people of God, invites all to undertake a profound interior renewal so that they may play their part in the missionary work of the church. (AG 35). As we have seen, small Christian communities have the capacity to prompt and sustain that profound interior renewal. They are of themselves places where the faithful are evangelized and formed as evangelizers to spread the gospel and participate in the transformation of the world.

Small Christian communities, therefore, do not exist for themselves alone, but to enable parishioners to participate more concretely in the mission of Jesus. "The mission of the parish is significantly enriched when it provides the people an opportunity to meet in smaller groups in which they can speak and better understand the meaning of their faith, and, by doing so, strengthen their commitment and celebrate their unity in Christ."[8]

In small communities people have the opportunity to observe various dimensions of the mission of Jesus, decide what aspect of the mission they can best participate in (based on their gifts and the needs or situations which arise), and then act on these decisions. If all small communities are formed for mission, evangelization, and justice and see these as intrinsic to their faith, what a marvelous transformation we would see in the church and the world.

This chapter calls for thinking big about something small. It calls for thinking in a big way about how the parish can be effected by the dynamism of many small Christian communities. Let us encourage imagination and creativity in this transformation!

Gary's Story

One individual whose life was touched by a small Christian community was able to expand his vision, to think big, and to influence many, particularly in the area of the development of lay leadership.

This man was Gary. At the age of twelve Gary received the only formal religious formation he would have in his lifetime. For two weeks Gary was instructed in the catechism and then received the sacraments of eucharist and confirmation.

When Gary first moved to his parish, he attended mass because of the staunch Catholic faith of his wife Monica. One of the parish priests invited Monica and Gary to participate in a small sharing group. As the young couple continued to meet with this small group, Gary's faith deepened and his gift for cutting through to the essentials became more and more apparent.

The following year Monica and Gary were encouraged to start a CFM group. They became the leader couple, responsible for visiting and inviting others to be part of their group and, later, leaders of all the CFM parish groups.

When the parish council was to be initiated, Gary became coordinator of a committee to prepare for it. For eighteen months this group of parishioners met with the pastor and staff to plan how to involve every spectrum of the parish in the formation of the council. As part of the preparation, people developed and wrote study materials based on the documents of Vatican II. Using his gift for writing, Gary contributed immensely to this project.

Gary had a wonderful way of challenging people. When three hundred signed up for small groups in preparation for initiating the council, Gary said, "That's not enough. Don't you think we should have gotten five hundred?" Gary said this not for the sake of numbers, but so that many more would have the experience of praying and learning through small groups. The challenge was met! Not five hundred but six hundred people were signed up to be part of the small-group reflection process. The small groups in the parish of which Gary and Monica were members had a great deal to do with the birth of RENEW. The roots of RENEW were planted and sprouted forth from this parish thirty years ago. Gary's challenge to think big is really part of the RENEW story.

Gary continued to be a leader. Extremely popular, exceedingly fair, he won the admiration of all. Gary was elected president of the parish council. He and Monica represented diocesan CFM groups on the Family Life Apostolate Board. Showing interest when the diocese was developing its pastoral council, Gary served on the planning committee and later was elected its first chairperson. Later, with a new archbishop, he served four more years as chairperson of the diocesan pastoral council. Gary continued to give untiringly of his service when called forth in many other capacities.

Gary had been formed by small communities when he studied and researched the documents of Vatican II. Respected by all, Gary was elected to the Regional Advisory Council and then the National Advisory Council for the National Conference of Catholic Bishops. From his humble beginnings Gary attained the highest elected office of the laity representing fifty million Catholics as chairperson of the Bishops' National Advisory Council.

In this capacity he was one of the advisors to the bishops in their writing of the pastoral *Economic Justice for All*. In seeking advisors, the bishops also contacted major firms to give their reaction to the pastorals. In an unusual turn of events, one of the firms contacted by the bishops' committee asked Gary to write its response. Gary was not only advising the bishops, but also advising those from whom the bishops were seeking advice. Who knows how far-reaching the influence of this one person was? In this instance Gary's spiritual and religious formation came from various small Christian communities and from Monica and their six children, his primary Christian community.

Gary died of cancer in September 1986. His small community wanted to remember him in a special way. They wrote letters to all of Gary's friends and associates and invited them to contribute to a memorial fund in Gary's name. More than seven thousand dollars were collected. The original intention of the community was to support Gary's youngest son, Tom, who was giving a year of service as a Georgetown student volunteer to the people of Samanco, Peru. The overwhelming response enabled the group to subsidize several students.

When Tom returned he wrote a letter to all who contributed. After recalling colorful memories of his amazing year with the young and the old, Tom closed his letter with these words:

> This brings me to the purpose of this letter, which is to thank you who believed enough in this program to support it. You did so for my father, which made the experience even more special for me. My father was someone who would have understood this program as you, his friends, have. I look at the long list of people who have contributed and I feel ashamed because I don't recognize all of the names. There are some I remember hearing only as a small boy, and others that I know very well—but I am struck by the mutual commitment to a shared community that goes far beyond the limits of this parish; a community that stretches around the world and beyond.

The small community of Monica and Gary, Dolores and Joe, Peggy and Art, Marilyn and Dan, in life and in death, continues to touch the world with their love.

CHAPTER 5

Approaches to Achieving the Pastoral Direction

Since every parish is unique, each will adopt its own way of implementing the vision of the parish as a community of many small communities. The successful implementation of the vision of the parish as a community of communities depends on two factors: (1) utilizing a combination of approaches, and (2) developing the core community which designs a precise parish plan and works it through to full implementation.

There will very likely be many kinds and varieties of small groups and/or small communities in each parish. There is need for more than one type of small community or one approach to implementing this pastoral plan. Flexibility is essential in meeting the pastoral circumstances of a wide variety of parishes. Therefore, from the many possible means of achieving the end, we propose three general approaches or categories as guideposts:

1. Seasonal small groups which provide parishioners the opportunity to meet periodically during the year to grow in their faith life;
2. Ministerial communities which provide those parishioners involved in specific ministries the environment needed for spiritual growth and support in order to grow effectively in their ministries;
3. Small Christian communities which provide parishioners the opportunity to meet on a regular basis for the purpose of calling one another to grow in openness to the gospel, transforming every area of their lives.

In our discussion of seasonal small groups, ministerial communities, and small Christian communities, we will try to highlight what is unique about each type of group or community and show why small Christian communities are an ideal to work toward.

Seasonal groups are purposely called "groups" because the style of meeting is not totally communal. The degree of commitment in shar-

ing is not as great as in small Christian communities. Bonds of friendship and support are not as strong as one would find in small Christian
communities where people come to know one another more profoundly. Yet great good comes from seasonal small groups. They provide a splendid opportunity for spiritual growth. Often those participating in seasonal groups begin to understand what community is and
experience a willingness to be open to community.

Ministerial communities help to move participants beyond the
experience of a "group" toward experiencing some of the basic elements of community—prayer, sharing, learning, mission, and mutual
support—while still placing its emphasis or focus on a particular
ministry.

Small Christian communities include the elements found in seasonal small groups and ministerial communities, but move beyond the
limitation of one specific ministry or a particular function. They are
aimed at a more integral and all-embracing experience of the gospel
way of life.

From one perspective these three groupings show a sense of progression toward the fullness of community, the third of which, small
Christian communities, shows a more complete understanding of
Christian community. Some parishes, in implementing the pastoral
direction, would even follow this order of developing, first, seasonal
groups, then approaching ministerial groups to adopt a more communal style, and, finally, promoting and establishing small Christian communities. Other parishes might start with all three approaches at the
same time or within the same year. It is not suggested that any one
approach by itself will necessarily develop the parish as a community
of many small communities; however, the use of a combination of
these three approaches will move a parish toward the fulfillment of its
goal of implementing the pastoral direction. Each parish will benefit
from studying these three approaches and setting realistic goals based
on the particular needs of the parish.

SEASONAL SMALL GROUPS

Providing opportunities for all parishioners to have a small group
experience is part of a massive approach toward developing the parish
as a community of small communities. Seasonal small groups provide
an opportunity for individuals to experience small groups for a limited
time, for example, during the six weeks of Lent. October–November,

Advent, Lent, and the Easter season are all appropriate times to invite people together in small groups. Lent is probably the best starting point because many parishioners are looking for a special way to prepare for the feast of the resurrection and the Easter season. Therefore, the Lenten season often seems to be the time when people are most willing to commit themselves to sharing in a small group.

Definition

A seasonal small group is a face to face gathering of six to twelve people who meet for a short period (four to six weeks) for the common purpose of growing in their faith life.

Purpose, Term, Challenge of Seasonal Small Groups

Seasonal small groups provide parishioners with both an opportunity to share faith and a supportive environment where spiritual growth can take place. The term of a seasonal group is usually a six week period in the autumn, in Lent, or in the Easter season, and a four week period during Advent. This experience can be repeated with new commitments made each time a group meets.

Providing seasonal opportunities may, in fact, be the best and least threatening way to give people a taste of a group that touches on small community. Many continue to meet seasonally in their small groups for years during autumn and during Lent. Bonds of friendship are strengthened, and they continue to support one another even during the times they are not meeting. For others, the seasonal experience furthers the desire to develop the communal experience in a deeper or more ongoing way. The members of the group may decide to focus on a particular ministry needed in the parish or larger community, and become a ministerial community, or they may decide to meet as a small Christian community in a regular way throughout the year, either weekly, every two weeks, or monthly.

The challenge for those who are in seasonal small groups is to move beyond the comfort level, to accept risk, and to move toward action and ministry. In other words, they are challenged to move to deeper levels of sharing, prayer, learning, mutual support, and mission.

Ministerial Communities

Another general category of small community can be called ministerial communities. Ministerial communities have great value in themselves and can also help people move toward small Christian communities as we have briefly described them (and will later describe them in more detail).

Small communities provide an ideal support for ministerial outreach. Jesus himself used a small community setting to prepare the apostles and disciples for ministry.

This special category of ministerial community does not imply that the other two approaches neglect ministry. Rather the development of ministerial communities is meant to focus on what already exists in abundance in most parishes, that is, all kinds of ministerial activity and committees. Parishes have put much creative energy into developing ministries, e.g. parish pastoral councils, social concerns committees, liturgy committees, etc. By helping these committees move toward being ministerial communities, parishioners can start to see the vision taking form without the overwhelming prospect of dismantling all the good that has already been accomplished or having to be about a whole new creation.

Definition

A ministerial community is a face to face gathering of approximately five to twelve people who meet on a regular basis with the common purpose of growing together in their faith life and supporting one another in a particular outreach or ministry.

Purpose, Term, Challenge of Ministerial Communities

The purpose of ministerial communities is to provide those parishioners involved in ministries the communal environment needed for support and spiritual growth. A good parish goal is to have all ministries in the parish come from a base of small community. If this goal is adopted, then each ministry group must clarify and agree to how they will live out each of the five elements of prayer, sharing, learning, mission, and mutual support.

Ideally there would be a stated length of time for each person in the ministerial community. Frequently this term is two years but could be renewed after evaluation or discernment. Often when people clearly state the length of time they are willing to be part of a ministerial community, there is greater commitment both to the ministry and to spiritual growth in the community.

As they strive to be a community, members of ministerial groups incorporate the five elements of community to a greater degree than is found in seasonal small groups. For example, it will be obvious that those in ministerial communities are striving to grow spiritually, especially through quality time spent in personal prayer as well as in prayer during their meetings. They are seeking to learn more about their faith and the skills needed for ministry. They are supporting one another more than previously in their lives and ministries. They are more at ease in sharing their faith. And lastly they are making a more conscious effort in their ministry to be about the mission of Jesus. Each of these five elements will be seen even more fully in small Christian communities where parishioners make a commitment to meet regularly and to grow together as a small faith community.

The challenge for those in ministerial communities is to deepen their sense of community, to develop in their specific ministry, and to begin to understand the ministerial implications of all areas of their lives (as we will later see are embraced by the small Christian communities).

SMALL CHRISTIAN COMMUNITIES

The particular type of small community that we shall be referring to as small Christian communities has particular characteristics that most completely embody what ministerial and seasonal small groups aspire to and have achieved to a degree.

Definition

A small Christian community is a face-to-face gathering of six to twelve people who invest time with one another for the common purpose of applying gospel values to every aspect of their lives.

These communities go beyond the limitation inherent in ministerial communities (that usually focus on particular ministries) and try to open members to see all of life as field for ministry. They move beyond a means of function to assume a style of relationship which speaks clearly about community. Moreover, whereas ministerial communities are usually just breaking into the experience of a communal style, small Christian communities, as they grow, explore greater depths of community.

Purpose, Term, Challenge of Small Christian Communities

The basic purpose of small Christian communities is to create an environment where people can grow in openness to the gospel, transforming every area of their lives. Members must initially have some understanding of this purpose in order to call one another forth in their spiritual growth. Through regular gatherings the full implications of being a small Christian community become increasingly apparent and challenging.

Those involved in small Christian communities commit themselves to meet on a regular basis: weekly, every two weeks, or monthly. Ideally individuals initially agree upon a three year commitment. This length of time allows them to develop the richness of community. After this period they reconsider whether they want to continue as a community.

The challenge for those in small Christian communities is to become increasingly wholehearted or unconditional in their commitment to the movement of God's Spirit within themselves, within one another, and within the world. They seek total openness to God's grace moving them to holistic spiritual growth.

Pastorally speaking, if small Christian communities were implemented in our parishes, they could make a significant change in our world. Small Christian communities can help parishioners take their call to holiness seriously and try to be more open to the Spirit of God working in them especially through their prayer and sacramental lives. They likewise enable people to start living out their faith more fully in the family, in the neighborhood, in the marketplace.

Why are small Christian communities an ideal to work toward? The mission of Jesus relates to every aspect of our lives—our work and ministry, our relationships in family and community, and our leisure times. If people lived the gospel fully in all concrete aspects of their lives, their lives would change and they would have a greater impact upon society.

Small Christian communities can help people to find time and space to pray and to think through a variety of life issues: family, neighborhood, community, parish, business, society, ecology, politics, economics, etc. Small Christian communities can help people to reflect

	Seasonal Small Groups	Ministerial Communities	Small Christian Communities
Definition	A face to face gathering of six to twelve people who meet for a short period (four to six weeks) for the common purpose of growing in their faith life.	A face to face gathering of approximately five to twelve people who meet on a regular basis with the common purpose of growing in their faith life and supporting one another in a particular outreach or ministry.	A face to face gathering of six to twelve people who invest time with one another for the common purpose of applying gospel values to every aspect of their lives.
Basic Purpose	To provide people an opportunity to share faith and a supportive environment where spiritual growth can take place during the various seasons.	To provide those parishioners involved in ministries the communal environment needed for support and spiritual growth.	To create an environment where people can grow in openness to the gospel, transforming every area of their lives.
Term	Usually six weeks, during the autumn, Lent or Easter season, four weeks during Advent.	Frequently two years, renewable after evaluation and/or discernment.	Usually three years, renewable after evaluation and discernment. Or the community may choose to divide, with each part taking in new members and starting new communities.
Challenge	To move beyond the comfort level, to accept risk, and to move toward action and ministry. In other words to move to deeper levels of sharing, prayer, learning, mutual support, and mission.	To deepen their sense of community, to develop in their specific ministry, and to begin to understand the ministerial implications of all areas of their lives.	To become increasingly wholehearted in their basic commitment to the movement of the Spirit within themselves, within one another, and within the world.

on the actual events of their lives as they experience them, to pray through them, to see any contradictions between their action and their stated values, to think through the Christian response to these events, and to move to appropriate positions and actions.

The communal style of meeting is a welcome relief from a totally task-oriented, busy, alienated, and even lonely life experienced by so many in our society today. The very way a small Christian community comes together already achieves much of its purpose. This communal style is in itself a way for the reign of God to be realized in our midst.

SUMMARY

The common purpose of seasonal small groups and ministerial communities is growth in the faith life of their members. In addition ministerial communities focus on the one "assigned" or favorite ministry. Constant challenge to growth, in the fuller sense of what it means to be a small Christian community, needs to be offered to these various groups. A balance needs to be achieved, therefore, in helping people to take ownership of and feel good about the commitments they have made in seasonal groups and ministerial communities, while at the same time challenging them to see the deeper gospel ways and call of the small Christian community.

The following chapters on seasonal small groups, ministerial communities, and small Christian communities will further expand our understanding of each while showing their interrelatedness. The variety shown here suggests the possibility of different combinations and a multiplicity of developmental approaches that could be utilized by a parish according to its circumstances. This variety and flexibility may offer more concretely realistic approaches than one uniform means to achieve this pastoral direction.

Many people will continue to progress through the three approaches presented here. The various ways that people are engaged in seasonal groups, extensively described in Chapter 6, obviously apply also to ministerial communities and small Christian communities. One approach builds on the other.

The formulation of a precise parish plan depends upon an understanding of basic approaches to small community formation and the work of a parish core community for small community development. Chapter 9 will offer guidance for the creation of a parish core community commissioned with the responsibility of small community development. Its tasks will be clearly delineated. The combination of clear guidance on parish-based small groups and communities plus the on-location creative planning and pastoral effort of the parish core community will result in a realistic and concrete plan for implementing small communities in the parish and developing the parish as a community made up of many small communities.

The accompanying chart summarizes the main aspects of the three types of groupings discussed in this chapter. It will serve as a good reference in understanding the differences among the three groups as well as the progression from seasonal groups to small Christian communities.

CHAPTER 6

Seasonal Small Groups

If the parish goal is to bring a large number of parishioners to experience community, then extensive efforts to introduce people to seasonal small groups must be made—both for their intrinsic value and for the implementation of a new pastoral direction. The methods suggested here for the development of seasonal small groups do not, therefore, stand in isolation but are very much part of the larger picture of developing the parish as a community of many small communities. All of the concrete means suggested here to involve parishioners in seasonal small groups are not only valuable in developing these groups, but can also be used in developing ministerial communities and small Christian communities.

Seasonal small groups serve a dual purpose. First, the groups, in themselves, offer a wonderful opportunity for spiritual growth for large numbers of people. Second, from the perspective of developing the parish as a community of many small communities, seasonal small groups offer initial steps in developing ministerial communities and small Christian communities. For example, seasonal small groups introduce people, perhaps for the first time, to the rich experience of faith sharing and give a taste of the possibilities open to them in ministerial or small Christian communities. Careful planning and implementation of seasonal small groups can reap a harvest of parish small communities in the future.

In order for a small group experience to be implemented for the entire parish, planning must begin about two months before the actual small group meetings are to be held. In parishes which do not have a core community, the parish staff and/or parish pastoral council need to form a "small group committee" which would be responsible for implementing this process. It is best if those who participate in this ministry do so in a communal and therefore supportive style. In moving toward the fullness of the vision of the parish as a community of communities, it is important to model the communal style in every way possible.

Such a committee is composed of five to ten parishioners who are able and willing to take responsibility for promoting and implementing the various aspects of seasonal small groups. One person serves as coordinator of the small group committee and also as a contact with parish staff, parish pastoral council, and small group leaders.

The following pages outline the responsibilities of such a committee and guide them in a step by step process to implement seasonal small groups in their parish.

The responsibilities of this committee fall into ten areas:

1. Establish a time line
2. Select materials
3. Publicize and communicate
4. Designate Sign-Up Sunday
5. Determine groups
6. Select and develop leaders
7. Designate Prayer Commitment Sunday
8. Evaluate small group experience
9. Hold a follow-up celebration
10. Evaluate the committee's work

At its first meeting the members of the small group committee discuss the above responsibilities and each member assumes responsibility for some area(s). A time-line is established and future meeting dates are scheduled. A check list is given at the end of this chapter to assist the work of the committee. (See Sample A at end of chapter.)

The ten areas of responsibility are described below.

1. TIME LINE

Establish a time line including dates for the following:

(a) Initial Small Group Committee*	Two months before small groups begin.
(b) Small Group Experience (Times given are for autumn or Lent.)	Begin first week of October for six weeks or week of Ash Wednesday through week before Holy Week.

* In parishes where a core community is in place, they will assume these responsibilities.

(c) Publicity and Communication	Begin at least four weeks prior to Sign-Up Sunday.
(d) Selection of Small Group Leaders	Four weeks prior to Sign-Up Sunday.
(e) Sign-Up Sunday	Two or three weeks prior to first week of small groups.
(f) Prayer Commitment Sunday	One week prior to beginning date for small groups.
(g) Leadership Development	Prior to or between Sign-Up Sunday and beginning date for small groups.
(h) Follow-Up Celebration	Soon after last week of small groups.

2. SELECTION OF MATERIALS

The small group committee is responsible for guiding the selection of the small group material. Booklets which incorporate five elements of Christian community (prayer, sharing, mutual support, learning, mission) are very helpful in the development of small groups. The small group committee is initially responsible for deciding what small group material is to be used. As the small groups continue meeting, they may wish to select their own materials with the guidance of the small group committee. The materials can be purchased by the parish and used by various small groups, or purchased by the small group members themselves.

3. PUBLICITY AND COMMUNICATION

Quality publicity and communication for the forthcoming small group effort is essential to parishioners' response to the invitation to join a seasonal small group. Parishioners with publishing or advertising expertise can be called upon to assist in this effort. In addition to a parish-wide invitation, existing groups such as school faculty, catechists, or single parent group members may be invited to meet for a small group experience for a period of time.

The following tasks to be accomplished together with a timeline are suggested to achieve maximum visibility while publicizing the event.

Publicity and Communication Time Line

Bulletin announcements	Each week for four weeks prior to Sign-Up Sunday
Pulpit announcements	Each week for three to four weeks prior to Sign-Up Sunday
Fliers, banners, letters to families, telephone	During the three or four week campaign prior to Sign-Up Sunday
Notice in a variety of local papers, including shoppers' newspapers; announcement on local radio station	Two weeks before Sign-Up Sunday
Communication with parish staff and pastoral council	Prior to and throughout process
Communication with leaders of every committee, organization, ministry and group in the parish	Immediately after first small group committee meeting

4. SIGN-UP SUNDAY

Designating one Sunday as "Sign-Up Sunday" is a very effective means to invite parishioners to be part of small groups. As indicated in the time line, Sign-Up Sunday is held two or three weeks before the small groups are scheduled to begin. The responsibilities for those working with this aspect include the following:

- select a speaker for Sign-Up Sunday;
- select and prepare persons to assist on Sign-Up Sunday;
- design, distribute, and collect sign-up cards;
- involve other parish groups in this effort.

Sign-Up Sunday Talk

During the eucharistic liturgies on Sign-Up Sunday, an invitation is extended to parishioners to sign up for small groups for the four or six week period. This invitation includes an explanation of why people join small groups, witnessing to the benefits of small group participation and the sign-up process.

The invitation can be made in the context of the homily or after the homily by one or two of the parishioners. It is desirable for the pastor to speak of his own conviction regarding the value of small communities and his desire to have everyone participate in small groups. He then introduces the person who will speak and encourage parishioners to participate in small groups.

Small Groups

The speaker explains that eight to twelve people gather in someone's home once a week for the six weeks of Lent (or October–November, etc.) and states the week they will begin (e.g. the week of Ash Wednesday, the first week in October, etc.). The speaker holds up the booklet to be used and tells the people it will be available for small groups and provides prayer, scripture reading, sharing questions.

The speaker also stresses that the atmosphere for small groups is relaxed, that no one will be forced to talk but each person will be respected. This will allay any fears that small group gatherings are sensitivity groups.

Motivation

People are attracted to a direct spiritual approach. The factors that most motivate people to join small groups are cited:

- satisfying our hunger for getting to know God better;
- meeting new people and being strengthened by these Christian friendships;
- growing as persons and improving ourselves;
- making the world a better place;
- making a difference through God's gracious action in one's life.

Witnessing to the Value of Small Groups

The most effective way to encourage others to sign up for a small group is through personal witnessing. Getting the right person to speak and to witness is important. Parishioners with high credibility in the parish who have been in a small group experience and can speak clearly with conviction and enthusiasm ought to be chosen. A team approach including a woman and a man will prove very effective. In order to encourage men as well as women to join small groups, it is important that one witness be a man. When parishioners share enthusiastically their experience of being a part of a small group, hearts are touched. Some starters which may be used follow:

"At first I was afraid . . ."
"Being in the small group has given me more self-confidence."
". . . has made Jesus more real in my life."
". . . has given me the strength to cope with a specific situation."
". . . has helped me live my faith at work."

Sign-Up Process

Toward the end of the talk the speaker pauses, holds up a sign-up card, and asks people to pick up a sign-up card and pencil in the pew. The speaker then invites all present to sign their names and indicate what day or night of the week is best for them to participate in this important activity. People are also asked to check if they are willing to host a small group.

- Allow time for people to fill out card.
- Tell people the ministers of hospitality will collect cards.

After an appropriate interval invite the ushers or the ministers of hospitality to collect cards. (If any people need more time, they may, if time allows, take cards home and return them to the rectory within the week.)

Sign-Up Cards

Prior to Sign-Up Sunday, sign-up cards are designed and printed. Included on this card is space for people to write their name, address, telephone number, and the times they are available for small group meetings. It is also wise to include on this card space for people to volunteer to host a small group. (See Sample B at end of chapter.)

In addition, if sign-up cards are to be mailed later to others who have not registered, the return address of the parish ought to be included.

Sheets and pencils are placed in pews before each mass and are collected by ministers of hospitality or other designated persons.

Support for Speakers

The person responsible for Sign-Up Sunday invites the other members of the small group committee to gather together in a small room before or during part of each mass to pray for the homilists and speakers and for the success of their efforts.

The small group committee members can also meet with the speakers after each mass to give their critique. This allows for further refinement or development of the talk between masses. Usually with this help the speaker gets progressively better as the day goes on.

Involving Others

Creative ways to involve parishioners generate a good spirit in the parish. Existing parish committees/ministries might be helpful and also feel more a part of the parish-wide effort to hold the small group experience if they are invited to help with some details of implementation. For example, the liturgical ministry might highlight the theme of "community" during the Sign-Up Sunday liturgy. The communication ministry might lend assistance with publicity, and the catechetical ministry might want to support the small group experience as an adult enrichment experience.

5. DETERMINE GROUPS

Immediately after sign-up cards are collected, the names of those who indicated their desire to participate are arranged into groups according to their stated time preference. It is possible that while trying to accommodate each person's choice there may not be enough people to form a group at a particular time. The committee then has to do extra work by calling and renegotiating with them to arrive at an agreeable meeting date and time. When this has been completed, those who have been selected and trained as leaders are assigned a group.

Lists are prepared for each leader with names, addresses, and telephone numbers of their group members together with the meeting time and place. If it is later discovered that a group is without a leader, a member of the group is invited to assume the role of leader. In the event that this happens there should be personal preparation of this leader.

6. LEADERSHIP TRAINING

Leadership training takes place before Sign-Up Sunday or at least two weeks before small groups begin to meet. The time needed for training is approximately four hours, usually two evening sessions of two hours each. A committee member, pastor, or a diocesan staff person facilitates the training sessions. (See Resource A of *Resources* for outline of sessions.)

Included in the training session are the following:

- prayer and faith sharing, based upon the scriptures;
- discussion of how to lead a small group;
- reflection of the responsibilities of being a small group leader;
- basic skills in using scripture;
- overview of booklets to be used;
- distribution of list of names, addresses, and telephone numbers of people in each leader's group (if not already done);
- distribution of booklets to leaders; the leaders can deliver booklets to their small group members before the first meeting;
- confirmation that each group has a meeting time and place which the leaders will communicate to their respective small group members (if not already done);
- explanation of small group evaluation and follow-up celebration;
- basic guide for small group leaders.

When leaders are given the list of people in their respective groups they are told to meet the people and give them the materials to be used. Many sign-up for small groups and never go to the first meeting. Perhaps they have fears which override their genuine desire to attend. The best way to avoid this occurrence is to have leaders visit the people in their group between Sign-Up Sunday and the actual first meeting date.

When leaders visit new participants in their own home, they are doing much more than handing over booklets or materials to be used. They are bearers of hospitality, warmth, welcoming, kindness, and caring. They carry the spirit of the parish to each home. There they can establish relationships immediately and can work through any difficulties their group members may have, e.g. getting someone to babysit or stay with sick or elderly family members, getting a ride to the small group meeting, etc.

When members are given in advance the materials they will use at their small group meeting, they will have time to reflect on the scriptures and questions to be used in the first session. This may also allay any apprehensions a member may have about being in the faith sharing group.

Many times leaders need encouragement to take the initiative to visit small group members in their own homes. It is not always easy dealing with the unknown. However, it is far better to extend oneself

before the first meeting than to be disappointed later when participants do not attend.

Leaders can be supported in this effort by the core community or
the small group coordinating committee. For example, leaders can
meet in groups of twos to role play, introducing themselves and welcoming their small group participants; they can be urged to prayerfully
prepare to meet their participants, etc.

7. PRAYER COMMITMENT SUNDAY

Prayer Commitment Sunday gives everyone an opportunity to be
part of the ongoing spiritual renewal of the parish by participating in a
prayer network. A prayer network is simply a group of people who are
bonded together by their commitment to pray for the renewal of the
parish during the seasons when small groups are held. The prayer network has the role of ensuring a strong prayer base for all small group
activity.

The invitation to participate is given on Prayer Commitment
Sunday, one week prior to the date for small groups to begin. Both the
celebrant and a member of the small group coordinating committee
may issue the invitation.

No matter what one's obligations or schedule might be, all are able
to be part of a massive prayer effort for the renewal of the parish.
Announcements in the parish bulletin and at the Sunday liturgy one
week prior to Prayer Commitment Sunday will alert people and prepare them to make a serious prayer commitment. On Prayer Commitment Sunday commitment cards and pencils are available in pews or at
church doors. The commitment cards need not elicit names or addresses. Sample C (at the end of this chapter) shows a prayer commitment card which may be copied or adapted for your parish. Completed
cards may be collected by the ministers of hospitality or placed in
baskets at the doors of the church after the financial collection.

8. SMALL GROUP EVALUATION/FOLLOW-UP

During the last session of the small group's seasonal gathering the
leader asks the members to evaluate their small group experience and
to consider becoming part of an ongoing faith sharing group. The written evaluation (see Sample D at the end of this chapter) is forwarded to
the small group committee together with the names of those who wish

to continue to meet in a faith sharing group on an ongoing basis. In addition other needs might surface, e.g. some might want a retreat day or evening and others might desire scripture study.

9. FOLLOW-UP CELEBRATION

Soon after the last small group meeting, participants in all small groups come together for a celebration. This session includes prayer, a time of sharing and witnessing, a time for refreshments, and a time for looking ahead.

Someone may give a presentation challenging those who participated in small groups to become involved in a particular ministry. Persons knowledgeable about ministerial communities may be invited to share their insights, the needs of the parish, and how these needs are being met through outreach. Those who wish to sign up for a ministry or a ministerial community are encouraged to do so. Those who wish to continue with their small groups are encouraged to resume meeting. Some may choose to be part of a small Christian community. Small group materials may be on display for perusal or someone could speak about available materials.

10. COMMITTEE EVALUATION

After studying the small group evaluations and experiencing the follow-up celebration, the small group committee meets to evaluate the small group experience and to discuss future plans. If a parish staff person is not present, committee members need to present the evaluation and projected plans to the pastor. This is an opportune time to explore and begin the development of a core community if one is not already in place.

Other Opportunities

- An evening of reflection for all small group participants during the small group sessions could be held to encourage the groups and show their unity with the parish.
- A meeting with small group leaders during the sessions and/or after the follow-up celebration is recommended to give them the opportunity to discuss their experiences. This time would also enable the small group committee to affirm the ministry of the leaders as well as to discover

the strengths and the areas to be strengthened either now or in future training sessions of small group leaders. If this meeting is held after the small group sessions, those interested in being small group leaders could express their availability and willingness to serve in the future. In addition, they could name members of their small groups who have the potential for being small group leaders in the future.

- A special evening could be held to explore further how groups could move into ministry.

Multiplication of Small Groups

Small groups can split or multiply in diverse ways. Some examples are given below which can be encouraged or adopted by each parish.

Every group leader finds an assistant within the group to share the leadership. The assistant leader is encouraged during a period of training to bring friends and prospects to the group he or she is in. After a period of time, e.g. six months, the assistant leader and friends spin off and form a new group. The original group leader seeks out a new assistant, and the cycle repeats itself.

Groups are encouraged to reach out to new people and invite them to their group. When their group reaches twelve members, they are challenged to divide and grow. Those using this model have discovered that healthy groups "give birth" to new groups. Groups that do not grow and multiply often have relational problems or other difficulties.

In church work we like to count numbers. However, an overemphasis on the multiplication of groups might lead to a certain amount of superficiality in the quality of these groups, especially in the area of mission.

CONCLUSION

As valuable as the experience of seasonal small groups may be, they obviously fall far short of the real potential for growth that small communities offer. Participants must now be challenged to move beyond the personal benefits of group faith sharing and connect this experience to their work of ministry in the parish or in other areas of their lives. Indeed, they are called to reflect on the implications of ministering in all of life's situations.

Our next chapter will explore the concept of ministerial communities and give some practical helps in developing them.

SAMPLE A

SEASONAL SMALL GROUP EXPERIENCE CHECK LIST

Small Group Committee

List names and telephone numbers of committee members on the back.

Dates for Small Group Committee meetings _____

Dates for parish-wide small group meetings _____

1. *Publicity*

   • what has to be done _____

   _____

   • by whom _____

   • when _____

2. *Sign-Up Sunday*

   • date _____

   • what has to be done _____

   _____

   • by whom _____

3. *Selection of Materials*

   • what has to be done _____

   _____

   • by whom _____

   • when _____

4. *Determining Groups*

- when _____

- where _____

- by whom _____

5. *Leadership Training*

- what has to be done _____

  _____

- by whom _____

- when _____

- where _____

6. *Prayer Commitment Sunday*

- date _____

- what has to be done _____

  _____

- by whom _____

7. *Follow-Up Celebration*

- what has to be done _____

  _____

- by whom _____

- when _____

- where _____

8. *Evaluation of People in Groups*

   - how _____

   - when _____

   - where _____

9. *Evaluation Committee*

   - how _____

   - when _____

   - where _____

SAMPLE B

SIGN-UP CARD

PLEASE INDICATE YOUR FIRST AND SECOND CHOICES FOR MEETING TIMES. (We will try our best to accommodate you.)

	Morning	Afternoon	Evening	Evening
	Adults			*H. S. Students*
Sun.	_____	_____	_____	_____
Mon.	_____	_____	_____	_____
Tues.	_____	_____	_____	_____
Wed.	_____	_____	_____	_____
Thurs.	_____	_____	_____	_____
Fri.	_____	_____	_____	_____
Sat.	_____	_____	_____	_____

_____ YES, I would like the small group (8 to 10 people) to meet in my home. (Scripture sharing booklets will be supplied.)

NAME _____

ADDRESS _____

TELEPHONE _____

SAMPLE C

Prayer Commitment Card

In order to ask God's blessings on our parish efforts at spiritual renewal, I promise the following:

- Attend one weekday mass   ———

- Offer one day of fasting and prayer   ———

- Prayerfully read the scripture readings for the following Sunday   ———

- Read and pray with the scriptures 15 minutes each day   ———

- Say the rosary once a week or each day   ———

- Other   ———

- Pray the following prayer each day   ———

Prayer to the Holy Spirit

Come, Holy Spirit, fill the hearts of the faithful. Enkindle the parish community of ———————————— with the fire of your love. Send forth your Spirit and we shall be created and you shall renew the face of the earth. Amen.

SAMPLE D

SEASONAL SMALL GROUP EVALUATION

(1) What were the strengths of your small group experience?

(2) How do you feel the small group experience can be improved?

(3) Of the *five elements of community* named below, which was most operative in your small group? Circle the appropriate one.

PRAYER   SHARING   MISSION

SUPPORT   LEARNING

(4) Which of the five elements did you feel needs to be more developed in your small group and why? Circle the appropriate one.

PRAYER   SHARING   MISSION

SUPPORT   LEARNING

(As a result of meeting in a seasonal small group, some parishioners express the desire to continue to meet on a regular basis either with the same group or with another group of people. We call those groups which meet regularly for the purpose of applying gospel values to every aspect of their lives small Christian communities.)

(5) Would you like to meet regularly in a small Christian community? If so, circle the appropriate frequency.

WEEKLY   ONCE EVERY TWO WEEKS   MONTHLY

(6) Other Comments

_____

Your Name

CHAPTER 7

Ministerial Communities

When we consider that the parish does not exist for itself but for the mission of Christ and that people are called forth to minister to one another in the parish community as well as to those around them where they live and work, we may very well ask, "How can we best enable people to minister?"

As mentioned earlier, small communities are being experienced as a means of deepening the spiritual life for many people today which prompts them to express their faith in action. The same principles which support small Christian community development can easily be applied to every parish group or ministry. In other words the elements of community building—sharing, mutual support, prayer, mission, and learning—can gradually be incorporated into every parish gathering or meeting. When groups consistently strive to include these elements in their meeting we say they are developing a communal style of meeting. When the value of a communal style as a base for ministry is clearly seen, then the development of all new ministries would likewise follow the model and be ministerial communities.

FROM COMMITTEE TO COMMUNITY

A close examination of the parish reveals a wide range of already existing parish groups, committees, organizations, societies, and ministries.

Many of these groups, though small in number and specific in purpose, are not communities. They are frequently groups or committees of people who come together more for a function than as a way of life. The parishioners in these committees are often highly motivated and are extremely hard working. Unfortunately some committee meetings are so task oriented they lack a sense of community.

Since a comparatively large number of people are involved in parish committees or ministries, the parish could easily begin to develop in a more communal direction by encouraging a greater sense of community in committees, ministry groups, parish staffs, RENEW small groups, peace teams, parish pastoral councils, Holy Name Societies, etc. It could be asked: Why move from committee meetings as we have known them in the past to a more communal style of meeting? The following explanations offer some insights.

- Many people who are committed to ministry also desire to grow personally and receive the support that comes from Christian community in order to continue effectively their ministry. Effective ministry includes awareness of the church's role in the world and the need to serve its mission.
- The ministries themselves will be more effective since they will flow from people who know the life and power that come from Christian community. The ministers will bring that life and energy to their ministry efforts.
- More people are willing to respond to the call to minister and continue in that call if they know that they will not simply be involved in a task, but that there will be a greater opportunity for them to grow spiritually.
- Many who engage in a prayerful, communal style of ministry experience that the task which needs to be accomplished not only is completed more quickly but also is accomplished in a spirit of greater joy and peace.

Parishioners, once having adopted the pastoral direction of the parish as a community of communities, realize the benefit of having all groups in the parish move toward community. Therefore, they encourage basic elements of community building—sharing, learning, mission, mutual support, and prayer—to be gradually incorporated into all parish committees concerned with ministerial service.

How Do Ministerial Communities Develop?

How do we encourage ministry groups within a parish to develop a more communal lifestyle? Significant to the development of ministerial communities are core community members and pastoral staffs who are convinced of the value of giving all those who minister an opportunity to grow spiritually through their ministry groups or committees. Once core community and staff members have themselves experienced a communal style of working together, they will speak more authentically and convincingly to others and be better able to motivate them to incorporate into their meetings and lives the five elements of community. The concepts of invitation and motivation are key factors in the development of ministerial communities. The groups or committees that can be approached include current parish committees/ministries, other small sharing groups, special interest groups, and short-term ministries. In addition, when the parish starts new ministries, they can begin immediately by using the five elements.

PARISH COMMITTEES OR MINISTRIES

Some parishes may wish to implement the pastoral direction in a gradual manner by identifying and working with one or more current parish committees that seem ready to implement this approach. Other parishes may begin by taking a broader approach and inviting all those involved in parish committees or ministries to an evening of reflection.

First let us look at how one would approach a current parish committee. Members of the core community may speak to the chairperson of the group in simple terms of incorporating into their meeting a time of prayer and a period of scripture sharing. In this way the parish is gradually bringing about a new style of parish activity. The members are encouraged to accept the fact that God will bless their work if they are more prayerful. A period of twenty minutes to a half hour at each meeting will contribute immensely to a greater prayerfulness in the group. A simple process could be used. The group would choose a scripture passage. After reading it and allowing some time for reflection, they would share what it means to them. The group can look at the implications of the reading in light of the circumstances coming up during the week. They can make applications for their particular ministry and then take some time for prayer together. As a group adopts this style it usually approaches its task in a spirit of faith and with a greater sense of support from one another.

Second, let us look at the possibility of holding an evening of reflection for all parishioners involved in ministries or committees. After the invitation has been sent out and responses received, the core community can arrange for those involved in the same ministry to sit together, preferably at round tables.

The agenda would include the following elements:

- welcome;
- a time of prayer and faith sharing;

- an explanation of the elements of community building;
- a reflection process to help participants examine their present ministries in light of the five elements;
- a time for each ministerial group to strategize how it can grow in each of these elements;
- a time for interested groups to make a commitment to develop a more communal style of meeting.

Either at this time or when ministry groups set goals and objectives for their mission or outreach, they can use the "Reflection Process on Five Elements of Christian Community" (which appears in *Resources*). This process can help determine which areas of community growth need strengthening. For example, committee or ministry groups which have as their focus social concerns, public relations, or finances may choose more time for prayer and sharing. Committees or ministry groups which focus on prayer, spiritual life, or worship may already spend time in prayer and sharing scripture, so they may decide to spend more time on learning or outreach.

OTHER SMALL SHARING GROUPS

In addition to ministerial communities, there may be other groups, such as small faith-sharing groups or Bible-study groups in the parish that have met for several years. They, too, can be approached and told about the benefits of incorporating the elements of community into their gatherings. Obviously, they will already be using one or more of these elements. Some groups may recognize that they as a group are called to ministry. They may have seen the need in their parish for a particular ministry, e.g. to the bereaved, to the elderly, to youth, to the homeless. After approaching the pastor and parish pastoral council about their ideas for beginning this ministry and receiving approval, they, too, can begin to incorporate into their meetings any of the elements not already present in order to provide the strength of community for their own lives and for their new ministry.

NEW MINISTRIES

When a parish starts new ministries, the core community can encourage those who will be working in these ministries to form ministerial communities from the beginning and not simply task-oriented committees. By integrating the five elements into their meetings, these groups will begin to be ministerial communities from their inception.

Several examples are given below. They simply show how new ministries may come into existence either by forming small communities for a specific ministerial outreach or by inviting existing small groups to assume a more communal style and a particular ministry.

Hospital Visitation

A small community could be formed to visit a hospital or nursing home in the name of the parish. The support, spiritual nourishment, and ongoing learning which people receive from their meeting as a small community can give greater vitality to these hospital/nursing home visits. This process can also help to make the volunteers more pastorally sensitive.

Hospitality

A small community could assume the ministry of hospitality. This ministry is multi-dimensional. For example, ministers of hospitality enrich the community experience of Sunday eucharist by welcoming the people who gather. In addition, they assume the role of reaching out by personal visitation to all new members in the name of the parish community. Their own involvement in a small community will help them to experience hospitality and strengthen them for reaching out to others. At the time of their visits they may present new parishioners with a booklet or brochure outlining all the services and opportunities of parish life, invite them to join a small group to meet other people, or simply be available to answer questions. By linking new as well as long-term members of the parish together, ministers of hospitality continue to foster the spirit of unity within the larger community.

Social Concerns

A small community may take on a ministry of direct service, e.g. collecting food or clothing for the needy, cooking meals for soup kitchens, or sheltering the homeless in church facilities or their own homes.

In addition to specific social concerns ministries where people are involved in direct service to others, small ministerial communities could be involved in action for systemic change. They may also pray about and study contemporary issues and church teachings and advocate for the homeless, the needy, or the oppressed.

The Elderly and Homebound

A small community might decide that more attention and care needs to be given to the elderly and the homebound. They might explore "Meals on Wheels," home visitation, shopping, transportation, and companionship needs of these parishioners. They would meet periodically to pray, to share ideas, and to support one another. During the liturgical seasons of Advent and Lent, they could lead a small sharing group in the home of one of the homebound or elderly.

Family Life

Many are concerned about the future of family life. A small community that prays and shares together could volunteer to work in building up family life in general, or in specific areas, such as instructing couples in preparation for marriage, assisting couples who are separated or divorced, helping to teach natural family planning, or promoting programs to foster parent/youth relationships. In addition, specific groups, e.g. Right to Life groups, could work on all aspects of community development.

Visiting Parents of Children (School)

A small community could visit and encourage parents of school children to take a more active interest in the parish and outline the various ways this could happen. The parents themselves could be asked to form a small group and explore the ministry of parenting. Visits by members of the small group could encourage parents of school children to explore church-related activities.

SPECIAL INTEREST GROUPS

Special interest groups, for example, Bible study groups, prayer groups, Pax Christi groups, Cursillo groups, Marriage Encounter groups, teachers, adult catechetical classes and catechumens, meet regularly because of a common interest or experience. Although the particular focus of these groups differs, their development as small communities is similar to that of ministry groups within the parish. While maintaining their unique focus (prayer, study, married life, a particular outreach, etc.) they could reach agreement as to how each of these elements would be integrated into their style of meeting or ministry.

Ministerial communities are ideally suited for teachers and catechists who recognize that the spark of religious living is ignited by the gift of faith. Learning assists religious faith, as St. Paul attests: "Keep on doing what you have learned and received and heard and seen in me. Then the God of peace will be with you" (Phil 4:9). In the sharing of faith among teachers and catechists the fire of the Holy Spirit engenders new life. Imagine the glorious impact upon students if teachers and catechists across the land centered their lives upon a loving and active relationship with Christ!

The reason for citing the above examples is obviously not simply to mention ministries, more fully explained elsewhere, but rather to consider the enriched possibilities of these ministries coming from a strong communal base.

SHORT-TERM MINISTRIES

Some ministries, for example, the ministry to the separated and divorced people in the church, are short-term ministries. People remain a part of these ministries while dealing with the trauma of transition from married life to single life. Although the term is short for those in need of ministry, there is usually an ongoing ministry group in the parish that schedules, organizes, and offers hospitality for them. The separated and divorced could find in a small supportive setting others with whom they can share their hurts and struggles. In realizing that others have gone through similar traumas they often find courage and healing and resolve to begin their lives in a new way. The Parish Project's Final Report on *Parish Life in the United States* claims that the features of this ministry are worth looking at for their relevance to other group ministries or peer ministries. When this ministry is well conducted seven basic traits are revealed:

1. *Critical issue.* Obviously the groups deal with a life-defining or shaping moment in people's lives.

2. *The whole issue.* Well done, the ministry allows for consideration of all aspects of the issue: psychological, social, legal, familial, religious, ecclesiastical and the like.

3. *Peer ministry.* Basically, people in the same experience minister to one another.

4. *Context of the church.* This peer ministry operates within the context of the church, its theology and worship, its ministry and broader support.

5. *Expertise.* The ministry can draw on relevant expertise when necessary (e.g. canon lawyers, psychologists, etc.).

6. *Reconciliation.* The ministry assures people of their worth and enables people to restore some wholeness to their lives.

7. *Clear norms.* Because the ministry accepts people as they are, it helps them to remain clear about ideals (e.g. of permanent marriage) and not minimize ideals out of defensiveness.[1]

These same traits could be used to fashion other small group ministries within the parish, for example, the ministry to the bereaved. Those who suffered the loss of a loved one—spouse, parent, child, relative, or friend—often feel isolated and need time and support to deal with their loss. Those involved in ministry to the bereaved can invite those who have recently lost loved ones to gather in a small group setting. Here through prayer and sharing, peer ministry again takes place as memories are recalled and tears are shed as part of the grieving and healing process.

BENEFITS OF COMMUNITIES

Many ministerial communities in the parish would contribute tremendously to the parish and beyond. Some benefits have already been stated in the preceding examples. Still others are revealed in the following examples.

A very important benefit would be that all ministries, committees, organizations would be more prayerful and imbued with the spirit of Jesus and his mission as envisioned by the church. Through prayer and scripture sharing an openness to the Holy Spirit would be encouraged in all parish deliberations. Parishioners formed through ministerial communities have added preparation to assume leadership roles within the parish, in the larger church, and in society.

If a parish strove to be a community of many small communities, worship would be enlivened by the depth of faith of all those participating. Liturgical ministers could gather in their respective ministry groupings to plan and evaluate their ministries. At the same time they would also pray and support one another. Ministers of the word, celebrants, eucharistic ministers, ministers of hospitality, the music director and choir or folk group, altar servers—all would feel a greater sense of community and communicate this to the worshiping congregation.

While family constitutes the most fundamental unit of church according to Vatican II, its very life would be strengthened in a variety of ways through support received in small communities. Parents trying to live and teach Christian values in their families would be strengthened in their endeavor when supported by others in peer ministry living the same values. Children, too, would benefit from small community support. Children suffering the loss of a parent through separation, divorce, or death or who have always been part of a single parent family benefit from the communal relations of their single parent. Yet many find a place to talk about their loss and receive support in small groups, e.g. in a program such as "Rainbows for All God's Children." The small community can become extended family for them.

Children experiencing catechesis in a small community setting often feel freer to pray, to question and to discuss their faith. Often a small community for children takes on a particular outreach (in the same way a larger group does) such as visiting the sick or making favors for nursing homes, running errands, or raking leaves for homebound persons.

More than periodic reunions are needed to follow through with teenage or young adult weekend retreat experiences (Antioch, Search, Crossroads, etc.). If small communities were implemented to complement these experiences young people would be helped to live out what they learned and experienced in an ongoing supportive atmosphere. Often young people return from these weekends full of enthusiasm, having made or renewed their commitment to Christ. Support is needed to sustain this commitment, and peer support is most influential for youth. A sound pastoral approach is to strengthen this conversion experience within small community follow-through and in periodic reunions of the larger group.

High school and college students alike would find support in a small community where they could talk through something they heard in class, a moral issue, their vocation, etc. Young people growing up in this style of church would have greater appreciation and ownership of faith. They would more easily feel a sense of belonging and most probably would remain a vital part of our parish communities.

Sick and aged people in their own homes, nursing homes, and hospitals would no longer say: "I used to be a parishioner in 'Hope Springs' parish." They would still be parishioners. They would know it, feel it, and experience it as ministers to the sick, homebound and elderly visited, prayed and shared with them. Some of their needs would be met by their friends in ministerial communities. They would no longer worry about who would drive them to stores or doctors' offices, help with meals, pick them up, or accompany them to the communal anointing of the sick. They could call upon their ministerial community friends as an extension of their family.

No longer would the unknown or forgotten parishioner have no one present at his or her mass of Christian burial, or, worse, be buried without any liturgical service. In a parish of small communities, hope-fully, everyone would either be a part of a community or would be touched by the loving outreach of ministerial community members. No one would be unknown or forgotten! Community is as important today as it was in the time of Jesus' own ministry. No one is meant to be alone.

Mindy's Story

Mindy and John were involved in a parish catechetical ministry in Colorado where several parents joined together to teach their own children the Catholic faith. Later they moved to Georgia, and because of the pleading of their three small children they began a similar ministry in their parish. Mindy reveals some of what this experience meant for her family and for others involved. In effect this is a ministerial community. Listen to Mindy's own words.

"After the first year we started to rely on each other and the six families became an 'aunts and uncles, cousins, nieces and nephews' sort of relationship. I can truly relate that to our prayers. We always started with a prayer—each person had a chance to state a special intention or thanksgiving as we went around the circle. So we learned to share our trials and triumphs—an important lesson for adults and children. I personally felt a lot of growth in this area. One of the fathers in our group would not be a part of the circle or teach or even be in the same room when we were doing anything religious. His wife has a deep faith and was able to pass that along to their daughter and still maintain a good relationship with him. After a year, he would come to someone else's house, and after a year and a half he would join hands and state his intention. By the time they came to visit us in Georgia,

they said they would go to the parish dances and socials and he loves
Friday night fish fries at the church. I truly believe he was able to see
other guys [fathers] say prayers and show their faith, and he now feels
more secure to share his growing faith. We were also there for them
when they lost their child to crib death. They felt the loving comfort of
our priest and our group helping them get through that time. We see
that his gradual acceptance of our faith is occurring. So our Colorado
group was a spiritual springboard for adults. If one of us had read a
good book we passed it around. Four of the six families had a non-
Catholic spouse, and they all taught (with the exception of the one
mentioned above). I think they were learning along with their children.

"Our children were delighted with the program. They would get
up in the morning and say, 'Do we get to go to our small community
today?' If it was 'yes,' the next question was, 'Do we have to go to big
church?' The answer: 'Yes, that's the part that starts it off right.' And if
their friends were at mass they were happy and relatively well behaved.
Support for the young is just as important as it is for us. I have often felt
that if the 'fallen away' had felt they had their friends there also, they
never would have left. But then they also have to get involved—a
commitment which comes from within."

From this excerpt of Mindy's story we realize the potential for
spiritual growth for children and adults alike when ministry comes
from a base of community.

SUMMARY

All committees or ministry groups which strive for balance in
incorporating into their meetings five elements of community building
are growing more in Christian community themselves and are contributing to the development of the parish as a community of communities. When this approach of the pastoral direction is implemented, it
enables many parishioners to be involved in ministry and, therefore,
many more people to be ministered to both within and beyond the
parish.

In Chapter 8 we will consider the basic commitment of those who
belong to small Christian communities, a detailed description of five
elements of community, and some concrete helps for implementing
small Christian communities in the parish.

CHAPTER 8

Small Christian Communities

Those parishes which adopt this pastoral direction realize the tremendous potential for spiritual growth and evangelization which small Christian communities afford. Therefore they make the opportunity to belong to a small Christian community a normative part of parish life much like religious education, sacramental preparation, and other parish experiences. Although seasonal small groups and ministerial communities offer countless opportunities for parishioners, ongoing small Christian communities still present an ideal to work toward. For it is in ongoing small Christian communities that people are especially helped to know and relate to one another, reflect on their life of faith in the company of others, and strive to apply the gospel to daily life.

GOD BUILDS COMMUNITY

Those involved in small Christian communities often realize that although they make a sincere effort to share community, it is actually God who calls us to community and God who builds community. In fact, community itself is

> first and foremost a gift of the Holy Spirit, not built upon mutual compatibility, shared affection or common interests, but upon having received the same divine breath, having been given a heart set aflame by the same divine fire and having been embraced by the same divine love. It is God-within who brings us into communion with each other and makes us one.[1]

The parish, however, can nurture community and help to create the environment where community happens. One pastor who has helped to develop small Christian communities in his parish describes their value:

Small Christian communities serve a parish in ways that are unique. The environment that includes prayer, caring friendship, learning more about faith, and reaching out to others is like an incubator to each of its members. For those who are new to the parish, it provides a sense of welcome and acceptance without the demands of organized ministry. For the person who wants to grow, it is an environment where experiences can be shared without confrontation and learned through personal insight. It can be a place where people who are burned out can be nurtured while experiencing new directions in faith life. In short, the small Christian community atmosphere is one in which one can relate, refocus, reflect, reform and personally contribute to the renewal of the world through faith in action.[2]

Those who join ongoing small Christian communities use the community experience to integrate a deep spirituality into every aspect of their lives rather than to center on a specific ministry. This spirituality finds expression in a basic commitment to God which we will briefly explore.

COMMITMENT OF SMALL CHRISTIAN COMMUNITY MEMBERS

Small Christian community members make a basic commitment to nurture faithfully a deeper relationship with God. People become part of small Christian communities for various reasons. Some enter into these communities with a clear understanding of the commitment. More often, they begin with general good will and a basic understanding that the small community is going to call them to a deeper spirituality and a more loving care for people. Gradually, through participation in the small Christian community, they come to realize, appreciate, and accept the very full commitment that is called for in these communities. When those in small Christian communities are faithful to this commitment the Spirit of God will be active in their lives and they will be prayerful, in good relationship with others, and committed to a better world.

Donal Dorr in his book *Spirituality and Justice* writes convincingly of the need for a balanced spirituality based on Micah 6:8. He speaks of three major spheres of spirituality: the personal, the interpersonal, and the public spheres. Simply outlined, he makes the following correlation.

Walk humbly with your God—personal relationship with God
Love tenderly—the interpersonal aspect
Act justly—the area of public life[3]

This correlation is an excellent way to remember the threefold commitment to which Christians are called. The basic commitment of being faithful to the Spirit of God in our lives is expressed in a personal relationship to God, a relationship with one another, and a relationship with the larger community (from the parish to the world). Together these three expressions indicate a commitment to spiritual growth and point toward a balanced spirituality. In a very real way these expressions are three aspects of the conversion process. Our spirituality must be rooted not just in one or two of these aspects, but in all three.

Although each expression of this commitment is integrally related to the others, it is appropriate to take each expression separately and examine its many facets.

Faithfulness to God

In small Christian communities people are called to seek God above all else and make the effort to grow in a personal, loving relationship with God. Since God ultimately is the source of community, it follows that people in small Christian communities are called to be deeply in touch with that source if they are going to become a community where the power of the Spirit is more fully alive. Put simply, am I able to say that I have a personal relationship with Jesus? Is that evident to others by the way I live out my life? When I awake in the morning how long is it before I consciously think of God? How often do I reflect on God's presence during the course of the day and how much does that relationship influence my decisions and actions?

Small Christian communities can help members express their commitment to God in a variety of ways. Through these communities members encourage one another to live in God's presence and develop their relationship with God. They challenge one another to see God in all people and live out that awareness especially in relationship to the seemingly less attractive, to the poor, the oppressed. They urge one another to find many other ways of expressing their faithfulness to God: by setting aside a specific amount of time each day for personal prayer and scripture reading, by developing a mature Catholic life through sound learning and reading, by embracing an integrated spirituality.

Faithfulness to One Another

When parishioners agree to be part of a small Christian community, they also agree to support the other members in living gospel values. This support is not just for crisis times but is often necessary on a daily basis. Small Christian communities call for a deep sense of mutual support so that people, in caring for each other, will grow in their ability to sense and rejoice in another's happiness and accomplishments as well as to detect any depression or frayed emotions.

They try to enable the other to speak about a difficult experience so as to uncover its root cause. Such personal caring will help people whose jobs are in jeopardy by helping them to find new employment, will help parents who are experiencing difficulties in raising children, will reach out in times of sickness and grief and times of celebration.

When small community members are committed to one another they will do extraordinary things. They will spend hours or days with a sick person in a member's family; they will help them to move or to build a home; they will adjust their own plans and schedules to join in a spontaneous celebration of an unanticipated joy. Because lasting spiritual relationships are formed in small communities, members begin to look upon one another as family. If perchance someone in the community dies and there are no close relatives, the members of the community might even have such a sense of responsibility that they would offer to assume responsibility for raising the children that were left.

Community demands openness to people as they really are, not as we would like to see them. In the early honeymoon stage of community people tend to idealize one another. As they continue to meet, they begin to know one another's faults and shortcomings as well as the good qualities. The real challenge is to remain open and patient with one another as irritating qualities surface.

When someone's aggressiveness or anger shows, friends need to be able to listen not only to the words spoken but also to the whole person (for example, voice inflection, body posture, facial expression) and then respond appropriately. Through active listening and loving responses members help, encourage, and effectively challenge one another. When members are truly committed to one another, trust, love, and honesty can eventually carry them beyond their difficulties and/or self-centeredness to new and deeper levels of relationship.

When looking at the qualities which community calls forth, it becomes evident that forgiveness is often the most difficult of all. It is easy to support one another when all is going well. The test of Christian community is the willingness to forgive and overcome deep hurts, and the willingness to be forgiven. Christian community is called to be the "forgiving community of the forgiven."[4] Forgiveness does not let hurts grow. When members of a small Christian community are committed to one another they need to review regularly how they relate to one another.

Accountability to one another has very practical implications. Among them is the responsibility of coming to meetings prepared. One aspect of preparation is praying during the week so that one brings the richness of God's Spirit to the meeting. If any neglect preparation frequently, they are called to their responsibilities by the others in a gentle, encouraging way. Members can be challenged while still affirming their goodness. To encourage and to challenge one another are not merely good things to do; such actions are at the heart of authentic Christian community.

Faithfulness to the Larger Community

Within this expression of the commitment to the larger community are two areas: the broader one of the world, the more focused one of the parish. Each will be considered in turn.

Parishioners often do not extend themselves beyond the parochial community, but rather confine their outreach to parish interests, activities, ministries. We will begin by reflecting on our commitment to the world first, in order to highlight the responsibilities of small Christian community members to reach out beyond the parish.

World

Commitment to the world means that small Christian community members strive to live and proclaim the gospel in every area of their lives. This brings the gospel into the family, the neighborhood, the marketplace, into areas of community life and politics, and eventually into every aspect of society—local, national, international!

Commitment to the world also means that small Christian community members have awareness about what is going on in distant places as they do about what is going on in their own area or country. Our interest in problems in our own neighborhood, city or town is often related to wider national and international problems. Through reflection and analysis members of small communities can become more knowledgeable about these linkages and about the basic unity of the human family.

Being committed to the world also means struggling to realize that all people are sisters and brothers. It means remembering them at prayer times, learning what can be done to address unjust structures, and acting to make this world a better place.

Parish

The small Christian community's mission to the larger community includes being part of the parish and part of the larger Catholic community. When members of small Christian communities do reach out in these areas they avoid the danger of becoming a closed group. When small Christian communities have a sense of mission there is less chance that they will be seen as elitist or separatist or in their own little church. Part of that mission is to be in service to the larger parish, the diocesan church, and the wider Catholic community.

The parish Sunday liturgical celebration is where all the people in small Christian communities come together with the other parishioners. Here it is extremely important that small community members reach out to other parishioners with a sense of hospitality. Hopefully, people will be able to say, "Look at these people in small Christian communities—see how they love one another and how they love us. What value there must be in what they are about." Small Christian community members can provide a beautiful welcome for the alienated, the stranger, the newcomer.

Members of small Christian communities need a wide vision to see where gospel values can be applied. From that vision they can discern where to put their efforts and where to advocate that others in the parish or in the larger community use their gifts.

In effect small Christian communities call people to respond to life-issues because the gospel, which has taken root in their hearts and minds, seeks expression. It creates in them an interest in making a better society and fostering the reign of God among us!

ESSENTIAL ELEMENTS OF COMMUNITY

In developing small Christian communities we emphasize five essential signs of communal life: sharing, learning, mutual support, mission, and prayer. These elements express a spirituality that acknowledges complete dependence upon God for creation of community. The use of these elements also helps to assure the growth of vital community while providing a structured format for meetings.

These elements are certainly not all-inclusive, nor do they attempt to fully define small Christian communities. They are listed not as static qualities but are intended to convey a sense of movement. The dynamic of small Christian communities is living, ever-growing and always deepening.

1. Sharing

Sharing means talking freely about God and about life experiences and reflecting on these in the light of scripture and tradition.

In an atmosphere of trust, members share the meaning of faith and the scriptures and reflect on how that faith and the scriptures relate to their life experiences. Often this sharing results in more profound insight and in strengthening the belief of others in the small community. As the realities of people's lives are brought forth they are measured against the word of God which becomes a two-edged sword demanding new hearts, attitudes and actions.

Personal sharing of faith empowers, challenges, and helps to transform lives. If people want to be in community, they have to be willing to share. Their commitment to one another implies a sense of openness. They make a conscious effort to build up the trust level within the community. Sharing in small communities encourages others to speak and often motivates people to change some aspect of their lives. In this setting people are often challenged to be totally responsive to the Lord. The role of the leader is key to helping people be open to meaningful communication, although all are responsible to make the effort and to draw others into sharing scripture, faith, prayer, and life experience.

In small Christian communities, attitudes are developed which carry over into every aspect of life. As these communities become life-sharing communities, lasting spiritual relationships are formed.

Consider the example of Monica who was deeply saddened at the news that her friend Dolores had several inoperable, malignant tumors. Reminiscing about their past, Monica recalled how their being part of a small Christian community for twenty-five years helped them cut through all the superficialities of life and get to the heart of the matter—Jesus. Monica's words, "We aren't just friends, we are spiritual sisters," show the powerful and profound relationships developed in small Christian communities.

2. Learning

Because small Christian communities are part of the wider church they are called to an ever fuller knowledge and understanding of the gospel, of the Catholic Church and its teaching on faith and morals, and of the relationship of that teaching to the circumstances and issues of their lives.

The term "learning" is deliberately used to connote a broad sense of learning. It includes catechesis, i.e. religious instruction for those already baptized; skills, e.g. communication and leadership skills; learning about the faith, gifts, and needs of others in the small community; learning about the parish, local, national, and international situations; learning simple methods of social analysis, etc.

The truly Catholic life of faith recognizes faith as a gift of God which comes, at the same time, from the faith life of others. Through scripture and tradition, as they have been kept alive and applied by the church community and its teaching authority over the centuries, faith is nourished and matures. Small community members are aided in their journey by the teaching of the church which offers an authoritative guide as they search the scriptures.

Small Christian communities have the responsibility of being knowledgeable about their faith. Catechesis can take place in and through small communities. For example, materials can be used which cover the formational importance of scripture, the nature of the church, the significance of the sacraments, the primacy of eucharist, and the basic call to holiness and mission. The very nature of small communities also calls for members to have a clear understanding of their role and connectedness with the larger parish, diocese, and universal church.

Through catechesis small community members can become more aware of how God is revealed in the world, in scripture, in the church, and in their own personal lives. As Christian people journey together to maturity in faith, learning also provides the means for discovering and developing gifts, discerning how gifts are to be used for others, and recognizing the diversity of roles that God has given, so that the body of Christ may grow to full stature. Commitment to learning acknowledges that the Christian is a seeker after truth and awakens the learner to the reality that one can never exhaust all there is to discover of the wonders of God, life, and the universe.

Because of the discipline and time required, realistic ways to learn are needed. If a small Christian community member hears a lecture on prayer, takes a course on scripture or theology, reads a good book, listens to a tape, attends a workshop, or participates in a peace march, and then shares some of the information received, the whole group will grow in knowledge. Some small communities decide to read an article pertinent to their life of faith and discuss it together. Others invite a speaker to the small community or to the parish to address an area of interest. Some parishes are discovering the importance of developing a resource library.

One of the most helpful ways for a small Christian community to grow in knowledge is to make a commitment to a long-term process of Christian formation. (See *Called To Lead: Leadership Development in a Small Community Context,* the companion volume to this work, for such a process.)

3. Mutual Support

In a society in which gospel values are all too frequently ridiculed and rejected, the believer needs a community which is supportive of these values. The small Christian community encourages fidelity to the gospel and also challenges itself and its members to a more profound and authentic commitment to Christian living.

Support systems that once existed, such as the extended family, the neighborhood, and the secure job, are for the most part gone. The church has found it difficult to provide a structure that offers sufficient support. In a society that tends toward hopelessness and self-concern, Christians need the encouragement and support of others who share their belief in God.

Some parishioners who desire to grow spiritually realize that they can do this best in a small community where they have the support of others. In fact, an experience of Christian community is becoming all the more necessary for the Christian who desires a deep faith life.

As individuals pray and share in their small communities the quality of the support they offer one another will grow. They come to know one another better and are more aware of both spoken and unspoken messages.

This support can be expressed in the form of mutual correction. When people truly want to grow, they are open to receive suggestions or corrections from others. They also gain courage to speak the truth in love as they offer their suggestions or corrections to others.

Mutual support flows very naturally out of prayer and sharing in a small community. It expresses itself in friendship, commitment, caring, and service. It is a response to Christ's call to love our neighbor as ourselves. Mutual support speaks to our human longing to be loved, encouraged, needed, respected, and challenged.

Marita, who had been in a small community for a year, spoke of the support she felt. "In that time," she said, "it's unbelievable. If something went wrong, I could pick up the phone and know I'd get help. I'd know that you, Sal, Chris, Frank . . . would help. You would do it without thinking twice. That's the beauty of community."

Mutual support can be the simple expression of letting a person know someone is only a telephone call away; it can be a promise to remember someone in prayer; it can be more concrete in helping a person with studies or work or ministry. Mutual support may even be offering financial assistance to a community member in need. The kind of support needed in any given situation will become evident through the prayer and sharing that take place in the small community setting.

As people meet in small Christian communities they grow in their support to one another. As their trust level increases, so, too, do the situations and events, beliefs and values, dreams and hopes they share. As these words are spoken people come to new realizations of how they can be more supportive. People who share community start to know they can count on one another in joyful and difficult times.

The following story illustrates the point more clearly. Bill, a member of a small group for some time, was troubled because his teenage daughter had run away from home and there was no indication as to where she was. He was so terribly upset, ashamed, and embarrassed that he told no one in his small community. One night Ed shared about his teenage daughter—she too had run away. Bill was totally disarmed by Ed's sharing. That sharing opened him up to a new experience and appreciation of the support of his community. The entire small community helped both men to express their feelings, tried to comfort them, prayed with them, and promised to support them in their search for their daughters.

(Much of what could be said under "Mutual Support" was expressed earlier under "Commitment to One Another." Those discussing or evaluating these five elements within their small Christian communities would do well to review that section.)

4. Mission

Authentic Christian communities are, like Jesus, committed to a life of loving mission or service. As a group and through its individual members, the community will work for compassion, justice, reconciliation, and peace within the group, in the family, in the workplace, in the neighborhood, and within the wider society.

The purpose of forming a small Christian community is to help people live more like Christ. Jesus both preached and lived a message that had social implications. He said that his followers would be known by their works, by how they love one another. Jesus' own example challenges us to feed the hungry, clothe the naked, comfort the afflicted, be life-giving to others. A small Christian community's journey together includes reaching out and serving the needs of others.

Mission or outreach provides a way for people to respond to their desire to make the world a better place. Mission includes direct service to others, advocacy, and commitment to systemic change. The realm of mission includes everyday life in family, work, civic community, parish as well as every area of human endeavor to which our lives are connected.

Small Christian communities differ from social, discussion, or study groups. Through the support received in their small Christian community, members strive to reflect gospel values in every aspect of their lives. They are not simply about service, but about being conscious in their daily lives of the implications of the mission of Jesus. For example, someone may be the primary care-giver for an elderly parent and through this care may come to see how the system deals with the elderly with regard to medical benefits, housing, Social Security, etc. He or she may then choose to put efforts into replacing an unjust order or policy with one that gives greater opportunity to the elderly.

Someone else may be working for a corporation that is failing to pay a living wage to its workers in the third world. Challenging that person to think through this situation and work to change the unjust policy may require much prayer, study, reflection, sharing, and support. To act on such an issue may cause many repercussions. The person risks losing position, salary, status, perhaps even a part of his or her identity. Community support after the person has acted on his or her convictions may be even more necessary and valuable than the support given previously.

In addition to individual life situations, small Christian communities can study, pray, and discern how to move beyond their local situations to address the needs of the wider community and the world, particularly the needs of the poor. Not only do needs have to be addressed but also the underlying causes of those needs. An examination by the community of a particular situation may uncover unjust policies that need to be addressed. Community members support one another in this effort to uncover and act upon both personal and structural injustice. Through their reflection and prayer they gain new insights about how they can bring the gospel message to bear on their decisions.

The very flow of communal meetings should be leading the small community to action decisions whereby they will be about the work of mission. The process of sharing can start with general concern, move people to reflection on their personal experience in relationship to that concern, and then logically enough to a point of deciding "what they are going to do" about the concern. The leader and all the community members themselves are vigilant in seeing that the community comes to a resolution of specific action. That sense of responsibility carries over to the next meeting when people report on how they carried out their intended mission action.

Hopefully the day will soon arrive when the notion of community cannot be spoken of without the implicit understanding of mission. In the long run small Christian communities will probably be judged more than anything else by their success (or failure) in carrying out mission.

5. Prayer

The element of prayer emphasizes the centrality of God's active presence in each small Christian community member's life and in the life of the community itself.

Prayer—both personal and communal—is emphasized here as a means of spiritual growth. One's prayer life and how one lives out the whole of life are very much related to the growth of small community.

As people open their hearts in prayer, they very often seek a deeper relationship with the triune God and with others. Prayer is an honest acknowledgement of our dependency on God's grace and of our inability to create community and be about mission by ourselves.

As community develops people must be constantly challenged to grow in their individual prayer lives and in communal prayer. Those coming to a community meeting can only contribute from the richness of their daily lives. The community offers a wonderful opportunity to learn more about prayer and to establish an accountability to one another that encourages growth in daily prayer.

In praying together the small community consciously opens itself to God's gracious action. As the community prays together, there can be a keen sense of that presence and a greater willingness to acknowledge dependence on God and on one another. In small Christian communities, then, people come to know God more profoundly—God who is at once near and distant, loving and yet hidden in mystery. The environment and dynamic of small Christian communities provide both a transcendental and an experiential dimension for participants to discover God through prayer, sharing, and outreach: transcendental in the search for God who remains mystery; experiential in discovering Christ in the midst of two or three or more gathered in God's name.

A wide variety of prayer forms—from quiet centering prayer to praying the Liturgy of the Hours, the official prayer of the church—are available today. Prayer can be as simple as learning to read scripture prayerfully and reflectively, perhaps taking one passage or one line at a time, savoring the word, letting it sink into one's heart and make its home there. The daily examen (a sample is included in the sessions on prayer in *Called To Lead*) can be an extremely effective way to become more conscious of the presence of God. In this practice one invokes the Spirit to see where God has been at work in one's life and where one has failed to be present to God. The use of the examen is a very beautiful and practical way to close one's day.

In a small Christian community setting members can share the prayer forms they use. By sharing how they pray, members can teach and inspire one another to develop new styles of prayer which may lead to a greater intimacy with God. Sharing about their prayer life at meetings can encourage all to be more faithful to prayer. In the small Christian community's atmosphere of trust, people may even feel free to admit that they have not been praying—an admission which may be the starting point in developing a prayer life. (See Chapter 17 for further reflection on prayer forms.)

Some may seek spiritual direction to assist them in their spiritual journeys. In this way they are enabled to look at the totality of their lives with a person experienced and knowledgeable about the spiritual life. Often through spiritual conversation with another, the "blind spots" of one's life are brought to greater consciousness, one is in greater touch with the conversion process in one's life, and a more profound sense of God acting in one's life is gained. At their gatherings small Christian community members can discuss the benefits of having a spiritual friend or spiritual director who shares a person's spiritual journey.

A small Christian community may occasionally bring in a guest speaker or hold an evening of reflection. By so doing they share a common experience which can be a springboard for further growth in the spiritual life. At a day of reflection they also have the opportunity to take quiet time to reflect on the quality of their life as a small Christian community.

Members can greatly benefit from spiritual reading and daily reflection on the scriptures. They can share and exchange spiritual books which they have read and recommend books and tapes to one another. Members can also call one another to frequent participation in the sacraments of penance and eucharist where they can encounter Christ in profound ways!

At their meetings participants can share the commitments they have made to spiritual growth since they last met, and how faithful they were to their commitments. In this way they become accountable to one another and challenge one another to growth.

In addition to the above practices small Christian community members can prepare for their meetings by prayerful reflection upon God's action in their lives since the last meeting and by attentiveness to the scriptures and other readings to be discussed during the session.

Through prayer small Christian community members acknowledge that the good they accomplished is a reflection of the presence of God.

As each of the above elements is incorporated into the daily life of the small Christian community members, spiritual growth will take place. The quality of small Christian community members' daily lives, how they live out their relationships, how they allow God's Spirit to operate in their everyday lives—all of these reflect on how God can act in a small community setting.

As participants share the commitments they have made to spiritual growth since they last met, and how faithful they were to their commitments, they become accountable to one another and challenge one another to further growth. They realize how directly God's action is involved in the creation of community and how deliberate must be their choice for deeper union with God for the realization of true Christian community.

HOW DO SMALL CHRISTIAN COMMUNITIES DEVELOP?

Key factors in developing small Christian communities include a wide range of actions.

Invite, Motivate, Witness

Among the first actions would be issuing an invitation to people to become part of a small Christian community. When this invitation is accompanied by some form of witnessing or sharing, people are more highly motivated to respond to the invitation. Sharing the value and beauty of small Christian communities and appealing to reasons why people are drawn to them can help to motivate people. Communicating a sense of what it means to be part of a small Christian community may effectively motivate others.

Develop Leaders

A second key factor in developing small Christian communities is leadership development. Once small community leaders understand their role and responsibilities, a major part of developing small communities has begun. Through their leadership they will help members to use a structured format in their gatherings based on the five elements of community. Gradually they will help members to understand their commitment to nurturing a deeper relationship with God. Together the leaders and small community members can explore how faithfulness to this commitment can lead them to be more prayerful, to build a good relationship with each other, and to be effective in working for a better world.

Establish a Core Community

The careful development of a core community would see to the above two areas as well as many others which would include providing ongoing pastoral care of leaders and suggesting resource materials appropriate for small Christian communities. (See Chapter 9 for other areas of responsibility.)

Give Support

Another important factor in developing and sustaining small Christian communities is staff support. Parishioners need to know that the pastor and staff believe in and encourage small Christian communities.

Since many of these and other aspects of developing small Christian communities are dealt with in different parts of this book, let us comment in more detail here on two aspects: (1) issuing an invitation and (2) support by staff.

1. Issuing an Invitation

The core community can encourage the development of small Christian communities in a variety of ways.

After the seasonal small group experience, participants are invited to complete an *evaluation form.* This form briefly explains the nature of small Christian communities. One question asks if parishioners would like to continue meeting on a regular basis in the style of a small Christian community. While completing the evaluation the entire group or some members may respond affirmatively and decide they would like to continue together. If there are sufficient members to continue as a small Christian community, their leader can help them decide on the most convenient time and inform the core community. If the number who wish to continue as a small Christian community is small, the core may arrange for others to join with them.

After holding seasonal groups, a core community may have a *follow-up celebration,* for example a pot-luck supper followed by time for sharing and witnessing by small group participants. Or at a large group gathering of all ministerial communities, the core community can ask for some time to speak with those involved in ministries. At such celebrations the core community can give a brief explanation of the nature of small Christian communities and issue the invitation to continue meeting on a more regular basis as a small Christian community. Sign-up cards may be distributed so that participants can choose the most convenient time to meet.

In addition the core community may extend a *parish-wide invitation* for people to become part of a small Christian community. This may be done at the Sunday liturgy or at a parish day of listening and planning where an explanation of the call to small Christian community is explained. Those who have been part of small Christian communities can be asked to witness to the movement of the Spirit in their lives through their experience. Parishioners can indicate their desire to be part of a small Christian community by completing a sign-up card. Those attracted to be part of small Christian communities can go directly into them.

In all of the above named cases parishioners are then grouped according to the times they have chosen to meet.

Other small Christian communities develop as a result of an *individual's suggestion or invitation.* The person issuing the invitation may be a member of the pastoral staff, a core community member, or a parishioner. The invitation may be given personally to an individual parishioner or to a group of parishioners.

For example, a pastoral leader can invite a group of parishioners together to talk about what it means to be a Christian. This simple invitation may interest and intrigue people since it is a call to meet new people, to grow with others, and to influence society.

Those who begin or join small Christian communities have various expectations and understandings. Some who respond to the invitation to small Christian community involvement come with a very rudimentary understanding of the commitments involved. They may start with a general willingness to see what small Christian community is about and gradually grow in *understanding the commitments* involved in small Christian community.

Others may begin with a very clear realization and appreciation of the full concept of small Christian communities and the commitments that will be involved, and be willing to grow through this experience.

Still others, who are invited after being involved in seasonal small groups or ministerial communities, may already see the importance of the basic communal approach bearing on all aspects of their life and the need for deeper commitments and respond in a wholehearted way. The initial experience they had reveals the depth of possibilities for spiritual growth, support and mission, and motivates and challenges them to continue as a small Christian community.

2. Support by the Staff

Small Christian communities need the guidance of the teaching church. As people discover or rediscover the power of the gospel, the teaching church can help them understand the true and full meaning of

God's word. Guidance from the pastoral staff and the use of good resources can help strengthen the understanding of our Catholic faith and tradition.

People in small Christian communities need to receive encouragement from parish leadership. People are basically good and often need some form of encouragement to put their goodness into action. Parish leadership is in an ideal position to offer such encouragement.

Small Christian communities need to experience a sense of belonging. Members of small Christian communities need to feel part of a larger believing, praying, celebrating, missionary church community. They need to be reminded by the staff that they are part of a long tradition in the church and that they have a role to play in the church. "They need to be tied into the life of the whole parish and they need to be kept from becoming self-enclosed cliques. This support from outside can help groups to be open to new members, to reach beyond themselves and to take leadership in forming other groups."[5]

SUMMARY

In these last three chapters we have looked at three related means which the parish can use in the process of becoming a community of small communities:

1. Inviting all parishioners to participate in seasonal small groups during the fall and/or Advent and Lent;
2. Encouraging all ministries to come from a base of community by developing ministerial communities;
3. Providing opportunities for all parishioners to be part of parish-based, ongoing small Christian communities.

In order to extend these opportunities for spiritual growth for all parishioners we recommend that a core community for small community development be established. In Chapter 9 we will explore this idea in detail. In addition we have included a six session process in *Resources* to assist the parish in the formation of a core community. (See Resource D.)

Let us close with Ann's story as told by her friend, which captures a sacred moment in the life of one small Christian community.

Ann's Story as Told by Her Friend

Our small community had gathered in my living room as we do every week to pray, share the scriptures, and make connections to our own lives. We quieted ourselves through sharing of spontaneous prayer and then someone read the gospel passage for the coming week. The faith sharing started in the direction of what it means to be a lost sheep. As the sharing went on, I looked to my left and saw my dear friend, Ann, begin to cry. Silently. No noise. Just streams of tears cascading down her face.

I was frozen. Ann and I talk every day. I thought, "My God, what could have happened since yesterday to make this very private, down to earth, perfectly together woman react like this right now?". . . "Just be with her," I thought. "Let her decide whether to share." "Oh God," I prayed, "be with her and help us to be present to her." No one commented on the fact that Ann was so visibly upset, but the miracle of the moment began to unfold as everyone in the room continued to share but gave Ann every opening to talk.

It became a climate of super sensitivity—serious conversation mixed with laughter. Ann was laughing too, and everyone was letting her set the direction of conversation. Still, she did not say what was the cause of her tears until we were ready to close the meeting with prayer and someone said, "Ann, I noticed that you were upset. Is there anything that we can do?"

"I hadn't planned on coming tonight because the day was so hard," she said, "but something made me come here. I thought I could handle it all by myself. Today I signed the divorce agreement and I saw twenty-five years of marriage go down the drain. I heard my husband say, 'I don't want to be married anymore.' We had so hoped that he would come back to us—but he's not. I feel so lost—just like that sheep in the gospel story."

As she continued to share, I was more than ever certain that healing was taking place; the dying and the rising that we remember about the death of Jesus and that we live over and over again in our own lives. It is not only the good things that we do in memory of him. It is the moments of resurrection that we also do in memory of him not only by choice, but as part of life.

It was an honor and a privilege to share that moment with Ann, and to end the evening with prayer for her husband, for her, and for all the lost sheep of the world—for the times when each of us feels lost and for the wisdom to allow ourselves to participate in God's time to gift us with newfound life.

Ann continues to be her usual "together" self as she moves forward in her life, but says she will never forget the love that she experienced that night, and neither will we. We are all different people now.

CHAPTER 9

Core Community Development

The implementation of the vision of the parish as a community of many small communities will certainly need to be a responsibility shared by committed people. Pastors and other pastoral staff members will probably be reluctant to embrace this direction if the full weight of its implementation rests with them. Therefore, it is recommended that a core community for small community development be started to foster opportunities for developing the parish as a community of small communities and to ensure a sound development of these communities. In this community willing parishioners are united with pastor and staff in a spirit of collaboration.

Since a core community of committed, prayerful people can work wonders for a parish adopting the pastoral direction, we will offer specific guidelines for the selection of the core community and outline its role and responsibilities. In addition a formation process for developing a core community is outlined here. The six sessions of the process can be found in the accompanying book, *Resources.* The parish staff will find these sessions helpful when they begin to form a core community. In the process of using these sessions, those chosen for the core begin to experience for themselves what it means to be a small ministering community.

DEFINITION OF A CORE COMMUNITY

A core community is a group of six to ten parishioners who come together to form community themselves and who are involved in the ministry of developing and caring for small groups and communities in the parish.

QUALITIES OF CORE COMMUNITY MEMBERS

The following qualities ought to be kept in mind when selecting core community members. Although each person may not have these qualities in the same degree, it is essential that all qualities be found in the core community as a whole.

FAITH-FILLED—a firm belief in the gospel of Jesus Christ and in the value of small communities to help people live the Christian life. The faith-filled person recognizes the importance of the church's sacramental life in maintaining Christian identity.

COMMITTED—a willingness and availability to commit time and energy to renewal and growth of the people of God through small community development. Commitment is one of the key elements of community development. The core community members envision their own community responsibilities as very important to a renewed church and worthy of deep personal commitment.

RELATIONAL—an ability to relate and work well with diverse parish groups, parishioners, and staff, e.g. priests, sisters, brothers, lay staff, and deacons.

RESPECTFUL—an appreciation for all those with whom they come in contact, an openness to differences of opinion.

ORGANIZED—the competence to accomplish the tasks related to the development of small communities.

SENSIBLE—the ability to use good judgment and to share laughter and joy with others.

SPIRITUAL—the ability to grow in adult Christian spirituality and to articulate their faith. Christians who are maturing spiritually ought to have an openness and respect for the diversity of ways that faith is expressed.

In essence, people of faith who have relational ability, believe in this pastoral direction, desire to see it implemented in their parish, and are willing to commit themselves to work for the gradual realization of it are needed.

SELECTION OF A CORE COMMUNITY

Once the pastor, staff, and parish pastoral council have accepted this pastoral direction as a priority for their parish, the pastor and staff, perhaps together with some parishioners, need to spend time in prayerful discernment to choose parishioners for this ministry. This group discerns the names of possible core community members, keeping in mind the necessary qualities.

If a parish has completed RENEW, some people from the Parish RENEW Team may well wish to serve on the core community. The remainder can be drawn from participants of the small RENEW groups themselves who have shown good leadership. An alert staff will find talented parishioners surfacing in these groups.

The means of selection ought not to be one of merely appointing people or asking for volunteers, but of truly asking the Spirit's guidance for potential members of this community. It is wise to list more names of people than are needed since not everyone may be able to respond affirmatively.

After names are surfaced an exploratory meeting will help these potential members to learn more about the core community. The pastor personally invites each person to this meeting and shares why they were chosen to participate.

SELECTION OF A COORDINATOR OF THE CORE COMMUNITY

There is great value in choosing a coordinator for the core community before the sessions for core community development begin. When this happens the group starts with clarity of leadership, stability, and a greater sense of direction. Having a coordinator in place beforehand will more easily engage the interest and involvement of highly qualified people, while a vague start could easily cause the loss of interest of the most valuable people. Some may fear that they may be pressured to fill the coordinator position.

As the pastor/staff and parishioners discern the core community members, they can also be alert to the person they believe would best coordinate the work of the core community. (It is best to have several names in order of preference in case the first person is unable to assume the responsibility.) The pastor then personally contacts the person chosen for the role of coordinator and encourages this person to accept this role.

If a coordinator is not selected before the process of developing a core community, the core community members themselves could select a coordinator through a process of discernment. If this selection process is used, it is understood that the person chosen by the core community would be acceptable to the pastor and the staff. (Cf. Resource D, Core Community Session 5 in *Resources* which devotes a section to the selection process of the coordinator.)

ROLE OF THE CORE COMMUNITY

The main role of the core community is to foster the development of small groups/communities in the parish. That effort must be sensitive to the ways in which the parish is already encouraging small group/community experiences. For example, if the parish has already used the RENEW process, some small groups may continue to meet periodically. Other groups may have already moved toward being small Christian communities.

Ideally the parish staff and parish pastoral council will clearly articulate the pastoral direction. Yet, practically speaking, the core community together with the parish staff members may assume this role and propose the pastoral direction to the council for affirmation. Once the pastoral direction has been articulated and affirmed, the core community, together with the pastor or other pastoral staff persons, assumes primary responsibility for its implementation.

In developing the parish as a community of communities, the core community plans and implements seasonal small groups, fosters the incorporation of five elements of community in the various parish groups, committees, ministries, and organizations, and initiates, encourages, and supports the development of small Christian communities.

RESPONSIBILITIES OF THE CORE COMMUNITY

The responsibilities of the core community are explained below. As the core community addresses these responsibilities in the parish, the pastoral direction begins to take shape in the parish and come alive.

Growing Together as a Community

The members of the core community commit themselves not only to the ministry of small community development, but also to forming community among themselves. Thus they incorporate the five elements of community growth into their meetings and way of life. Absolutely essential among these elements is prayer. Through both personal and communal prayer, the core community discerns the implications of the pastoral direction for the parish.

As the members of the core community increasingly open themselves to being filled with the Spirit of God, they become more life-giving to others and have greater potential for building Christian community. They experience first-hand the joys and disappointments, the struggles and hopes of striving for community and are better able to understand the growth of other groups and communities.

Developing a Climate of Acceptance

The core community works to develop a climate of acceptance of the pastoral direction throughout the parish. It presents the direction to various groups in the parish. A variety of means, including a parish process for listening and planning, can be employed to present the direction to the entire parish. (See Resource F in *Resources* for a sample process.) Since the core community members are concerned about a style of parish, working toward total acceptance continues to be part of the ongoing ministry of the core community. For example, as the membership of the parish pastoral council changes through the years, the core can make a presentation to the council as well as to committees and ministerial groups so that new members can understand the value of holding seasonal small groups, ministerial communities, and small Christian communities.

Planning

The core community begins planning by setting long-term goals. In order to set goals, the community may focus on the question: "Considering the pastoral direction, what do we want our parish to look like in five years?"

One possible goal would be to have twenty-five percent of the parish in small communities within five years. After writing goals, the core community sets yearly objectives as stepping-stones toward achieving the long-term goals. Some examples of first year objectives toward a five year goal could include the following:

1. To hold seasonal, small groups during Lent;
2. To work with two ministerial committees which seem most receptive to growing from committee to community;
3. To initiate five new small Christian communities.

The second year objectives could include increasing the number of times for holding seasonal small groups, e.g. in both the autumn and Lent, scheduling a large group experience for all participants in ministerial communities, or doubling the number of new small Christian communities.

The core community ought to have a good sense of accomplishment in achieving their yearly objectives. By following a planning process the core community moves step by step toward implementing a new vision of parish. It is recommended that the core community coordinate its yearly objectives/plans with other parish ministries.

Development of Leaders

The development of small community leaders may very possibly be the most important way to ensure that the pastoral direction of small communities will take root in the parish and succeed. A well-formed lay leadership is needed to guide parish-based small communities. While great strides have been taken in recent years in the formation of lay people, more emphasis can be given to the specific role of small community leadership formation.

A prime responsibility of the core community is to plan and coordinate training for small group/community leaders. Development of small community leaders is imperative if the small community is to be focused. The leader has the responsibility for guiding the community through the faith-sharing, prayer, and action response of the small community sessions. The leader keeps the community on the topic with charity and flexibility, gently includes hesitant members, and develops a warm, accepting, open climate and group cohesiveness.

A leadership development program contained in *Called To Lead,* a companion book of *Small Christian Community: A Vision of Hope,* has been specifically designed to enable leaders to fulfill their role more effectively. Core concepts of the Catholic faith, such as a basic understanding of scripture, church, sacraments, mission, spirituality, and prayer, are presented simply and clearly in a process that takes place within the context of a small group. In addition there are sessions on stages of community growth, communication skills, and group dynamics. The participation of group members in discussion and sharing of experience, prayer, and reflection is a critical part of the process. The information presented is basic and yet is developed to enable participants to become more comfortable in sharing some of the most profound beliefs of our faith. Also through participation in these sessions leaders will more fully recognize the importance of the communal dimension of Christianity, deepen their awareness of the presence and action of the Spirit in their lives, and increase their realization of the social responsibilities of their faith.

When these sessions are used in the formation of small Christian community leaders, the potential for prayer, learning, mutual support, and mission is boundless.

With *Called To Lead* and with other materials found in the *Resources,* the parish has ample resources to develop leadership for small communities. Once core community members have participated in these sessions, some of them ought to be able to prepare and conduct the sessions for small community leaders.

In addition the core provides continuing support for small community leaders in a variety of ways, including the following activities.

Providing Materials

The core community coordinates (and at times may develop) resources for small communities to use during their gatherings. Often the core will have a bibliography of available resources or have sample copies from which the small community leaders may choose their materials. Some parishes may buy booklets in quantity and lend them to small communities for a period of time.

Good materials are essential in enabling small Christian communities to grow. Materials which touch on various aspects of our faith, the moral and social teachings of the church, the Sunday readings, and those which open up possibilities for prayer, reflection, sharing, and action are recommended. The most important materials are not necessarily those with which people are most comfortable but those that stretch their thinking and help them to relate the gospel to all areas of their lives.

In these materials a progression of questions is important for the gradual engagement of small Christian community members. The best materials for small community members to use are those which go from objective thought to reflection on personal experience to a determination of how to grow spiritually or what to do about a problem or situation. The flow of the meeting naturally leads to an action step.

Materials can be found within the *Pilgrimage* Series published by Paulist Press and the International Office of RENEW, and small group booklets published by Sheed and Ward that skillfully interweave the key elements for small Christian community growth. There is still a great need to develop materials that will open people and help them to express their faith in all areas of life.

In addition to knowing key materials for small Christian community development, the core community needs to be aware of materials that will facilitate development of ministerial communities. It is important to select materials that will be non-threatening and easily used by current parish committees or ministries. Two booklets written by Lois Kikkert, O.P. are highly recommended: *Prayers to a God of Surprises* and *Prayers for the Seasons*. Each of these booklets consists of twelve prayer services that include the opportunity for reflection and sharing. The purpose of these booklets is to foster and facilitate a prayerful and supportive environment through which all types of ministry within the parish can be enriched and empowered. Both booklets are available from the International Office of RENEW.

When members of any conceivable committee, ministry, group, or organization in the parish spend the first thirty minutes using these materials, they would move in a gentle way toward the community values of which we have been speaking. Using such resources may offer the first opportunity for many in the ministry to share scripture and spontaneous prayer in a small group setting. When a particular parish committee begins to use prayer services such as these on a consistent basis, they will help people become more present to themselves, to one another, and to God. Also they will gain comfortability in sharing scripture, faith, and prayer. As community develops among participants, more positive outcomes for ministry can certainly be projected.

Other materials which focus on the groups' particular ministries, touch on matters of importance for those in this ministry, and present possibilities for prayer, sharing, and action are appropriate.

Coordination of Activity

In many ways the core community coordinates the activities of the various small communities. The core sponsors occasions which will bring them together for large group experiences—weekend retreats, picnics, Christmas parties, pot-luck suppers, rallies, etc.—and sees that overall harmony is maintained through a good system of communication.

Pastoral Care

The ministry of pastoral care is one of the most beautiful aspects of the core community's work. The members foster the growth and development of all the small communities in the parish. Their ministry includes encouragement, caring, looking after, tending to, challenging, developing, and nourishing growth with leaders and small communities themselves. Because of its importance this responsibility is more fully developed in Chapter 13.

Communication

The core community maintains good communication with parish staff, council, and other groups working in the area of community building and tells parishioners of its activities and efforts through appropriate channels.

Other Responsibilities

Other responsibilities of the core community to help implement the pastoral direction include the following:

- coordinating recruitment efforts for new members and leaders of small communities;
- evaluating progress of parish small communities and encouraging continuing evaluation;
- ensuring that small communities relate closely to parish RCIA efforts;
- guiding and encouraging existing small groups, ministerial communities, and small Christian communities to incorporate five elements of Christian community in their meetings.

Accountability

The core community is accountable to the pastor and/or parish staff and the parish pastoral council. Some possibilities for facilitating this accountability include the following. (1) The core community could become one of the standing committees or ministries of the council. (2) The core community could be a sub-committee of the spiritual life committee. (3) If a council of ministries has been developed, the core community may function as one of the community building ministries. It is recommended that parishes develop whatever structure most effectively facilitates good communication. Some see that in a situation where the parish strongly advocates the pastoral direction, the parish pastoral council and the core community could eventually become synonymous.

The significance of having a prayerful, resourceful core community is crucial in bringing to life all the facets of the pastoral direction. If the pastoral direction is to become well integrated into all parish pastoral approaches, it is important that the pastor and staff make an initial and ongoing effort in the formation and support of their parish core community for small community development.

The presence and ministry of a core community can ensure that the vision of small communities will remain constant in the changing circumstances of a parish. If by chance the pastor is changed, the coordinator needs to communicate with the new pastor about the ministry of the core community, invite his involvement, and work in close harmony with him.

FORMATION PROCESS FOR CORE COMMUNITY

A formation process has been developed and used successfully in the development of core communities. This process is outlined below and given in greater detail in Resource D in *Resources.* The following outline briefly describes this formation process.

Session I: A Pastoral Direction of the Parish as a Community Made Up of Many Small Communities
- a way of being church that is rooted in our Christian tradition.

Session II: Responsibilities and Qualities of Core Community
- rationale for small communities
- definition and need for core community
- responsibilities and qualities of core community

Session III: Hopes and Expectations
- tasks involved
- time commitment
- frequency of meetings
- prayer life of core community
- knowledge and skills to be gained

Session IV: Developing Goals and Objectives for Core Community (This session usually requires two meetings or an extended meeting.)

- ministry goal and objectives
- core community life goal and objectives

Session V: Discernment of Gifts
- prayerful reflection on gifts
- obstacles to identifying gifts
- reflection on the Holy Spirit, gift-giver

Session VI: Reflection on the Mission of Jesus
- the reign of God
- the meaning of the mission
- being "sent forth"

This formation process may be done in a number of ways:

- six consecutive two-hour weekly sessions;
- six two-hour sessions, every other week;
- two six-hour sessions.

SUMMARY

We began this chapter with a definition of the core community, qualities to look for in the selection of core community members, and some recommendations for the selection process itself. Then we looked at the role and responsibilities of the core community. As these responsibilities are lived out, the development of seasonal small groups, ministerial communities, and small Christian communities will gradually take place. As these various approaches to achieving this pastoral direction are put into practice, the whole life of the parish can be affected in a positive way.

Of course, the task of implementing this pastoral direction is never fully accomplished, but becomes a way of being church. Core communities will always be able to invite parishioners to be part of seasonal small groups because of the mobility of people and because of the varying circumstances of parishioners' lives. Some people will become available and open to this kind of invitation for a short term small group experience at different times in their lives.

As parishioners become involved in the various ministries of the parish, the core community, together with those already involved in ministry, can introduce them to a communal style of meeting. In addition, the core community will always find ways to support small community leaders and the small Christian communities themselves as they strive to apply the gospel to all areas of their lives.

In conclusion, let us emphasize that core community members will fulfill their responsibilities with much greater spirit and support as they continue to grow as a small Christian community themselves.

CHAPTER 10

The Priest and Parish Staff

If this pastoral direction of the parish as a community of small communities is valued, then what kind of pastoral leadership is necessary to implement it?

Parish life is challenged to bring about deeper commitments to Christ and to enable faith life to be a leaven in our world. In our post-Vatican II era there seems to be more varied and increased expectations for priests. For the priest, there is often "a weariness that comes from 'standing in the breach' during a time of profound transition both in our culture and in the history of the Church."[1] Small parishes may no longer have the presence of a priest on a daily basis and larger parishes try to expand their pastoral staffs in striving to meet the needs of parishioners.

Given these circumstances, could not small communities offer great pastoral hope and promise? By utilizing the small community approach the pastoral staff does not have to be present to each person individually, but can multiply a pastoral presence many times over. Small communities are an ideal place for parishioners to come to "know" God and be led to deeper conversion and mission.

Ultimately what do priests and other pastoral staff members want for their parishes? To create a climate for faith development where people are supported and challenged to make a greater commitment to living the gospel? To make the reign of God more alive and visible in their parishes? To help people discover and experience a more personal relationship with God? To encourage people to become more prayerful and to share about their relationship with God? To create an environment where people are supported in mission? To increase participation in the Sunday liturgy? To help parishioners make connections between the Sunday liturgy and their daily lives?

IMPORTANCE OF LEADERSHIP

In so many ways the leadership of the pastor and pastoral staff is significant in achieving the pastoral direction of the parish as a community of small communities. For these communities to develop as Christian communities within the structure of the Catholic Church, there must be clear ecclesial relationships between the small communities and the local pastor and pastoral staff.

The importance of the priest and leadership cannot be stated too strongly. As the Second Vatican Council admonished, "the wished-for renewal of the whole church depends in large measure on a ministry of priests which is vitalized by the spirit of Christ" (OT Preface). For this pastoral direction to flourish, strong leadership and encouragement is of utmost importance.

Obviously a key element to implementation of the small community pastoral direction is the attitude of the pastor and staff. Attitude is contagious. If there is an enthusiasm and a commitment to the vision of small community, then it can become a reality in the parish.

A pastoral direction of small community, a positive attitude, strong leadership—in theory, this all looks good, but let us look for a moment at the reality of some of the circumstances in many parishes today.

For many years the pastoral cry has been: "The same people are doing everything." The annual events such as the men's communion breakfast or the women's bazaar provide good experiences for people, but how often the burden of responsibility managing these events rests on the same people over and over!

Has not the experience often been that a few people do everything? Understandably they often complain about having to be the ones who always do the work. However, sometimes new people arrive on the scene and do not find it easy to break into the circle of the involved. Sometimes the "overworked" do in fact love that role so much that they do not want to give it up. This can also be true for the pastoral leadership of the parish, who can find it difficult to give up some of the things they have been doing.

Let us look at leadership in the parish. In many parishes there is no really discernible parish pastoral plan. This is not because of any ill intention or lack of desire for a pastoral direction, but often because the daily reality of rectory and parish life is dictated by telephone calls, emergencies, funerals, problem solving needs—in other words, crisis management. How often does a priest plan to accomplish a task or go out for a day only to have his plans thwarted by an unscheduled visit from a parishioner? How often does one telephone call change the events of an entire day?

In most instances the parish is a very busy place. Many parishes have "in place" numerous good activities and ministries: educational programs, hospital visitation, liturgical planning, prayer experiences, outreach to the needy, etc. "Managing" these along with the "emergency needs" offers a pastor and staff more than enough to feel overburdened. Thus, beginning to think about implementing a pastoral direction which could be seen as requiring additional time or some concrete changes, no matter how small, can be seen as theoretical or at least "not realistic in our situation."

Besides the busyness, the number of active priests has diminished considerably. There are fewer priests to do even more work than before. The average age of priests is older, and recent surveys of priests seem to indicate that many are "overwhelmed" and "burned-out."[2]

Despite all these problems, however, with all that has been said in the previous chapters about how Spirit-filled this pastoral direction of small communities is, why aren't all pastors and staffs eager to implement it? Certainly some of the above reasons are obvious, but perhaps there are some deeper reasons that cause hesitation.

CHALLENGES TO IMPLEMENTATION

What kind of leadership is needed for the implementation of this pastoral direction? One of the key challenges will be for pastors and pastoral staffs to focus to a greater extent on the relational aspects of their ministry. That is not to say that pastors and staffs have not been relational in the past. In fact, many leaders feel "burned out" from all the requests and needs of people with whom they relate. However, this direction does necessitate a partial shift in the style of relating.

This "shift" is not entirely new in terms of the importance pastors may already attach to relationships in the parish. In fact, a great degree of the current pastoral ministry is relational. However, with the small community approach, there are times when the pastor makes a shift in his "stance" toward relationships with parishioners. For the most part, he is clearly exercising his role of teaching, forming and "educating in faith." However, at times, precisely for the sake of "forming genuine Christian community" (PO 6) in his work with small communities, he sees himself as walking "hand in hand" with parishioners on this faith journey and recognizes his own need for spiritual growth and spiritual nurturing. He shares his own human and spiritual needs with a small community in the parish and receives their love and support. He enters into a more open sharing with people which supports their spiritual growth, and he increases his love of the Lord, thus making him an even more effective minister to the parish.

The recent Vatican document, *Apostolic Exhortation on the Laity,* speaks to this loving, supporting relationship among laity, priests and religious:

> In the formation that the lay faithful receive from their diocese and parish, especially concerning communion and mission, the help that diverse members of the church can give to each other is particularly important. This mutual help also aids in revealing the mystery of the church as mother and teacher. Priests and religious ought to assist the lay faithful in their formation. In this regard the synod fathers have invited priests and candidates for orders to "be prepared carefully so that they are ready to foster the vocation and mission of the lay faithful." In turn, the lay faithful themselves can and should help priests and religious in the course of their spiritual and pastoral journey.[3]

For some priests, there may be some discomfort with this more communal style of church which has not been a part of their family or of their seminary training. The priest may feel a certain uneasiness that the implementation of this pastoral direction may cause factions within the parish or that a certain amount of elitism may occur. Maybe persons involved in these small communities will see themselves as "super Christians."

Another fear may be that small groups could slip into heretical thinking. Maybe they will just "wander around" the scriptures or will become fundamentalist. Perhaps the priest fears that the groups may become "therapy groups" and not faith sharing communities.

BENEFITS TO IMPLEMENTATION

The wonderful benefits of small communities, however, far outweigh these fears. In regard to seminary training, is it ever possible to say that training and education have totally ended? A changing world requires new thinking in regard to pastoral practices. A post-Vatican II church challenges leadership to adopt approaches to meet the needs of the people.

No pastor wants the parish divided or controlled by a few. In fact one key role of the pastor is to unify the parish. With the type of guidelines offered in this manual, small Christian communities do, in fact, grow in their sense of mission and service to others. With effective training, parishioners in small communities are hardly elitist, but have a better sense of the larger church, are more loyal, and thus are willing to be of greater service to the larger church and the world.

While those in small Christian communities share from a feeling level, they do not do so to the exclusion of sharing on all levels. Very authentic conversions are happening in small groups. People are not just experiencing "feeling good" together, but are having an experience of who God is in their lives. In fact, much catechesis takes place in the small community. It is a profoundly spiritual and intellectual experience.

Through these communities pastors can provide sound formation, ongoing development and education for their people. Small community leaders are trained to bring any issues of doctrine to the attention of the pastoral staff, so there is little danger of heresy. Another great benefit of the small community is its ability to motivate participants to learn more about the scriptures. Through increased interest and hunger for knowledge about the scriptures, staffs have eager learners who are highly motivated and thus they can provide educational and formational opportunities.

One very real fear that most people have is that of losing control of situations in their lives. For priests and other staff members this may be the fear of losing control of what is happening in the small group and in the parish. On the other hand we know that if we do not provide people with a means for satisfying their spiritual hunger, they may leave the parish. That is a real loss of control. When a pastor and staff members are in a spiritual relationship with the people, they will not ordinarily lose parishioners. Not meeting the needs of people by failing to provide some of the basic spiritual elements of scripture and communion found in small communities may, in fact, ironically be inviting a loss of control. Nothing is more out of control than the number of people who have left parishes and opted for various fundamentalist and non-denominational groups. This is not a matter of control then, but rather a matter of love and respect.

OTHER CHALLENGES

Fear is a common human emotion, and an unconscious fear of change can be deadening. When we speak of this new pastoral direction, one of the roadblocks is that it calls for change. Even though the gains far outweigh any negative effects of change, still the most common response often is unconscious fear.

In our society, education is prized, and attitudes of dominance can easily "slip in." How often might a staff member who has struggled through long and tedious graduate work feel that the "people in the parish do not as yet understand"? Or how often may there be engendered an air of superiority because of having a "clearer vision of the people's needs" or "that others are not as well equipped as I am"?

It may appear more subtle, but some active and faithful lay persons may actually be hurting the development of lay leadership by being the "super lay leader" who can do it all. The power of the Spirit is most alive when all members of the church are encouraged to share in the mission of Jesus and to belong to the church as true disciples of Jesus.

The point is that parishes can hire larger staffs and actually add to the number of people who are already burned out. In fact as staffs get larger there is even a greater temptation to take more responsibility away from parishioners.

The issue is not just larger staffs. The system itself can be improved. New ways to enable people are needed. Are there not better pastoral approaches that do not burn out people? The small Christian community pastoral approach is a vision that boosts morale with hope precisely because it involves many more in the ministry of Jesus and enables the parish priest and other staff members to touch more lives than ever before by bringing so many into an effective means of spiritual growth.

Thus far issues of fear and control of leadership have been identified. Some of these are conscious and others reside in the unconscious.

The parish as a community of small communities is a distinctly relational model of church. One of the concrete challenges of this type of leadership is the human difficulty of establishing right relationships. Psychologists speak of the human struggle for intimacy and unconditional love which is a part of human longing. Human beings battle to let go of their own ego needs and to live in harmony with those around them.

Expectations can lay heavy on anyone who tries to live up to the image of a leader who is without fault. For this person, to be left wanting or to be without the right answers for all situations can be disconcerting. In a culture which requires competence and administrative skills, what about the priest or other staff members who feel uncertain about being able to implement this new style of parish life, or who feel that closer bonds with parishioners will find them spiritually wanting?

Challenges Can Be Met

Our church teaches us that we are to be in communion with each other. We have the beautiful biblical symbol of the vine and the branches which "reveal the mystery of communion that serves as the unifying bond between the Lord and his disciples, between Christ and the baptized."[4]

We are invited into this beautiful relationship with one another. We don't need to impress one another; in fact, sharing our imperfections can make us more lovable! The gospel stories and the message of Jesus is that we are only strong when God's strength shows forth in our weakness. Often, however, leaders in parishes will do anything to appear in control. Jesus did not say "Blessed are those who are in control" or "Blessed are those who have all the answers." No, he spoke of the blessed as those who are poor, those who hunger and thirst, those who are single-hearted.

Jesus emptied himself and became little. Poverty of spirit may at times be the most painful human experience for the priest or pastoral staff person, and yet spirituality happens where there is great honesty and dependence upon God—honesty about who we really are as "little ones" in relation to God and who we are in relationship to one another. We are all simply on a journey together, a journey of faith where we need one another to love and be loved.

No one needs to have all the answers. No one has to carry that burden. At times it may feel like a loss of status, but people can best relate to leaders when they find them to be mutual journeyers. Rather than lessening the role of priesthood and ecclesial leadership, sharing the spiritual journey enhances the appreciation and love for the religious leader.

In most instances, priests become priests because of their deep love for people and the church. Pastoral staffs enter into their ministries for the same reason. We all need to be loved, understood, and accepted. Loving and the need to be loved—that is certainly the very substance of spirituality!

Way of Being Church

The development of small Christian communities in the parish offers an effective way of doing what the church asks. It provides a safe format for priests and other staff members to develop a more collegial and relational style of ministry. It shifts the emphasis from the leader seeing himself only as *the expert* to the leader recognizing he is a learner as well; from being the answer person to being someone seeking an experience of God; from feeling "I have arrived" to being a pilgrim; from providing prayer formulas to knowing God better; from doing for people to enabling; from ministering all by oneself to doing it with others.

Confidence is the issue! Often the priest or pastoral staff person will say: "People will be upset if I join a particular small community." "I'm too busy." "I don't know how I'll be received by parishioners in that kind of relationship." "How will it be taken if I share my own spiritual growth journey?"

Is not the real issue: "I'm not confident enough in myself and my parishioners; I really don't know how to enable others"? Confidence grows in the doing. Small Christian communities offer a safe, gentle way to move into enabling relationships. Confidence comes also as staffs recognize that they do not have to do it alone. There are many parishioners who are both supportive and talented and who will love and respect staffs all the more because of the open and sharing stance that is taken.

So the challenge becomes how to scout for that talent. In every parish there are numerous parishioners who are capable and talented. Whether it be the poorest parish in the city or an affluent parish in the suburbs, the gifts of the Spirit are alive and present. So many of the skills needed for the implementation of this vision are "naturals" to some people.

Most pastors and staffs know their parishioners well, or at least have enough contact to keep scouting for the right people to work toward this pastoral direction. In some ways it could be compared to college football scouting. Those responsible for scouting are constantly "on the lookout" for talent and commitment. When a talented player is spotted, the scout does not wait until the player expresses an interest; rather he pursues the player and interests him in coming to the college. The player knows why he is wanted. Pastors and staffs could well utilize the skills of scouting!

In many ways a key role of pastors and staffs is to empower others. The Whiteheads in their book *The Emerging Laity* describe a cycle of empowering people to action. They begin with the notion of *recognition:* recognition and ownership of the unique gifts and abilities a person has been given. For the priest and professional staff person these may be gifts such as: "I am kind." "I am a caring person." "I am willing to be of service." That kind of recognition is so essential to begin the process of empowerment, and also allows for the awareness of personal vulnerabilities.[5]

The second phase of the cycle is *receptivity*. This includes the conscious awareness of, and choices and decisions for, the direction of life. For the priest this may be the positive choice of becoming a priest. In his priesthood he then makes many other choices which could include the decision to start small Christian communities.

The cycle cannot be complete, however, without the third component: *purified recognition*. This necessitates an ongoing self-awareness, particularly about human failings.

For example, having made the choice for priesthood and small communities, the priest comes to realize that he is not using his gifts as well as he had hoped. He may have intended to empower a small group of people but finds himself dominating the group. He may come to realize that he cannot do everything by himself. Perhaps this pastoral direction is so clear to him that he begins impatiently to overpower people in his need to move the pastoral direction forward. In this third phase of the empowerment cycle, he then comes to a point of purifying his pastoral approaches.

For a priest to be purified he must constantly recognize that the work of the church is God's work, not his. He needs to call upon others to multiply the pastoral presence needed in the parish. The cycle does not end; rather it begins once again as even deeper bonds of relationship are established and more people are empowered to experience the fullness of the Spirit.

SMALL CHRISTIAN COMMUNITY PARTICIPATION

To be priest means to be part of the Christian community. Father Robert Lauder, in his book *The Priest as Person,* describes it this way:

> A person's horizon or world is a network of meanings that are real to an individual. In other ages, the world or horizon of many people was Christian. Not so today. The contemporary priest functions in a post-Christian world. This reality puts special pressure on both him and those to whom he is ministering. No one can be a person alone. For better or worse, we need one another. We will influence one another. The crucial question is: how will we influence one another? Will we influence one another for better or worse? The answer for the believer is to enter as deeply as possible into the Christian community. The contemporary priest must experience Christian com-

munity in at least two ways: he must help to form a Christian community as part of his apostolate, and he must be part of a community if he is to grow or perhaps even survive as a Christian minister. In a Christian community, persons try to coexist precisely as Christians. The community is rooted in truth and love, and its members try to serve one another in these two areas.[6]

In the initial implementation, the pastor and staff will need to spend time not only exploring the pastoral direction, but also adopting a communal style for all their staff meetings and retreat experiences. By so doing, their communication with the parish about the pastoral direction will be authentic because they will speak from experience and not mere theory.

In addition to incorporating this pastoral direction into all parish meetings, it is essential that all staff members themselves be participants in small Christian communities. There are many benefits to being a part of a small community. The most obvious is that personal experience is the best teacher. By knowing the benefits first-hand, staff members can encourage others with greater conviction. This will only enhance the development of the vision in the parish.

There may be some initial concern on the part of a few parishioners that one of the priests or other staff members is giving priority to a particular group of people (i.e., their small community), but if the staff explain their own personal commitment to spiritual growth and how this is enhanced in the small community, fears will be quieted.

For any staff members who are in small communities, the following *guidelines* may enhance their participation:

1. *Communicate clearly why you will be a participant in this particular small community.* Generally this would include the fact that one is free on a certain evening or at a certain time of the day. Thus, you joined this small community because it was available at a convenient time for you. You may wish to explain that you are not "playing favorites," but being a member of a small community is a top priority and this particular small community meets at a convenient time.
2. *Don't allow the group to make you the "answer person."* You may need to explain that there is a time and place for the important role of teaching, but in this instance you are there to share your own faith story and listen to others just like any other member of the small community.
3. *Be yourself.* It is not necessary to be anyone but yourself. People love people who are most themselves.

4. *Follow rules of good participation, i.e. do not dominate.* As a leader in the parish, it is sometimes difficult to be a member rather than the leader of the group. It will be necessary to be particularly vigilant in this area.
5. *Be a good listener.* Many times in their positions and with their responsibilities staff impart information. The small community offers the opportunity to take a listening stance.
6. *Be open to requests for priestly/staff ministry, i.e. evenings of recollection, retreats, etc.* Being a member of a small community does not preclude providing reflection experiences for the small community or for a number of small communities. These requests frequently help priests and other staff members be what they are called to be.

Likewise, it is essential that other small community members are clear about the role of the priest or other staff persons in their communities. Important *guidelines* for them include the following:

1. *Understand the priest's or staff's background.* Understanding and acceptance are always the best ways to create an atmosphere of trust and warmth. Small community members need to understand some of the concerns the staff persons may have, particularly coming from certain educational styles and background preferences. This is true in regard to all participants in the community. Each person comes from a different background and needs understanding and acceptance.
2. *Be welcoming but not pushy.* It is easy when persons are in positions of authority to look to them for increased participation and with higher expectations than are given to the rest of the members. The priest or staff member is welcomed and encouraged as are others, but no special pressure needs to be given the staff member. Constant pushing of anyone to become a participant is counterproductive. All people want to be with friends, not to be "worked on."
3. *Respect their calendar and other responsibilities.* It is essential that basic respect be given to the busy schedules of all concerned. In many ways this may be an opportunity to identify with the many responsibilities and demands of staff persons.
4. *Love and support are key.* Love draws people to involvement. For the pastor or staff person, the message needs to be: "We would enjoy having you with us." Not: "You need this."
5. *Do not make the priest or other staff members the "answer person."* It is important for the entire group to recognize that in this particular setting the priest or other staff members do not want to be called on as the "expert" but rather want to be regular participants in the community.
6. *Be realistic in expectations.* Others may need to miss meetings and so may the staff person.

7. *Do not be judgmental.* Judgment is not appropriate for any member. In the final analysis, even though there are many benefits to small communities, the quality of participation or non-participation is not for one to judge.

MANAGING TIME

Obviously, new pastoral practices will not become a reality unless there is some change in the way ministry is carried out. Let us look at the manner in which many priests spend their time. For most priests, ten to twelve hours a day of direct service could be the norm. But the question becomes: "Is all ministry relating back to me? Am I making myself indispensable?"

Direct service ministry has many pluses, and for the priest and professional minister there are many positive returns for caring for the sick, counseling the troubled, solving problems for people who are needy and vulnerable. But is direct service in all instances the best way to create community? If others were empowered, could not many more people minister to one another and thus multiply the amount and quality of ministry?

The question is one of balance. We need both. We need direct service ministry, but we also need a healthy balance of empowering. The old adage is appropriate here: "It is better to teach the hungry how to fish than to give them a fish."

Pastors and staffs do not need more tasks; in fact, most are already overloaded. At a time when there are fewer priests and the median age is rising, it is impractical to suggest even higher expectations and demands on an already overburdened clergy. Might not, rather, a restructuring of some current time commitments be helpful?

A dramatic change in time commitments is not suggested, but rather a gradual and clearly communicated change. Initially the pastor and pastoral staff will need to spend at least some percentage of their time in developing this pastoral direction as they work with a core community and with the leaders of the small communities. With a positive attitude and quality time commitment, a pastor and staff will begin to experience some success in the implementation of this pastoral direction.

As small successes are realized in becoming a parish community of many small communities, an appreciation of collaborative ministry ensues. The pastor and staff understand that they are moving beyond "activating the laity" and "shared responsibility" to a greater sense of "the collaborative ministry of pastoral care" that is "to enable others to minister to one another, to become part of a people, and to extend their Christian commitment to everything they do."[7]

When small community leaders begin to assume their role within their small communities, a reduction in the number of people the pastor and staff need to relate to directly occurs. Life becomes more manageable with a clear pastoral direction. While small community ministry will itself require time on the part of the pastor and staff, the pastoral results are most encouraging. Pastors and staffs experience great fulfillment from their efforts. So many parishioners are growing spiritually. This approach to pastoring and management is a concrete way to avoid burnout and give needed hope to and boost the morale of parish staffs.

Imagine how the efforts of one pastor could be multiplied if some quality time was devoted to developing a core community for small Christian community development whose members in turn would be at the service of twenty-five small group leaders. These small Christian community leaders would, in turn, be at the service of small groups, each comprising about ten people. In effect, with this network, one person would be reaching two hundred and fifty people in in-depth spiritual formation. It would be difficult to find another parish model in which so many could be benefiting in this manner. And these efforts themselves can be multiplied. Certainly at the initial stages of development, the core community needs special attention and involvement on the part of the pastor. However, once the overall direction is set and the core community is adequately prepared for this ministry, the pastor's role becomes less demanding.

The pastoral direction calls for developing ministry from a communal base. Let us say that the pastor spends ten percent of his time visiting the sick. During this visiting time, he can perhaps make ten calls per week, but is unable to spend much time with each person. If the pastor focused his efforts on the development of small communities, he could gather small groups of people together who feel drawn to this particular ministry and enable and support them in becoming ministers to the sick both at home and in the hospital. If ten people gathered for prayer, sharing, learning, and support, they could visit many more people each week and offer more quality time. At the same time, the pastor who also wishes to maintain direct ministry will himself have more quality time for the visits he is able to make.

Developing a more communal approach to ministry does not necessarily mean spending more time. Shifts of time and emphasis will result in maximizing pastoral effectiveness.

Obviously, it is not necessary to change time commitments in all areas of ministry. Initially it could mean only a five to fifteen percent change in the use of time. The key elements are supporting the core community, being a part of a community oneself, and making a firm commitment to personal prayer and spiritual development. As pastors and staffs make their own deeper commitments to prayer and a more intimate relationship with Jesus, the vision will flourish. As the pastoral direction grows in the parish, pastors and staffs will recognize that more and more of their ministry flows from a communal base.

ROLE OF THE PASTOR AND PASTORAL STAFF

With the increasing number of small communities developing in the parish, the role of the pastor and pastoral staff becomes crucial to the long-term success of developing the parish as a community of communities. In summary, the following are ways to support this development:

1. Becoming involved in a small Christian community. There is no greater witness than personal participation and there is no greater means of learning the value of small communities than a personal experience.
2. Visiting small Christian communities. Pastors and staffs need to be aware of the small communities and their aspirations and needs and can learn a great deal from regular contact.
3. Encouraging those involved in small Christian communities, e.g. by recognizing their efforts and giving feedback either publicly or privately. People need support from leadership.
4. Establishing good lines of communication between small Christian communities and the parish pastoral council.
5. Recognizing the leadership of small Christian communities as a ministry within the parish.
6. Expressing personal interest by calling people to find out how things are going.
7. Providing opportunities for the entire parish to understand the place of small Christian communities in the parish through the pulpit, the bulletin, a letter, and/or through a parish process of listening and planning.
8. Initiating the development of a core community as the first step to implementing this pastoral direction.
9. Being part of and maintaining ongoing communication with the core community.

10. Participating in a communal way in core community development and leadership development.
11. Participating in the yearly goal setting and evaluation sessions of the core community.
12. Providing continuing support and supervision for core community and small community leaders.
13. Helping small Christian communities to be connected with each other and to the parish as a whole.
14. Challenging and supporting small Christian communities in outreach, mission and evangelization. Initially, small communities will need help in growing in this awareness and moving toward action.
15. Joining in celebrations where many small communities gather. When small communities celebrate, it is so important for staff to enter into the celebrations.

Vatican II has challenged and encouraged priests to not only provide care to individuals, but to provide for the "formation of genuine Christian community" (PO 6). Rather than weighing them down, formation of genuine Christian community can free priests and staffs. Meeting the current needs of people enriches the ministerial work of priests, and allows them to move toward roles more fitting their priestly nature. Priests and other pastoral staff members want to see their people grow spiritually. They want to enable people to effectively live out the Christian life in their families and in the world in which they live.

Is this pastoral direction, this more communal style of church, that different from the early church? Not really; in fact it is very similar to the way Jesus and his disciples ministered. The Spirit continues to lead us in the ways of Jesus.

CHAPTER 11

The Parish Pastoral Council and Pastoral Direction

Parish pastoral councils differ from parish to parish, from diocese to diocese. Each council may see its role in a different light. However, the main purpose of a parish pastoral council remains the same: to ensure that the life of the parish reflects the mission of Jesus, and that all parishioners are provided the opportunity to share in that mission.

The parish pastoral council is called to invoke the Spirit to seek God's truth for the parish and to know more clearly how the mission and ministry of Jesus is to be lived out in the local community at this time. Councils are guided not only by their own "articles of understanding" or constitutions but also by the norms and directions of the universal and diocesan church.

When a parish becomes interested in implementing the pastoral direction, the parish pastoral council plays a key role. Therefore, parish pastoral councils need to be knowledgeable about small Christian communities. If a diocese has incorporated the development of small Christian communities in its pastoral direction, obviously a parish pastoral council needs to take this into consideration when planning to ensure that small Christian communities come to fruition in the parish. One way for this to happen, as we have explained in Chapter 9, is to designate a core community for small Christian community development which will work toward developing the parish as a community of communities.

The parish pastoral council can through its own convictions and commitment help parishioners realize the benefits of developing the parish as a community of communities. When it is understood that the pastoral direction is directed toward evangelization through small communities and is meant to enliven the faith life of all persons within the parish, and enable them to live fully the Christian vocation in the world, most parishioners are readily open to sharing in its implementation.

The parish pastoral council can be a key instrument in bringing the pastoral direction to reality. Its first task is to study and understand the concepts contained in the pastoral direction, to educate council members on its principles, and to enable these principles to become part of their life and ministry.

From a very practical standpoint, the council through its purpose, role, style, and structure can influence the acceptance of the pastoral direction in the parish. As a starting point, the council can begin as soon as possible to incorporate into its meeting format the elements necessary for the development of Christian community: prayer, learning, sharing, mission, and mutual support. Thus they will themselves model the communal style of meeting.

Father Mike Hammer of the archdiocese of Milwaukee tells a poignant story of conversion through a parish pastoral council. He was working with a parish that was starting a new parish pastoral council. As part of prayer formation Father Michael urged the council to spend twenty minutes in prayer and reflection during each meeting. Paul, the parish custodian, felt that this was "too much time to spend on prayer and not enough on action." Reluctantly he agreed to go along with the suggestion, but said he would not take a turn preparing the prayer. Several months later at an agenda meeting he changed his mind. It was now his responsibility to choose a reading for the next meeting.

When it came time for the prayer, Paul read the story of Martha and Mary. Father Mike says, "We were feeling he was kind of putting us in our place." But when it came time for Paul to share his reflection, he surprised them when he said, "I have always been a Martha. This is the first time I was asked to be a Mary and I really like it." Later Paul recounted, "My wife told me that since I came on the council there was a difference in how I responded at home." How often do we neglect the opportunity to help people to grow spiritually? Father Mike's suggestion that prayer be given priority time during council meetings led to a conversion of heart for at least one person, Paul, and his story has since touched many hearts.[1]

ROLES OF THE PARISH PASTORAL COUNCIL

The parish pastoral council assumes many roles in its ministry: visioner, evaluator, recommender, implementer, coordinator. Several examples follow which show how the council, in these respective roles, may foster the parish direction.

Designer/Visioner

When a council focuses on long-range planning, it is articulating future needs based on current trends within the church and world. When planning, the council can incorporate small Christian communities into its present and future direction. Small Christian communities can, in fact, be the main focus of a future pastoral direction.

Evaluator

Since one of its major roles is to evaluate the parish with regard to its mission and/or its pastoral direction, the council has the responsibility of periodically reviewing progress on these matters. This evaluation may be done directly by the council; it may elect to coordinate the work of other groups or assign the task to a specific ad hoc group within the parish.

When exercising its evaluating role the parish pastoral council may review the work with the core community and present its assessment to both the core community and the pastor.

Recommender

In the case where no core community has yet been developed, the council may, in light of its evaluation, recommend a core community for the development of the communal approach in all aspects of parish life.

Implementer

When the council takes direct responsibility for carrying out a specific action in the parish, either through its own membership or by designating specific persons or groups, the council serves as an implementer. If the council designates parishioners to serve as the core community, or if the council assumes responsibility for implementing the pastoral direction of the parish as a community of many small communities, it is acting in the role of implementer. Ordinarily, however, council members enable others to be implementers.

Coordinator

In its role of coordinator the council maintains an overview of parish services and activities and draws attention to duplication of efforts and/or areas of need or neglect. In this regard the council may realize that a particular group has been overlooked, e.g. the homebound, the bereaved, or that there is a need for advocacy, e.g. for the homeless, for low or middle income housing in the local community or beyond it.

Once a core community has been established and small communities are meeting, the council can invite the core community members to meet with them in a sharing session several times a year. In this way areas of need may be explored. The core community members, in their turn, can approach small communities to see if any would be willing to pray, study, and discern whether or not their community would accept responsibility for a particular ministry.

In this situation a process of communal discernment could be used which would help the small community members to recognize and follow God's will for them. The goal would be for the small community to arrive at a "shared decision"—shared both in the information that comes from all the members and in the final acceptance of the decision by all the members.[2]

This process of approaching small communities to ascertain their desire, availability, and commitment to assume a particular ministry can be initiated by meeting with individual small communities or by meeting with all small groups/communities when they gather for prayer, witnessing, learning, support, and socializing at a large group celebration. Individual small communities can then choose the appropriate time for them to discern God's will for them.

Accountability

Accountability of the core community to the pastor, parish staff and council is essential for two basic reasons:

1. If the council is to live its purpose fully it needs to be aware of the ministries that small groups are involved in and call upon the core community to assist in discovering and inviting ministries to flourish.
2. If the core community is to develop small communities in the parish it needs information from the council in a number of areas.
   (a) What small communities/groups are in existence in the parish?

(b) Which organizations, ministries, committees would be open to learning and using a communal style or evaluating their style of meeting?

(c) Which needed areas of ministry have been discerned by the council (in order that the parish reflects the mission of Jesus) so that connections can be made between small communities and ministries?

Councils will do well to develop whatever means or structure most effectively facilitates good communication between the core community and the council. Three suggestions for this accountability follow:

1. The core community may become one of the standing committees, commissions or ministries of the council.
2. Where a council of ministries has been developed according to the ministries of word, worship, community building and service, the core community may function as one of the community building ministries.
3. The core community may become a sub-committee of the spiritual life committee or the community relations committee.

Reflection Questions

To function well the council must constantly focus on its purpose. Frequently reflection and discussion on three questions will help it to remain faithful to its purpose.

1. What is my (our) understanding of the mission of Jesus?
2. How can we best ensure that the life of the parish reflects the mission of Jesus?
3. How can we provide opportunities for all parishioners to share in this mission?

The purpose of the council would be admirably fulfilled by focusing its understanding and action on the parish becoming a community of many small communities. For in small communities there is greater possibility that more people will be formed and involved in the mission of Jesus as they minister to one another, the parish, and beyond as part of their outreach.

CHAPTER 12

Communicating to the Parish

How can the pastor and pastoral staff most easily and effectively communicate the pastoral direction of a community of small communities to the parish? Communication, even in the best of circumstances, is a challenge. Webster defines the verb communicate: "to impart or to transmit knowledge, information, thought, or feeling so that it is satisfactorily received or understood." In this chapter we will address not only ways to share about this pastoral direction, but also how to help parishioners receive and understand the concept of their parish as a community of small communities. We will look at various styles of communication, methods of communicating the pastoral direction, and specifically three concrete ways to communicate: from the pulpit, with the parish pastoral council, and through a parish process for listening and planning.

KEY CONCEPTS TO COMMUNICATE

For most pastors and pastoral staffs the primary concern is how to truly serve their people. An underlying concept that the pastor will continually want to communicate is that shifts are being made so that there will be more effective service and ministry in the parish. What kinds of shifts? Shifts in certain time commitments; shifts in those who will be visiting the sick; shifts in time, in order to allow the staff to participate in a small community themselves, etc. When these shifts are made, the priests and other staff members will be better able to serve the pastoral and spiritual needs of parishioners.

Parishioners need reassurance that things will not get chaotic and change rapidly; thus sharing specific new choices that staffs are making in the daily use of time will be helpful. To declare that the parish is going to go through some dramatic changes would not benefit the parish. Instead, it would be more beneficial to begin change slowly, but deliberately, carefully communicating each step along the way.

149

Communicating a shift in the way in which visiting the sick will be handled in the parish is an example of this direct, simple communication. The pastor could explain as follows:

> Ordinarily in the past, _____ and I tried to do most of the visiting of the sick and elderly in our parish. That has had many advantages as well as some disadvantages. Often we have had to hurry through the visits because we felt we had so many people to see. Usually those who are sick and elderly like to have someone stay longer and pray and share with them. Besides, we know it is the responsibility of all of us as a parish to care for the sick. So, in order to multiply the number and quality of visits to the sick that can be made, we are inviting interested parishioners to join in this ministry.
>
> The group of parishioners who will participate in this ministry to the sick will be meeting regularly. We will be praying together, sharing the scriptures and our faith reflections, as well as providing support for each other in order to bring the love of the parish community to the sick.
>
> This will allow so many more visits to the sick, the homebound, and the elderly to be made. Each person will have fewer people to visit and will have more time for prayer and support.
>
> The small group of us will grow together in this ministry. Of course _____ and I will still do some visiting, but through building a faith community of visitors, we will be able to better serve more of the sick of our parish.

Such a gentle explanation will help people receive and understand how a community approach to ministry can be effective.

Obviously much communication is verbal; yet we also communicate through non-verbal messages. There is no greater communication tool than honest personal conviction about the value of small Christian communities. Parishioners know when the pastor and the pastoral staff are supportive and enthusiastic about something.

One pastor who was beginning RENEW in his parish spoke about his own belief in small groups and strongly encouraged his entire parish to join a small group. He was a member of a group himself and shared honestly and openly his own positive experience of the faith sharing group. He did this not only from the pulpit and through the bulletin, but also in informal conversations with parishioners. Simple questions such as "How is your group going?" and "What's happening in your RENEW group?" were a regular part of his exchanges with parishioners.

This pastor was communicating that he was interested and committed not only to his small group, but to the development of small groups throughout the entire parish. As was stated in the chapter on the priest and parish staff, one of the key components for parish "ownership" of this pastoral direction is the attitude of the leadership.

STYLES OF COMMUNICATION

Let us look now at various styles of communication that could be utilized to communicate this pastoral direction in a parish. Thomas Sweetser and Carol Wisniewski Holden in their book *Leadership in a Successful Parish* list five styles of pastoring which we will translate for our purposes here into five styles of communication.[1]

1. Telling

In the telling style, the communicator feels he or she knows what is best for the parish and sees to it that it is carried out. There is the attitude: "I know what to do and I am happy to tell you." The assumption of the communicator is that the stance of the parish is: "Just tell us what to do and we'll be glad to do it." This may have been effective at one time, but as we in the church have grown as church in our understanding of the advantages of participation, this style has become less effective.

2. Selling

A second style of communication is that of selling. This is based upon a sense of influence. The purpose is to give people a reason to be interested. It might sound something like this: "Have I got an idea for you!" In some ways the pastor and staff become salespersons with a message. As Sweetser and Holden observe, such an approach can work for a while, but eventually people see through this approach and begin to feel they are being used. They then often react with passive resistance.[2]

3. Testing or Evaluative

The testing or evaluative style is more of a "fishing" style of communication. The pastor or staff checks out ideas with others. It may sound something like this: "I have an idea; what do you think?" The person then can agree or disagree, but unless there is real ownership on the part of those receiving the message, the second part of communication, which is making sure the receiver understands and accepts the message, may be lacking.

4. Passive

The passive style of communication is one without energy in which the communicator expresses an idea, but with little or no personal commitment. It sends a message that is lethargic, and there is no ownership of the idea. In this model no one has many ideas. Obviously in this model a new pastoral direction could not be communicated with any enthusiasm. This fourth style of communication is relatively ineffective.

5. Participatory or Mutual

This communication style creates a climate of "joining." The leader says: "I have an idea." Others say: "Let's hear it; we have ideas too." Mutual sharing occurs. There is joint reflection and the purpose is the overall good of the parish. According to Sweetser and Holden: "In the participatory style the pastor still exercises strong leadership. However, the emphasis is not on making the final decisions, but on creating the most conducive environment and climate for people to participate in identifying the problems and choosing the best solutions. The pastor makes sure that everyone has a part to play. He establishes an appropriate process for gathering the necessary information, for helping people stay with a decision until everyone can own and accept the result, and for dividing up the work so that all are included and are given areas of co-responsibility. Everyone becomes a co-owner of the task and co-minister of the parish as a whole. But it does take skill, time, and much patience as people try to understand and practice this new approach to shared leadership of the parish."[3]

Which of these styles will be helpful in communicating a pastoral vision in the parish? It is unlikely that the telling, testing, or passive styles will be of much benefit. Rather a healthy combination of the selling and participatory style will be most effective.

Let us clarify the selling style. We are not talking about selling this pastoral direction as a salesperson may try to sell a vacuum cleaner or a new car. However, with shifts in a style of ministry, parishioners will have to begin to take ownership; thus they will have to be convinced themselves. Communicating a more communal style of parish will need more than a psychological or sociological approach. It will include communication about the power of the Spirit alive in the church today.

Earlier we spoke about the communitarian nature of the church and the power of the Spirit at work in the church. Thus the primary message to communicate is the beautiful power of the Spirit at work in the parish, bringing parishioners more deeply into a loving relationship with God and with one another. It is always the Spirit who gives us words to speak.

Empowered by the Spirit, the pastor or staff do not so much "sell" the pastoral direction as witness to it, sharing how it will empower the parish to loving, knowing, and better serving God and one another. In many ways the pastor is sharing about God's own self-communication, the Trinity, a loving community. Thus the witnessing of the pastor and staff to community becomes an expression of who God is and calls people to be.

A second approach to communicating the pastoral direction is that of the participatory style of communication where all parishioners are included in a process of ownership. Obviously participatory communication is an adult form of communication and can be most effective. It requires commitment and maturity on the part of everyone involved. Not only are ideas shared, but their implementation is carried out by parishioners as well as staff.

Our church calls us to this co-responsibility: "Because the church is communion, there must be participation and co-responsibility at all her levels. This general principle must be understood in diverse ways in diverse areas. . . . From Vatican II has positively come a new style of collaboration. . . . The spirit of willingness with which many lay persons put themselves at the service of the church is to be numbered among the best fruits of the council. In this is experienced the fact that we are all the church."[4]

The following reflections on methods of communication utilize this participative approach.

METHODS OF COMMUNICATING THE PASTORAL DIRECTION

A. The pastor and/or pastoral staff person begins by introducing the concept of small Christian communities for the parish at a staff meeting and/or parish pastoral council meeting. The person initiating the idea must have both a clear sense of the pastoral direction as well as personal conviction about the importance of this approach.

B. Secondly, the pastor assembles a group of people (hopefully this group will be or will develop into the core community), who are open to the pastoral direction, to gather information and plan for parish small community development. (Information on the core community was developed in Chapter 9.) As this group is formed and begins the first steps of implementation, the group continues ongoing communication with the entire parish about its efforts.

C. It is essential to speak with the parish pastoral council about implementing the pastoral direction. They are a very important group in the parish and carry leadership responsibility. (See Chapter 11.) Ideally, in the early stages of looking at the pastoral direction, the parish pastoral council is consulted. One practical way to help the parish pastoral council reflect on this vision of the parish as a community of small communities would be to have the council use a reflection process. (See Resource E for a sample Process for Parish Pastoral Council Reflection.) If a core community has already been established, the core community could assist the council with this process. If no core community has yet been established, the council may wish to set one up.

At this time, the pastor and core community are not asking the parish pastoral council to make a decision on implementing this pastoral direction, but rather to reflect on how to help the parish participate in reflection on it as a future direction for the parish.

D. In order to help the entire parish reflect on this pastoral direction, the core community may choose to hold a process for listening and planning. This process would be a gathering of parishioners for the specific purpose of gaining input into planning for the parish to move in this pastoral direction. It would also assist parishioners in their reflection and response to the pastoral direction.

Why have a parish process for listening and planning? The primary purpose of this process is to provide an opportunity for parishioners to listen to one another. It allows for shared responsibility, a time for the gifts of all to be used; it allows all parishioners to share their thoughts and feelings; it helps develop leadership; it can be a beautiful spiritual event. It is an experience of being church. The process for listening and planning can help parishioners connect with the pastoral direction and see its practical implications.

It is important for the pastor to take a key role in inviting the entire parish to participate in this process for listening and planning. The pastor could speak at all the masses, inviting people to pray for the upcoming process for listening and planning in which there will be more reflection on the parish's experience of small groups. Everyone interested is invited to come. The pastor will want to offer a great deal of encouragement and motivation. (See Resource F in *Resources* for sample parish process for listening and planning.)

E. Following the process, the pastor will again wish to speak from the pulpit and share the events of the process. He may wish to say something like this:

I want to share with you the reflections of the parish process for listening and planning which was held last week to help us all better understand the small Christian community vision and what it could mean for the future direction of our parish.

Over the years since Vatican II, we have matured and have gained a greater sense of our own call to mission and ministry. We are very aware of the power of the Spirit at work in the church, bringing parishioners into a growing, loving relationship with God and with one another.

Now many more parishioners are better prepared to participate in the ministry of the parish. For example, in regard to baptismal preparation, we as a staff, will be meeting with parishioners who will in turn be gathering with small groups of parents preparing to have their children baptized. We will be using a more communal model with much of the preparation done in living rooms, sharing scripture, praying, learning about the sacrament of baptism, and finding support from each other.

I also want to give adequate time to my own small community in the parish. Some of my time will also be given to the development of the small community leaders. Again we're doing this in order to "multiply" the service that can be given in the parish. What I most want to say is that there will need to be some shift in the way the rest of the staff and I spend our time in ministering to and with you.

Actually, the movement in this pastoral direction is not only happening here at _____ parish. Following our RENEW experience (or whatever small group experience has been a part of the parish), the reflection of our parish pastoral coun-

cil, and the input of the parish process for listening and planning, we know that our parish is not having an isolated experience. The development of small communities is a phenomenon in other parishes as well. Our diocese is helping and supporting these efforts, and it seems to be a strong reality, not only here, but in many parts of the world.

The question for all of us on staff is: How can we best serve the parish? Through your reflections and the call of the universal church, we feel this is the best way we can serve you now. Let me close with a reflection from the Final Report of the 1985 Extraordinary Synod of Bishops: "Because the church is communion, the new 'basic communities,' if they truly live in unity with the church, are a true expression of communion and a means for the construction of a more profound communion. They are thus cause for great hope for the life of the church" (Evangelii Nuntiandi, 58).[5]

This is an exciting time in our parish. We will be learning together how to live out this call from our church in our everyday parish life.

WHAT WE COMMUNICATE

In many different ways, we communicate what we believe! If the pastor and staff truly believe in this pastoral direction, it will be communicated not only through means such as the pulpit, through the parish pastoral council, and in a process for listening and planning, but also through less formal exchanges. How important it is to give clear, simple, direct messages about the implementation of this pastoral direction in the parish. The message is simple: God calls us to be a people who love and care for each other in community. Together in all aspects of parish life we want to pray and grow spiritually, support and love one another, learn and deepen our faith, reach out in mission and ministry, and care for each other in community.

CHAPTER 13

Ministry of Small Community Leadership

No book on the vision of small Christian communities would be complete without a rather extensive exploration of the kind of leadership necessary to help groups grow into Christian communities of faith. Each small community has a leader who is a person of faith and is trained in various skills.

What does it mean to provide the ministry of leadership for a small community? How does this leadership fit into the ministry of leadership of the entire parish and the larger church? These are questions which will be addressed in this chapter.

The ministry of small community leadership which is provided by lay persons, while different from the ministry of the ordained priesthood, is, in fact, quite complementary. Each person has received a call from God through baptism. The 1989 document *Apostolic Exhortation on the Laity* speaks of this call. "The lay faithful participate, for their part, in the threefold mission of Christ as priest, prophet and king."[1]

However, the apostolic exhortation goes on to clarify the differing roles of the lay faithful and the clergy. "The ordained ministries, apart from the persons who receive them, are a grace for the entire church. These ministries express and realize a participation in the priesthood of Jesus Christ that is different, not simply in degree but in essence, from the participation given to all the lay faithful through baptism and confirmation. On the other hand, the ministerial priesthood, as the Second Vatican Council recalls, essentially has the royal priesthood of all the faithful as its aim and is ordered to it."[2]

The ministry of leadership in small communities is a very specific service that lay persons can render. All persons, by virtue of their baptism, receive a call, a personal vocation to holiness. Ordained ministers have a special sacramental and unifying role in the body of the church. However, it is not the responsibility of the ordained ministry to build up the church community and the responsibility of the lay community to transform the world. Rather it is the responsibility of both ordained ministers and the laity to build up the church and to help transform the world. It is a question of emphasis. The laity, as well as ordained ministers, are called to "communio,"[3] to building up the body of Christ.

It is not a matter of dependence or independence in ministry but rather a matter of interdependence. The church is not a mere organization, but the mystery of the Lord's continuing presence in and for the world. The church is the body of Christ in time and space. We are all responsible for bringing the awareness of the mystery of God into our world today. We can call it collaborative ministry or shared responsibility. It is that, but it is much more. As ordained ministers and laity, we all minister together for the purpose of living out "communio," making God's word more alive in our world today.

Small community leaders share in the pastoral care of their small communities. What does pastoral care mean? The word "pastor" is taken from the Latin root word "pascere" which means "to feed." *Roget's Thesaurus* offers another expression of the concept of pastoring or shepherding: "to guide" or "to show the way."

Very simply, for the leader, the ministry of pastoral care is caring for the small Christian community. The leader of the small community "feeds," "guides," and "shows the way." That is not to say that the leader is the only person responsible for pastoral care in the group. In fact, as the community grows, each person learns more about caring for others and the mystery of a communal church becomes a greater lived reality.

As was stated in a previous chapter, priests and pastoral staffs often see great value in having others share in the ministry of pastoral care since even a very energetic staff cannot offer adequate pastoral care to everyone.

Every group needs good leadership. Let us look specifically at the role of the leaders of small communities.

ROLE OF A SMALL COMMUNITY LEADER

The leader is sensitive to each of the following responsibilities. However, the leader does not handle these totally alone, but also enables and encourages other members of the community to share in these responsibilities.

To Welcome

A small community leader is welcoming and hospitable to others. In our culture, there are many "acceptable" signs of etiquette and politeness. Some of these may be motivated by a desire to please, to look good, or to be accepted by others. While that is not entirely poor motivation, the kind of hospitality that a small community leader offers comes from a deep and honest love and respect for the other person, not mere politeness. Ideally, everyone is welcomed to be a member of the community, not only those of a particular social class, ethnic background, or educational status. The leader is constantly aware of any new person and gives special attention to introductions and welcoming to strangers.

The leader is conscious of the difference between being truly hospitable and being overbearing.

> The paradox of hospitality is that it wants to create emptiness, not a fearful emptiness, but a friendly emptiness where strangers can enter and discover themselves as created free; free to sing their own songs, speak their own language, dance their own dances, free also to leave and follow their own vocations. Hospitality is not a subtle invitation to adopt the life style of the host, but the gift of a chance for the guest to find his own.[4]

The leader knows that it is important to recognize each person every time a gathering begins. Each person is highly valued. As the small community grows in comfort the leader continues to offer hospitality, particularly if there is anyone in the group who may feel "left out" or uncomfortable.

To Be Sensitive

A small community leader is sensitive and caring. The leader is responsible for developing sensitivity to the needs of the other members of the community. If one member is hurting or unusually distressed, the leader notices and recognizes the pain. For example, one of the small community members has not been feeling well and is going for medical tests. In the course of the sharing, this person says that he is going for tests on Wednesday and acknowledges his anxiety. As a sensitive and caring response, the leader could call this individual on Thursday to inquire about the medical tests. The leader could also encourage others in the group to minister in a similar manner.

In another situation, some community members may be absent from the meeting without letting anyone know the reason. The leader would call after the meeting to let them know they were missed and to find out if everything is all right.

Some community members may be more shy than others. Even after groups have grown together a long time, there may be some members who are still hesitant to speak. The leader will want to invite the shy or fearful person to share.

In some ways the small community leader may be likened to an orchestra leader. At times it is necessary to quiet down some of the trumpets and basses and at other times to bring in the quieter flutes and piccolos. At all times the orchestra leader is aware of the value of each instrument and how the song is to be played. He is not a controller but rather allows the music to be played in harmony.

At some times people may become discouraged or fearful about some personal issues. Again the leader supports and allows for the sharing of feelings about personal crisis. Any response to someone's feelings is not conditioned by a judgment, but rather by acknowledging the validity of the feeling. Being sensitive to people is not always an easy task; however it is very much a part of the pastoring role. Very simply, the leader "pastors" the group by recognizing, respecting and showing care for all members.

Because of the uniqueness of small groups and the open process of sharing personal experiences, it may happen that someone tries to use the sharing as an opportunity to unburden a deep-seated emotional problem. The leader ought to be ready to identify and respond to this possibility. Faith sharing naturally involves the expression of personal stories and feelings. Tears are sometimes shed. But there is a point beyond which personal sharing becomes an attempt at therapy. How does the leader recognize that the group is going beyond that point? It will probably be evident to the leader that the group is feeling uncomfortable, embarrassed, or even fearful because someone is revealing aspects of his or her life that are inappropriate for this gathering. The sharing is no longer about faith at all. It does not stem from the scripture reading or the focus of the evening's theme. What may have begun as faith sharing has become an occasion for venting one's emotions.

An individual's use of the group for therapy is really unfair to everyone involved. This kind of sharing deters the group from its task, which is faith sharing. It discourages reluctant participants and prevents them from sharing their stories. It places an undue burden on the leader who is expected to respond as a professional helper. And, finally, it is unfair to the troubled individual who obviously needs more help than the group can provide.

What is the leader to do? Here are six suggestions:

1. Try to prevent this kind of inappropriate sharing from happening in the first place. During the initial meeting of the group, an explanation of what faith sharing is and what it is not will establish ground rules and fix boundaries.
2. Anticipate dominating types who take control of the group and divert it away from faith sharing toward their own agendas.
3. When an individual sends signals for help, and if you feel personally capable of responding, meet or call that person. Express your concern ever so gently and give the other an opportunity to respond, e.g. "Joe, I noticed last evening that you seemed a little down. Am I correct? Is there something wrong?" This form of response and questioning is well within the role of leader and demonstrates effective pastoring.
4. If the preventative measures described above do not work and an individual begins to unburden his or her problem inappropriately during the meeting, try to stop the behavior before it goes too far. Use phrases or questions that redirect the group to faith sharing. When all else fails, simply stop the person carefully and gently, but firmly. For example, say, "Peg, you are really hurting. I want you to know that I care about you. Let's talk about it when our faith sharing is over, after the meeting. All right?"
5. Recognize the signs of deep personal trouble, such as the following:
   a. severe depression evidenced by the repeated admission of being depressed, sleeping disorders, and difficulty accomplishing ordinary life tasks;
   b. uncontrollable tears in inappropriate circumstances;
   c. serious parenting problems;
   d. alcohol or drug related problems.
6. When a person is obviously in need of help, and if you judge that you can be heard, arrange to meet with the hurting person. During the conversation, you can say, e.g., "I've heard you express a lot of pain in the last three weeks. You said that you've been very depressed. Have you thought about getting some help from a counselor?" This intervention can help the person recognize the need for help. You might refer the person to the pastor or a member of the pastoral staff. No matter what happens, confidentiality is observed. (Material adapted from *RENEW Small Group Leader's Workbook*, Maurice Monette, author.)

To Listen

A small community leader is a good and active listener. In a world where there is so much noise and activity, it is difficult to cultivate the skill of listening even in a small group of ten people. Good listening often means setting aside one's own thoughts in order to focus completely on the person speaking and what he or she is saying. The leader can best challenge the community to good listening by modeling it.

One important responsibility of the leader is to ensure that there are no unnecessary outside disturbances. For example, if a telephone is constantly ringing, it is difficult for the group to pay attention to what is occurring in the group sharing. Quiet is a wonderful gift a group can be given, especially for prayer and reflection on the scriptures.

Another responsibility is helping the community to listen to one another. Researchers in human communication tell us that over eighty percent of what is communicated is done non-verbally. The leader needs to be aware of non-verbal signals. If the non-verbal communication is very different from the words being spoken, the leader may wish to ask about it directly.

In one small group a young woman who had been divorced was speaking about how powerfully God had been working in her life. She shared about some of the earlier pain of her life, and how, after a few years, she could feel that God had been with her all the time. As she spoke she began to cry. One group member assumed that she was crying because she was still upset with some of those earlier circumstances of her life. After the group member spoke to her and asked what she was still upset about, the leader asked the young woman why she was crying. Her response: "Because right now, as I am sharing this, I feel so loved by God. I don't feel sad, but I am crying because of the joy I feel." Good listening includes testing one's assumptions.

To Challenge to Growth

A small community leader challenges the community to growth. No matter how long members of a community have known each other, there is the constant need to challenge one another to growth. The leader plays a gentle, encouraging role, and does not dominate, but ensures that the group is growing in Christian community and not just becoming a comfortable "cozy" support group.

In some instances leaders would prefer to call themselves facilitators. Small community leaders certainly do facilitate the gatherings of the community, but there is much more that is asked of the leader.

The leader constantly evaluates with the community. If the community members have moved into too much discussion and not enough real sharing about their lives, the leader invites the community to reflect on that reality. Perhaps they will take a full meeting to talk about sharing from the heart. Maybe the community has lost its prayerfulness, so there is need to bring that to the attention of the group.

A key responsibility of the pastoral minister is the ongoing spiritual development and learning of the community. The leader may wish to bring in speakers on particular areas of interest or tapes which could help the community grow in knowing and utilizing various forms of prayer. Suggesting spiritual reading books or tapes as well as informing the community of opportunities for spiritual formation in the parish or community is also an excellent means of catechesis.

Small community leaders can encourage the community to share prayer experiences together. They can provide input on various styles of prayer and urge daily scripture reading by community members. By inviting the members of the community to witness to their personal prayer, greater commitments to prayer can be generated in others.

The small community leader will also need to encourage community members to be prepared for the meetings and gatherings in which they share and support one another. Each person is called to be a contributing member, and thus preparation for the meetings is essential.

The area that is often most difficult for a community to remain faithful to is that of mission or action. For many Catholics there is a tendency to settle for a safe sanctuary, a privatized religion in which prayer and action are not integrated. The leader will constantly want to raise the question of action, application, and the integration of word and deed. Each gathering of the community should contain a time for planning action and evaluating past commitments to action.

As has been stated before, often these actions will take place within the daily circumstances of life, e.g. more patience with a child, reaching out to a neighbor whose wife recently died, making just decisions at the office, etc. At times they may also include some concrete action to help the parish grow, e.g. being greeters at some of the Sunday liturgies, planning a prayer vigil for the entire parish, hosting an evening of reflection on social concerns, etc. The community is strongly encouraged to reach beyond the parish into the community or into the larger world.

One small community initiated a "twinning" experience with a Central American basic Christian community. They not only became acquainted and developed a prayer network between them, but actually got to know one another and offered needed support. They communicated through mail, and some members visited the base community in Guatemala. As community members became more familiar and comfortable with one another, a special bonding took place. People were sharing as people. Now in addition to watching the evening news and trying to sort out the "Central American situation," people were knowing and loving a group of Central American Christians.

The point of this reflection is that the leader is constantly growing in awareness of the needs of the church and world. While the leader is not totally responsible for the ideas and implementation of action, if the community is weak in that area, the leader challenges the group to growth.

The small community leader helps the community see that these actions are not isolated good deeds but rather a response to their call to mission. As members of the church we are all sent to transform the world, to be on mission. Thus, concrete actions are not an optional choice for Christians but a response to their baptismal call.

To Set the Stage

A small community leader sets the stage for growth in faith. No detail is too minor for the leader. For the sharing itself, the arrangement of the room is important. A circle or some similar arrangement allows people to see and hear each other without strain. The Bible is given a place of prominence. A candle or a symbol reflecting the theme of the scripture reading can also be utilized.

Most communities find that refreshments add to the social and communal bonding of the group. Serving coffee or refreshments during the sharing can often be distracting, but serving such refreshments following the sharing would be most appropriate. Again the leader may wish to arrange who will bring the refreshments or delegate this to some other members of the group.

Often the question is raised about the participation of children. The decision of how and when to include children may be dictated by cultural norms and preferences. Some groups may wish to include children in all aspects of the gatherings; others may wish to have a babysitter and include the children in the social part of the gathering. In some instances, it may be a difficult distraction to have children at the meeting itself because most adults cannot concentrate well when they have children to watch. (This issue will be addressed in greater detail in Chapter 16 on the domestic church.)

To Be Humble

A small community leader is humble. As was stated previously, the leader of the small community is not in charge or in control. The small community leader has a humble heart, and, like Jesus, takes on the attitude of servanthood. St. Paul describes the attitude of Jesus in Philippians 2:6–8:

> Who, though he was in the form of God,
> did not regard equality with God
> something to be grasped.
> Rather, he emptied himself,
> taking the form of a slave,
> coming in human likeness;
> and found human in appearance,
> he humbled himself,
> becoming obedient to death,
> even death on a cross.

Servanthood then is the attitude of a true leader of a small community.

One human tendency a person may have when given authority or leadership responsibilities could be to control or "to make sure things happen the way I think they should." Since leaders in other areas of life sometimes focus on "taking control" and "moving up the ladder," small community leaders might be tempted to believe that the life and growth of the small community is totally dependent on them.

In fact, leaders do have a very unique "pastoring role." However it is the type of leadership role that Jesus spoke of when he told his followers "not to lord it over one another," but rather to be servants, to be humble. Humble leaders constantly rely on the power of God. These leaders recognize that "nothing is impossible with God" and that truly loving relationships are possible only with the power of God in one's life.

Humble leaders do not believe that everything depends on them. In fact, with an attitude of humility, leaders know that others have good ideas, and have very unique gifts to bring also. Humble leaders do not compare others' gifts, do not make judgments on the motivation of others, and are willing to share how they have worked out difficult situations and how God has helped them in their lives.

Humble leaders do not dominate and do not teach in the traditional sense of knowing more than others. Humble leaders are truly wise and share from life's experience and past learnings. These leaders are not threatened if others in the group share more experienced wisdom or even if others in the group have more natural leadership ability. Humble leaders pray constantly for guidance.

Let us look at two different reactions of a leader. At certain times there may be the need for a new person to assume leadership in the small community. If the previous leader feels overly responsible for the group, it will not be an easy transition. The leader will find fault with the new ways things are being done. There may even be some undermining of the new leadership. This could all be very subtle and hardly recognized by the former leader.

Humble leaders, on the other hand, will undoubtedly experience some of the same feelings of "letting go," but will support the new leadership. If the previous leader finds that things are not going the way that is most beneficial for the group, he or she takes a quiet, reflective stance and brings up the issues or concerns when appropriate. The humble leader does not govern the group. The leader is servant.

To Be in Relationship with the Larger Church

The small community leader is clear about the small community's relationship with the parish and the larger church. Small Christian communities are part of the parish. Small community leaders are clear that as leaders they are a necessary link to the larger parish. Leaders know that these small communities exist in order to be at the service of the parish, the larger church, and the world. As leaders they are sent to serve by the parish and they serve the parish.

Small community leaders are always encouraged to have respect for the teaching authority of the church and to recognize that it is through the body of the entire church that truths are revealed. To be truly pastoral means to have a firm commitment to the church and to look to the church for guidance.

Christian leaders are called to interiorize their Catholic heritage. According to Catholic teaching, each person has the right and responsibility to grow in one's relationship with God according to one's personal conscience, but the Christian conscience can only be properly formed through the scriptures, tradition, and the teaching authority of the church. The Vatican II Constitution on Divine Revelation states:

> It is clear, therefore, that sacred tradition, sacred scripture, and the teaching authority of the church, in accord with God's most wise design, are so linked and joined together that one cannot stand without the others, and that all together and each in its own way under the action of the one Holy Spirit contribute effectively to the salvation of souls (DV 10).

Small communities are at the service of the parish. Leaders understand that a large part of the small community's mandate is to serve and to respond to the needs of the parish and larger community. Small community leaders recognize the importance of Sunday liturgy and active participation in the celebration of the liturgy. They encourage community members to see the church building itself as a very important place of worship and welcome.

The leader assists the community in learning they are to be hospitable not only to one another but to the parish as a whole. Small community members ought to be the first ones to extend a hand of welcome to a newcomer in the parish or to those visiting. Small community members ought to be the ones who circulate during doughnuts and coffee to meet and reach out to those who are not active in the parish.

A large part of the pastoring role of the leader is to communicate with the pastor of the parish. The leader ought to strive to work within an open, respectful, and caring relationship with the pastor and staff.

Sometimes issues of doctrine or church teaching may arise. The small community leader need not handle these alone, but may take them to the pastoral staff for their input and expertise.

There may be circumstances when a pastor who has supported the model of small Christian community in a particular parish is changed. Ideally, the new pastor would support this pastoral direction and the communities would continue to flourish.

In many instances, the new pastor will be coming from a parish background that did not include small communities. In time his experience in the parish may lead to a deep conviction of their value. In other instances, the new pastor may stress other priorities and be non-supportive of small communities. Dialogue and a welcoming invitation to small community involvement may in time lead him to be appreciative of the value of small communities. In all cases the leadership of small communities is encouraged to maintain an attitude of respect for the new pastor and to foster parish unity.

To Be Prayerful

A small community leader is a person of deep prayer. We have often heard the adage "Pray always." What does praying always mean for leaders of small communities? Part of ministry to the community is to pray for each person regularly and for the entire group. Prayer helps leaders remember that God works in people's lives. The small community in its fullness is an experience of God. Only personal prayer and commitment to meditation will assure this.

Leaders play a large part in helping the community become and continue as a praying community. The meeting itself ought to have a conducive atmosphere for prayer.

Another aspect of the pastoring role is to help community members become more comfortable with the scriptures. Therefore, leaders themselves know how to read and pray the scriptures. Daily reading and meditating upon the scriptures is of utmost importance for leaders. Through a daily commitment to the Bible, leaders learn first-hand the powerful way that the word is able to transform lives.

To Forgive

A small community leader is open to forgive and be forgiven. As the community matures, it will go through various stages of growth, some easy and some difficult. There will be moments of conflict, and, as is true in any intimate human relationships, some alienation and fragmentation. No leader can be totally disengaged from the conflict. Small community leaders will recognize vulnerability, both their own and others, and will find it necessary to forgive and to be forgiven.

The small community leader takes Jesus seriously when he says that "if someone wrongs you seven times in one day, and returns to you seven times saying, 'I am sorry,' you should forgive him" (Lk 17:4).

This does not mean that the leader avoids conflicts; quite the opposite. Conflict and differences of opinion are not necessarily negative; they expand sharing. However, when conflicts elicit deep anger or emotion, they need to be addressed. Despite the fear of anger many may have, conflict must be acknowledged by a leader. The challenge is to maintain a respectful atmosphere. If arguments ensue, the pastoral response is to clarify that opinions on many issues can be diverse.

It may be helpful for the leader to assess the symptoms of the conflict. Is the conflict the result of normal group growth patterns, a power struggle, personal insecurity or the threat to a person's self-image, transference from an area of someone's personal life, philosophical differences, or perhaps differences of method or approaches? If an assessment is accurately made, it allows the leader to deal directly with the conflict. If the situation concerns the group's growth or differences of approaches, it may be helpful for the leader to address the issues openly in the group setting. If, on the other hand, the conflict is the result of personal insecurity or transference from an area of personal life, the leader may wish to address the conflict with the concerned individuals outside the group setting. (For more reflection on conflict and forgiveness, see *Called To Lead,* a companion volume to this work.)

To Celebrate

A small community leader has a positive attitude, the gift of joy, and a celebrating spirit. People create climates of acceptance and joy. For people to be open to the Spirit and the power of God's Word in their lives, the environment ought to create open hearts and souls so that God can speak. Sharing positive experiences of God and the beautiful world of the Spirit provides all with the personal knowledge of God's love in their lives.

Leaders help create this atmosphere by personal attitudes of joy and spiritual wonder. Leaders help the community in an awareness and acknowledgement of the power of God in its midst. This realization leads to a sense of joy and celebration. It may take the form of a party, of a prayer experience which celebrates some occasion, such as a birthday or significant anniversary. Cakes are baked, candles are lit, songs are sung. Pastoring is sensitive to all aspects of life.

Much emphasis has been placed thus far on the meetings held by the small community. There are, however, numerous other means of celebrating, bonding, and creating communal experiences. Ideally, other gatherings include families of small community members, so that the bonding happens not only among adults, but among entire families and significant other people in community members' lives.

These could well include the following:

- Christmas parties
- summer picnics
- Sunday afternoon outings
- an annual weekend camping trip
- pilgrimage trips
- an annual retreat together
- vacations together
- apostolic endeavors, i.e. inner city soup kitchen or a social justice response to an issue

This list is not exhaustive, but merely suggestive.

EXTENSIVE TRAINING FOR THE MINISTRY OF PASTORAL CARE

The development of leaders for the pastoral care of small communities is so essential that a separate companion volume to this work, *Called To Lead,* has been designed. Each leader is asked to participate in this development process.

Briefing

Briefings are meetings in which there is an opportunity for small community leaders to prepare for their upcoming gathering. Through briefings small community leaders can dialogue about pastoral considerations for their communities, evaluate previous meetings, become better prepared in understanding the materials they will be using, and discuss any areas of concern they may have in regard to their community gatherings.

In addition to leadership development sessions, it is recommended that regular briefings be planned for leaders prior to each small community gathering. Members of the core community, a parish staff person or priest holds the briefings or makes arrangements for others to do so. On some occasions a member of the core community could meet with a group of small community leaders, although generally it is done on a one-to-one basis.

Since one of the pastoral responsibilities of the core community is to provide support and direction to the leaders of the small communities, these individual briefing sessions allow for that ongoing, regular support and direction. Briefing is especially recommended for these groups which are developing a more intense community life.

Aspects of Briefing

In a first organizational step, the core community decides who among them will assume the responsibility of briefing, to which small community each will relate, and how often. It is necessary to consider the number of small communities as well as the number of core community members who have the qualities, gifts, and time necessary for this role.

Geographic location and personal relationships among small community leaders and the core members is also an important factor. It is necessary to have an openness to this kind of ministry as well as the positive support and recognition of the pastor and staff.

Specific qualities are important for those doing the briefing:

1. **Respect for Diversity:** Persons need a receptivity to different personalities and an openness to different expressions of spirituality.
2. **Common Sense:** Any person doing briefing needs an instinct for what seems appropriate or inappropriate in a given situation or relationship. In addition the person needs a facility to recognize and help small Christian community leaders acknowledge when a person's behavior is abnormal and requires care beyond their pastoral skills.
3. **Emotional Stability:** Those doing the briefing ought to be emotionally stable themselves.
4. **Trustworthiness:** Each person concerned must have the ability to keep confidences.
5. **Credibility:** Those doing the briefing must have a level of acceptance within the community.
6. **Humility:** "Briefers" need to realize that they do not have all the answers and must be willing to seek advice from others with more experience and knowledge.
7. **Availability:** Briefing will take time; it is important to be able to give adequate time and attention to small Christian community leaders.
8. **Desire for Growth:** Persons doing briefing also need a desire for continuing faith and skills development in their own lives.

What Happens in Briefings

The spiritual growth of the individuals and the group as a whole is key to developing as a small Christian community. Growth in personal relationship with Jesus and commitment to the gospel way of life is the foundation of any authentic Christian community. The briefing meeting gives the small Christian community leader time to discuss the needs for spiritual development experienced within the group and ways to meet those needs. The core member can suggest resources that are available and also bring the needs of the groups to the core community meeting for long-range planning.

Suggestions that a core member may offer to a small community leader include the following:

- simple instructions on how to keep a journal;
- basic techniques for sharing faith at a deeper level;
- resource persons who may be available for spiritual direction;
- an evening of reflection on themes pertinent to the needs of the small community: God's love, forgiveness, prayer, ways to deal with feelings of jealousy and anger, etc.;
- spiritual reading suggestions;
- instruction and experience with different styles of personal and group prayer;
- ways to do outreach and concretize mission.

It is important that the core community person and the small Christian community leader have a good understanding of any content and materials that small communities are using at a given time. During the briefing session, small community leaders share their understanding of the content and the direction of the next small community meetings. During this time, any questions in reference to content could be raised. If the core community member is not familiar with the material there is still time to consult a resource person or the materials for clarification.

Specific Issues for Briefings

There may be some things happening or not happening in the group that the small Christian community leaders need to discuss in the briefings which would help them better deal with the situation. The briefing meeting provides the opportunity to review the dynamics of a particular group, what might be causing certain behaviors and what the appropriate responses could be. Issues may be matters such as the following:

1. *People are not showing up for the meeting.* It is important that the individuals themselves be asked the reasons for this occurrence. The following questions may be helpful points of reference:

- Is the meeting location easily accessible to everyone?
- Is there a genuine atmosphere of warmth and hospitality?
- Is the content meeting the needs of those involved?
- Does the content relate to their life experiences?
- Do individuals realize that their commitment to be present at the meeting is very important to the growth of the group?
- Have expectations been discussed?
- Are meetings too frequent? Are meetings frequent enough to allow a true sense of belonging or commitment to growth?
- Is the leadership style meeting the needs of the group or is it too dominant or too non-directive?
- Is there a member who is too dominating or controlling?
- Are there personality conflicts?

2. *People in the group are in conflict; they have begun to wonder why things are not as "loving" as when they first joined the group.* The core member could review with the leader some of the points regarding conflict resolution. Reviewing the stages of group development might help determine if the problem is emerging as part of the natural growth process. Should this be the case, encouraging the group to see their experience as a growing one and challenging the members to the next stage of growth is vital.

3. *Someone in the group is having a personal difficulty in some area of his or her life (e.g. sickness in the family, job loss, or other emotional upsets).* The best response might be to encourage the person to share the difficulty with the rest of the group so there can be a pastoral response (meals in time of sickness, suggestions about job opportunities, words of encouragement). It is crucial that sound judgment be exercised in this area.

Small communities cannot provide for all of the therapeutic needs of their members; however, the person experiencing the difficulty might be helped by the leader, by some trusted person in the group, or by the group as a whole. In some cases, the person may be encouraged to go to someone outside the group who has a particular knowledge in the area of difficulty (counseling, Alcoholics Anonymous, Alanon, Weight Watchers, etc.). Naturally, it is everyone's responsibility, but in particular it is part of the role of the small community leader to pick up the signals that indicate someone is experiencing extreme difficulty. Briefing meetings can help a leader sort out various options.

4. *Someone in the group is dominating or being non-participative.* Reviewing some of the leadership skills and group dynamic insights

and deciding which applies in the given situation may alleviate this problem.

Community Development

During the briefing meeting the core member can help the small community leader explore various ways to increase the sense of community within the group as well as ideas to help with the bonding of families and close friends of the small community members. This is especially important if the group itself is not already taking the initiative in this regard. Some suggestions previously stated include: an annual weekend retreat involving families and other significant people in the small community members' lives, parties, picnics, or even a mystery trip.

Relationship to the Parish

The briefing session provides time to relate to what other groups are doing also. It is important that each small group in the parish develop an appreciation and value for all the various types of groups in the parish. It is a time when the core community can assess with the small community leader the need for a large gathering of the small groups (or at least the leaders of the small groups) in order to network and develop a sense that each group is only a small part of a much larger vision. During the briefing session, small community leaders can better learn how to serve or be served by the larger parish community.

Support for Mission

As was stated previously, living out mission and ministry is an important component of the small community effort. The small community leader needs to be encouraged to call individual members and the community as a whole to a sense of mission to which the church has been entrusted by Jesus. Matthew 25 speaks strongly of the importance of living out our relationship to God through our relationships with one another. The briefing time provides the opportunity to reflect on ways to help people make these connections between their everyday lives and the call of the gospel. Briefings offer the opportunity to reflect together on the larger needs of the parish and the world at large. Briefers can help leaders be aware of the social justice efforts in the parish and other resources which would help the community respond to parish and community needs.

Briefing Summary

The areas covered during the briefing sessions relate closely to the five elements of Christian community: prayer, mutual support, sharing, learning, and mission. The small Christian community ought to have an opportunity to evaluate in an ongoing manner how it is developing in relationship to these elements. The briefing meeting provides the opportunity for mutual communication in which encouragement can be given, suggestions made, and resources cited that would assist the community in growth in certain areas.

THE GIFT

The call to ministry is ultimately the call to receive a great gift from God. The leaders of small Christian communities are truly gifted by God, for their call is to love people in a very real manner. They are invited to enter people's lives with humility, concern, and skill and to be vital links between the small community and the larger church. They are called to enable and empower others. Like all Christians, small community leaders are challenged to live a Christ-centered life, embodying the exhortation of Jesus: "Love one another as I have loved you." With their loving attention, communities will flourish and God's reign will be experienced.

CHAPTER 14

Evangelization and Small Christian Communities

In Chapter 4 we spoke about evangelization and the conviction that small Christian communities provide an ideal vehicle to move the parish toward becoming an evangelizing parish. In fact, we suggested that by restructuring the parish into a community of small communities, the parish could move beyond sporadic, periodic evangelization events to becoming a consistently evangelizing parish. Why this strong emphasis on the parish becoming an evangelizing parish? In this chapter we will take a look at that very question.

In these years before the turn of the century and in the twenty-first century, there is and will continue to be a great emphasis in the Catholic Church on evangelization. Pope John Paul II consistently speaks about a "reevangelization" or a "new evangelization" of all Christians. The year 2000 has been designated as the year of great jubilee in which the church will focus particular efforts on the task of bringing Christ to the world. In preparation for Evangelization 2000, this decade has been set aside as a time of preparation through prayer and penance in an effort to call all Christians to renew their commitment and fidelity to the mission of evangelization.

Vatican II set the stage for this rejuvenation. Pope Paul VI then took the vision of evangelization articulated by Vatican II and clarified and explained it further in his apostolic exhortation "On Evangelization in the Modern World," promulgated on the tenth anniversary of the closing of this historic council. This document provides a challenging and inspiring understanding of evangelization. Pope Paul VI writes: "The church, 'striving to proclaim the gospel to all people,' has had the single aim of fulfilling its duty of being the messenger of the good news of Jesus Christ—the good news proclaimed through two fundamental commands: 'Put on the new self' and 'Be reconciled to God.' "[1] This document, literally a twenty-five year plan to help us become an evangelizing church, summarizes the direction of all evangelization efforts.

WHAT IS EVANGELIZATION?

Evangelization! What is it? To the "average Catholic" it may seem like a foreign term, something that has more to do with television evangelists than with their lives. It could mean for others something that the priest does from the pulpit or professional staff do in the parish. For many Catholics it is something for Protestants to do rather than an active response they have to their baptismal call and commitment. Some still "hanker" for the "good old days" when the priest administered the sacraments and took care of everything. But those days are gone, and through the challenge of Vatican II, Paul VI, John Paul II, and the current documents of the church, we now understand with greater clarity that all baptized Christians are called to this responsibility of evangelization.

What then is evangelization, and if all Christians are called to evangelize, how do we engage more parishioners in this effort? The word "evangel" comes from a Greek root word, meaning "good news." Evangelization then means spreading the good news joyfully, sharing the story. What story? The story of Jesus and what he has done in our lives. The story of those who were healed and loved by Jesus, the story of how God has entered our lives, healed and loved us.

> Evangelization implies outreach to those who do not yet know and love Jesus Christ or realize how much he knows and loves them. It implies enthusiasm and apostolic zeal in the proclamation of the gospel, a passionate desire to help people fall in love with Jesus and commit themselves to him forever. More than a program, evangelization is an attitude. It is a mentality of sharing, of inviting, of welcoming people into the joy of communion with Jesus Christ.[2]

Pope Paul VI provides a broad definition of evangelization. He states that "evangelization means bringing the good news into all the strata of humanity, and through its influence transforming humanity from within and making it new."[3] In Pope Paul VI's definition, evangelization is broader than "getting people to come back to church" or even converting the unbaptized. It is both of these, but so much more. Evangelization calls us to the transformation of humanity and making all of creation new.

Evangelization begins with each person accepting the word of God. As we come to accept that word more fully, deep, radical conversion happens, and not only do we speak that word verbally, but we live it very concretely. We look to Jesus to see how evangelization occurs. Jesus evangelized through his life. He healed the sick and cared for the poor and downtrodden. People were attracted to him because he "spoke with authority." In other words he spoke about God from his own knowledge and experience of God. He touched people where they were in their lives. If they were sick or hurting, he comforted them; if they were frightened, he reassured them; if they were righteous, he challenged them.

That is the kind of evangelization to which we as Christians are also challenged. As a part of living out the values of Jesus in our daily lives, we need also to share our stories. We need to give one another hope by telling how God is acting in our lives today. We need to share the wonderful miracles that are part of our everyday lives, the times we were blind but now can see, the times we were downtrodden but have been lifted up. Often those miracles will be in very ordinary, but powerful, experiences. How often have our broken relationships been healed or our tears wiped away!

As we come to know Jesus better and share his word with others, we will also want to welcome them. We invite them to share their stories. There are so many stories of faith, but so few people who yet understand that that is what their lives are. Just as through the centuries the stories of Jesus have fed and nourished us, we can feed and nourish each other through our stories of faith.

In this chapter we will be looking at evangelization and small Christian communities and then return to thoughts about what we mean by an evangelizing parish. Small Christian communities are an ideal way for the work of evangelization to be accomplished. It is precisely in small Christian communities that people are sharing their stories and seeing how God is acting in all aspects of their lives. These communities are able to reach out to the unbaptized and alienated with conviction and welcome them to their community of faith. The question is not, "Do we focus on evangelization *or* the development of small communities?" Rather we see that small communities provide a fertile environment for the overall task of evangelization to occur most effectively in the parish.

"EVANGELII NUNTIANDI"
AND SMALL CHRISTIAN COMMUNITIES

In "Evangelii Nuntiandi," Pope Paul VI speaks of the importance of small communities in the process of evangelization. He calls them "a hope for the universal church." He then speaks of some important aspects of small Christian communities if they are to be truly evangelizing:

- that they seek their nourishment in the word of God;
- that they avoid the ever present temptation of systematic protest and a hypercritical attitude;
- that they remain firmly attached to the local church in which they are inserted, and to the universal church;
- that they maintain a sincere communion with the pastors whom the Lord gives to his church;
- that they never look on themselves as the sole beneficiaries or sole agents of evangelization;
- that they constantly grow in missionary consciousness, fervor, commitment and zeal;
- that they show themselves to be universal in all things.[4]

Paul VI describes the need for a radical conversion, a profound change of minds and hearts in people if they are to be effective evangelizers. He highlights key elements of evangelization: *interior change, renewal of humanity, witness of life, explicit proclamation, inner adherence, entry into community, acceptance of signs and apostolic initiative.* We will explore each of these elements, and see how small communities can play a vital role.

Interior Change

Evangelization cannot happen without ongoing conversion in the lives of evangelizers. For Paul VI, this is *metanoia,* or a radical conversion which affects both the mind and heart of the believer.[5] This happens in such powerful ways in small communities. As people share about their life in faith, they begin to see their life in a new light. They break open the scriptures and become aware of the discrepancies between how they live and the call of the gospel. They are inspired by the ways God is acting in their own life and in the lives of other community members. They are filled with gratitude recognizing how God is working in every aspect of their lives. The Spirit is alive in the community and moves community members to a graced moment of metanoia.

An excellent example is that of Jim, a man in his early thirties who lives in a tough neighborhood in New Jersey. Jim had little church or religious experience, but somehow got involved in a RENEW faith sharing group. He took over some leadership responsibilities and his love for the Lord became real and obvious. When his pastor was asked about this newfound leader and where he got all his leadership skills, he smiled and said, "Jim was head of the local drug traffic here before RENEW." It was in the context of the small group that Jim had a real metanoia, a deep conversion.

There is story after story about changes in the lives of people who have participated in faith sharing groups. Stories will only be multiplied and deepened as these groups grow into communities, where support for conversion becomes ongoing and normative.

Renewal of Humanity

Paul VI's vision of evangelization is interior change in order to transform society. The challenge is to bring the good news of Jesus into all parts of our culture and society.

In the sharing of their own stories and real life situations with other people, those in small communities develop keener observational powers. The caring in the group helps members become more compassionate toward people they interact with daily. Community members also grow in sensitivity to keeping abreast of world news events that influence human lives. Small communities, in fact, are the perfect context to connect the gospel message to any life situation. Communities not only help members "see" better, but also help them refine precise and explicit ways to act in complex life situations. Communities give people the courage to take concrete action and provide a context for accountability and evaluation of those actions.

Witness of Life

The gospel will be best proclaimed by effective witnesses. The small community provides an excellent environment for people to become effective witnesses. It provides the kind of environment where people can come, reflect, be healed, and know there is security and support as they live and work in a world which may seem hardened against gospel values. People offer an example to one another regarding concrete situations and allow the gospel to influence aspects of their lives that previously may have been unconnected to gospel values. Small community members begin to understand their responsibility to exemplify these values, and they begin to witness in a more holistic way.

Explicit Proclamation

How does the average parishioner proclaim the gospel in an explicit manner? Only through an authentic faith experience. Proclaiming the good news must come from a heart alive with the message of Jesus. The small community provides this type of formation. In communities people learn to speak about Jesus. What may have been fears or inhibitions start to break down and people begin to speak freely about Jesus and what he has done in their lives. The joy of discovering and the confidence that comes when small community members take ownership of their faith call for expression. This is carried beyond the community and leads to a natural expression of faith in everyday life.

Inner Adherence

Paul VI also speaks about the need for all Christians to develop an inner commitment to the gospel. As small communities gather, they come together as a group of believers. Because for many Catholics faith has been inherited, they need to think through and articulate their faith in order to assume personal ownership. The witnessing to one another builds up the faith commitment of each, and they begin to see that not only were most of them "born Catholic," but they have a deep conviction about their faith. Perhaps even to the surprise of small community members, they share their "beliefs" in conversations with family, friends, acquaintances and co-workers.

Entry into Community

As the small community grows, they expand their understanding of mission. The tightly knit group realizes that they need openness and expansion. The good news of Jesus cannot be contained. There is a growing desire to bring others to share the wonderful experience of being disciples of Jesus. The community is open to inquirers. In fact, they attract others.

An excellent example is the story of a man who approached the pastor of a large Catholic church. The man was walking down the corridor in the parish community center and asked if he could buy a ticket to the upcoming parish picnic. The pastor, not recognizing him as a regular parishioner, sold him a ticket and asked the gentleman if he was a member of the parish. The man said he was not and had not been to church for a long time, but his family wanted to come to the picnic. The pastor invited him to join a group that was meeting that very evening, the "Re-Membering" group, a small group adapted from the RCIA experience. The gentleman seemed pleased to be asked and joined the group.

As people began sharing their stories, the gentleman began to feel a bond with the group. He had a taste of a receptive and honest small community. One of the people said that she had been away from the church for many years, but had been back now for the past five years. Others had varying lengths of time of separation from the church. The gentleman who had come to the parish to buy a picnic ticket said, "I've been away from the church for twenty years and I've been back for fifty-eight minutes." In the experience a kernel of this man's faith had come alive!

Acceptance of Signs

Another key element that Pope Paul VI discusses is the acceptance of signs. As people change, they themselves become signs of transformation. They participate more fully in the life of the church. Any privatized view of faith begins to break down in the context of community sharing. Connections between difficult areas of life and faith are made. Small community participants not only participate in the church, but become living signs themselves, visible sacraments of salvation which is very attractive to others.

In the upcoming chapter on the RCIA we will look at the ways the small community becomes a very real sign of the larger community for the inquirer. In small communities inquirers can sort out their own questions and concerns. The strong, loving, communal quality of the small community serves as an ideal entry point for the inquirer and also provides strong support for anyone approaching full reception of the sacraments of the church.

Apostolic Initiative

"Finally the person who has been evangelized goes on to evangelize others."[6] One of the important elements discussed earlier to help a group grow to become a Christian community is that of mission. True faith in Jesus cannot be "hidden" but must be shared.

Many Catholics grew up with the notion that faith is a personal matter. People's many personal needs can easily absorb their energy. As communities share, the message of the gospel compels people to greater concern for others. A sense of urgency is created as well as compassion for suffering humanity and the suffering Jesus endured for the redemption of the human family. As people grow they become more open to the power of the Holy Spirit and allow that power to take root in their hearts, much like the Pentecost moment. As with the early disciples, they receive fire which cannot be quenched and begin spreading the good news of Jesus to the whole world. People who may previously have been fearful or passive begin taking apostolic initiative. Even the timid are transformed as they proudly boast of Jesus and his gracious and healing way of life.

Reflecting on Pope Paul VI's words, it is so apparent that small communities provide an excellent approach to evangelization. They provide an environment for sound growth, which allows many people to have a change of heart. What greater way to free people to proclaim the gospel! What greater hope for the universal church this could be!

WHY EVANGELIZE?

We live in a world desperately in need of the good news of Jesus. There are many who have not as yet been introduced to Jesus, and there are others who have been members of the church, but have disconnected themselves. We hear the desperate cry from the third world for freedom from oppression and poverty. We hear the cry from the second world, asking for freedom from domination and freedom of expression of their religious beliefs, and we hear the cry from the first world, longing for spiritual meaning. No matter what the culture, there is a strong cry for the good news of Jesus.

In the recent document from the Synod on the Laity, there is significant emphasis on the call not only to evangelize, but to reevangelize. In the United States, there is great need for evangelization as well as reevangelization, with fewer than half of our baptized Catholics attending church every Sunday. With much of our first world culture focused on materialism, individualism, and consumerism, there is a call to open our hearts to those who are in our midst and in need of renewed faith. Rare is the family today which has not experienced some family members withdrawing from the sacramental life of the church. Young people are often looking for spiritual experience, but often do not look to the church. The synod reflects that the hour for reevangelization has come.

> Whole countries and nations where religion and the Christian life were formerly flourishing and capable of fostering a viable and working community of faith are now put to a hard test and in some cases are even undergoing a radical transformation as a result of a constant spreading of an indifference to religions, of secularism and atheism. This particularly concerns countries and nations of the so-called first world, in which economic well-being and consumerism, even if co-existent with a tragic situation of poverty and misery, inspires and sustains a life lived "as if God did not exist." This indifference to religion and the practice of religion devoid of true meaning in the face of life's serious problems are not less worrying and upsetting when compared with declared atheism. Sometimes the Christian faith as well, while maintaining some of the externals of its tradition and rituals, tends to be separated from those moments of human existence which have the most significance, such as birth, suffering and death. In such cases, the questions and formidable enigmas posed by these situations, if remaining without responses, expose contemporary people to an inconsolable delusion or to the temptation of eliminating the truly humanizing dimension of life implicit in these problems.[7]

Some interesting studies have been conducted to look at this need for reevangelization in the United States. Looking at the results of some of these surveys gives us an opportunity to see how small communities offer the opportunity to meet many of our needs for reevangelization.

In a 1978 Gallup survey on unchurched Americans, it was found that most inactive Catholics had received religious training as a child and most of them pray. Their doctrinal beliefs were only slightly different from active Catholics. In fact eighty-seven percent of inactive

Catholics would like their child to receive religious instruction. In many ways while inactive Catholics may not have been going to church most of them were not really "fallen away."[8]

In 1979 Father Alvin Illig, the Director of the Paulist National Catholic Evangelization Association in Washington, D.C., and the bishops' committee on evangelization commissioned a new empirical study of the process of dropping out of active church life. The researchers found that many people drop out of active church life at some time or other. In fact about forty-two percent of all Catholics drop out at some point of their lives, but the majority of them return at a later time. An estimated forty to forty-five percent of those who had dropped out were twenty-two or younger at the time of withdrawal.

An interesting fact: their decision was almost always the result of interpersonal factors, seldom because of philosophical or intellectual influences. In fact the researchers suggest that the key to understanding "dropping out" is mostly in the area of relationships with other people and inward needs. Another interesting finding was that those who drop out from active church life seldom drop out from Catholicism as self-identity. Most still call themselves Catholics.[9]

The study also looked at why people return to active church life. Two conditions were identified: people felt a general sense of need or readiness and their reentry was facilitated by a personal relationship with an active Catholic. Since few returnees had left the church due to philosophical problems or doubts, they returned not through philosophical teaching, but in most cases through interpersonal and spiritual factors—friendships, family, love affairs, loss of loved ones, personal or family crisis, illness or a sense of "coming to themselves."[10]

These studies are very useful in helping us to understand why people return to church. They tell us it is often through other people. If one of the key "dropout" factors has been interpersonal problems, then it makes good sense to initiate reentry through positive relationships. Small communities play an extremely vital role in providing good relationships. With so many inactive Catholics coming back to the church as a result of interpersonal and spiritual factors—new relationships, loss, friendship, pain—the small community is an ideal reentry point.

EVANGELIZATION TODAY

As was stated in Chapter 4, the U.S. bishops have articulated four aspects of evangelization. We will look more closely at how these aspects can be lived out through small Christian communities.

1. Calling Active Believers to Even Deeper Faith

In the past we had a rather clear definition of what it meant to be a Catholic. It included attendance at mass on Sunday, adhering to the rules of fast and abstinence, observing the moral teachings of the church, bringing children to Catholic schools, refraining from meat on Friday—to name some of the most obvious. However, today we seek a faith response which touches every aspect of our lives.

Small communities provide a place and opportunity for church-going Catholics to support and love one another in their faith. One gentleman who had been a practicing Catholic all of his life shared his fears about his wife's impending death in his small community. It was indeed a transforming moment when the healing and compassion of Jesus was so alive in the other members of the community. They held him as he cried and wiped his tears, promising through their actions the deep love and comfort of Jesus.

Small communities also provide an opportunity for church-going Catholics to see how forces such as individualism and materialism within the secular world have tended to neutralize their faith commitment. Sharing and witnessing to one another about the gospel message challenges and moves people to deeper conviction, mission and outreach. That beautiful dynamic life cycle we spoke of in Chapter 3, life, community and worship, becomes a greater reality.

But what about active Catholics who do not participate in parish life over and above coming to mass? Are they open to small group participation or becoming members of small communities? Over ten years ago, Phase One of the Notre Dame study of Catholic Parish Life in the United States showed that only about twelve percent of active Catholics were involved in parish life beyond attendance at Sunday liturgy. However, in Phase Two of the Notre Dame Study of Catholic Parish Life in the United States, new data was found. In the past ten years a significant change has occurred and largely as a result of small groups. Now about twenty-four percent of active Catholics are participating in spiritual renewal groups or prayer groups.[11] These spiritual renewal groups or prayer groups are the seeds of small Christian communities where conversion and evangelization will be normative in parish life.

We are faced with a challenging task: evangelizing the active Catholic! The bishops of Texas reflect:

> The biggest task may very well be that of inspiring active Catholics to fall in love with Jesus, to be converted to him, to make him central to their lives, to imitate him, and to share their experience of him with others. After all, our greatest resource is our own Catholic people, and so much of evangelization is encouraging one another to appreciate the breath and length, the height and depth of the Catholic experience of Jesus Christ.[12]

2. Bringing the Message of Christ to Alienated or Inactive Catholics

We have spoken about alienated Catholics earlier in this chapter in our reflection on the need to evangelize. Suffice it to say here that those who are a part of small Christian communities are discovering a deeper faith and love for God and wish to share that good news. They become empowered and encouraged by the community to speak to alienated Catholics who often may be relatives, friends or co-workers. They are not offering an invitation merely geared at building up numbers. Rather they are sharing an invitation which comes from a deep faith and joy. That can be very attractive.

An exciting model for welcoming the alienated and inactive Catholic back to the church is the "Re-Membering Church." In the "Re-Membering Church" people who have been alienated or hurt are invited to come together as a small community themselves to reflect on scripture, share their stories, and experience healing through the community.

If small communities are in place in the parish, individuals returning to the church could become part of one of the already existing small communities. They could be welcomed into an existing community by hearing the stories of others in the community and sharing their own stories. As alienated persons experience these communities of disciples gathered to learn and to share the word, they can become more comfortable in being reunited to their deepest faith roots.

Father Patrick Brennan in his work *The Evangelizing Parish* reflects on the role of the parish with inactive or alienated Catholics:

Parishes should approach the inactive member with an attitude of care. Care should be focused on the inactive member as a person—a hurting person. Some of those hurts are related to the Church; others are deeply rooted in the fabric of the person's personal life.

We do not get people back to church by trying to get them back to church. Rather, people may return to church if they meet and relate to Christian people who have genuine concern and compassion for (the other) person.[13]

What better way to relate deeply with other Christian people than in a small faith community!

3. Inviting People to Join in the Church's Belief and Worship

The Sunday liturgy and sacramental life of the church provides nourishment for our spiritual journeys. "The liturgy, particularly the eucharist . . . is the focus of Catholic evangelization. All missionary activity must flow from the liturgy and be directed to the liturgy."[14] To be an evangelizer means inviting others into the full experience of Jesus' life, death and resurrection. What better means than inviting others to be fed with the eucharist?

The conversion experience that so frequently takes place in a small community opens people to a whole new experience of life. Primary in this is a deeper appreciation of the Sunday eucharist. The word which has enriched small community members during the week also becomes a rich source of nourishment at the liturgy. Because the liturgy is the summit of our Christian faith, those in small communities want to share it with those they love and those who are hungering for a relationship with God.

4. Making the Gospel Real by Applying It to the Issues and Conditions of Our Lives

Small communities assist Christians in their efforts to proclaim the gospel in all aspects of their lives. Again we see this is not an option, but an essential part of the Christian call to holiness, for as Pope Paul VI has said, "evangelization means bringing the good news into all the strata of humanity."[15] We as Christians are called to evangelize the culture.

But how do we do this if we have not "eyes to see or ears to hear"? The dynamic of small community sensitizes and teaches us how to see the world about us as never before. As we said previously in reflecting upon Pope Paul's call to apostolic initiative, the small community can help people develop creative thoughts regarding specific applications of the gospel in their lives. It can give them courage to take action, and offer a means of accountability and evaluation of these actions.

There is probably no greater challenge for us as Christians today than evangelizing our culture. Living in a society where the world's values are often at odds with gospel values calls for vigilant and persistent efforts on the part of committed Christians to "proclaim the good news of Jesus." Where there is poverty and injustice, the voice of Christians must be heard. Where there is homelessness, hunger, unemployment, and disease, the message of Jesus is desperately needed. As Christians gather together to share and love one another in small communities, they can bear the weight of their mission in the world together.

CALLED TO BE EVANGELIZING PARISHES

We began this chapter by stating that by restructuring the parish into a community of small communities, the parish could move beyond sporadic, periodic evangelization events to becoming a consistently evangelizing parish. Often parishes may hold rallies or even assign evangelization efforts to a committee or a team. As good as these efforts are, the difficulty can often be that only a few take responsibility for the evangelizing efforts in the parish. In order to be an evangelizing parish we need to call large numbers of parishioners to responsibility for evangelization. Like the universal call to holiness, the call to be an evangelizer is not an option for the Christian.

Through small communities we are able to have large numbers of people involved in evangelization efforts. A network of people will create a climate of evangelization for the entire parish. Imagine the impact of so many small communities actively engaged in evangelization.

All these small communities would provide members with courage and a sense of being sent forth. Successes and failures could be evaluated and people reenergized for evangelization outreach.

Whatever the focus of a particular small community might be, participants could be formed to see that they have an intrinsic call to evangelization. The key to successfully becoming an evangelizing parish is to move beyond passing and temporary efforts and create a style and structure of parish that is always about the work of evangelization. The pastoral vision of the parish as a community of small communities would achieve this. "If evangelization is indispensable to the church, then small Christian communities are indispensable to evangelization."[16]

Recall that beautiful Pentecost moment in our church when the disciples were gathered as a small community, frightened and confused. The Holy Spirit came upon them and gave them the power to go out into the whole world to proclaim the message of Jesus. There was power and mystery. That moment is happening again today. We too are called to be transformed and changed. We too are called to go forth, as Christians supported and inspired by other Christians, to the whole world to *Proclaim the good news that Jesus is alive, he is risen, he is here!*

CHAPTER 15

The RCIA and Small Christian Communities

In this chapter we will be looking at the Rite of Christian Initiation of Adults, how it is a style or model of parish life, the relationship between small Christian communities and the RCIA, and some practical suggestions for relating the two in parish life.

The modern RCIA was born in 1972 on the feast of the Epiphany and came into existence as the *Ordo Initiationis Christianae Adultorum.* It became a part of the English-speaking world in 1974, and has been written in its latest form in 1988 as The Rite of Christian Initiation of Adults: The Roman Ritual. This document invites all parishes to enter into a process of welcoming new members into a caring community of believers, the church.

"Being in the RCIA has helped me to learn how to share and to love more." "The catechumenate opened up a whole new area of thought processes for me. It made me more spiritual and helped me grow closer to God." "I loved the way we shared our faith; the catechumenate helped me learn how to pray more and sharing in the small groups was 'my favorite part.' " "I began to look at my entire life as a journey with God." "People loved me. It was wonderful and very spiritual." "I became ready to share my faith in my everyday life."

These, and many more comments like them, come from newly baptized people who have experienced the RCIA process. The voices of the newly baptized and those brought into full communion in the church are the voices of true disciples of Jesus. They are alive with the good news of Jesus. They long to share their faith and the new power of the Holy Spirit that is so vibrant within them.

The Rite of Christian Initiation of Adults gives us a process in which all Christians who are enthusiastic about their relationship with God and with one another in God can invite and welcome people into the marvelous experience of being church. Within the rite the basic model of church is community. Through the RCIA the entire Christian community is called to be "on mission" and to be primary ministers in providing welcome and hospitality, to share personal faith in the Lord Jesus, to live gospel values, to evangelize, to catechize, to enter more deeply into the paschal mystery (the life, death, and resurrection of Jesus), and to celebrate all of life as a worshiping community.

The RCIA document itself is a liturgical document, but has numerous pastoral implications. While the RCIA process is a beautiful way to bring catechumens into the church, it is much more. The RCIA provides a framework for parish life. Msgr. Thomas Ivory in his work *Conversion and Community: A Catechumenal Model for Total Parish Formation* states: "I believe we can develop a model of Church as catechumenate—that is, the Church as the environment in which people hear the good news of God's plan for them in Jesus Christ, and in which believers are nurtured and formed in their faith and seek to live out their relationship with Christ in a Christian lifestyle."[1]

Neither the RCIA nor small Christian communities are "one more activity in the parish." Rather, they are "a way of being parish," a means by which spiritual formation is enhanced and evangelization can happen. The style of church suggested throughout our reflection on the parish as a community of small Christian communities is the same style suggested by the catechumenal model of church.

THE RITE OF CHRISTIAN INITIATION OF ADULTS

The roots of the RCIA go back to the early church, in which the followers of Jesus initiated new members into the community through a single celebration of baptism, confirmation, and eucharist. Basing its method on the experience of the early church, the RCIA has four sequential periods. Each of these periods is described below.

Pre-Catechumenate or Inquiry Period

The first stage is the time for getting acquainted. It is a time for interested persons to come to know Jesus or to continue their search for a deeper relationship with Jesus. In this initial step, adults come to the church to inquire about Catholic beliefs, and to search out their journeys into the Catholic Church. Parishioners share their own faith stories and listen to the inquirer's story, questions, and hopes. Through the dialogue the church shares its traditions and history. It is a time for inquirers to reflect and ponder.

In essence the pre-catechumenate is a time of inquiry and evangelization. From evangelization come the faith and initial conversion that cause a person to feel called away from sin and drawn into the mystery of God's love. The whole period is set aside for this evangelization, so that the genuine will to follow Christ and seek baptism may mature.[2]

Catechumenate

In this second stage, inquirers begin the process of making a decision. Inquirers, as they enter the catechumenate, state their desire to formally begin the process of belonging to the family of Catholic believers. "Catechumen" is a Greek word meaning "one who thoroughly sounds out something."

The catechumenate is an extended period during which the candidates are given suitable pastoral guidance aimed at their development in the Christian life. This step includes an explanation of the doctrines and traditions of the Catholic faith. In this way the dispositions manifested at their acceptance into the catechumenate are brought to maturity. Through word, worship, service, and community building, the catechumens come to know the revealing presence of God in their lives. The catechumenate concludes with the Rite of Election on the First Sunday of Lent.[3]

Period of Purification and Enlightenment

The third period or stage is the deepening of the commitment or a time for the catechumen to engage in spiritual purification and enlightenment. It continues during Lent and culminates at the Easter vigil. Lent is an appropriate time for retreat and reflection and calls all parishioners to live more fully the paschal mystery.

The period of purification and enlightenment, which is a period of more intense spiritual preparation, is intended to purify the minds and hearts of the elect as they search their own consciences and do penance. This period is intended as well to enlighten the minds and hearts of the elect (those preparing to receive the sacraments of initiation) with a deeper knowledge of Christ the savior. Holy Saturday is the day of proximate preparation for the celebration of the sacraments of initiation, and on that day the rites of preparation may be celebrated.[4]

Period of Mystagogy or Post-Baptismal Catechesis

In the fourth stage there begins the celebration of the great gift. This final period of initiation, mystagogy, coincides with the Easter season. Together, the faithful and the newly initiated (neophytes) unfold the mysteries to understand them more fully. This is a time for the community and the neophytes to grow in deepening their grasp of the paschal mystery and in making it part of their lives through meditation on the gospel, sharing in the eucharist, and doing the works of charity. The period of post-baptismal catechesis is of great significance for both the neophytes and the rest of the faithful. Through it the neophytes, with the help of their godparents and sponsors, should experience a full and joyful welcome into the community and enter into closer ties with the other faithful.[5]

The steps by which a person moves forward on this faith journey are marked by liturgical rites.

(a) *First Step: Acceptance into the Order of Catechumens*
The Rite of Acceptance into the Order of Catechumens is the liturgical rite, usually celebrated on some annual date or dates, marking the beginning of the catechumenate proper, as the candidates express and the church accepts their intention to respond to God's call to follow the way of Christ.

(b) *Second Step: Election of Enrollment of Names*
The Rite of Election, usually celebrated on the First Sunday of Lent, is the way by which the church formally ratifies the catechumens' readiness for the sacraments of initiation and the catechumens, now the elect, express the will to receive these sacraments.

(c) *Third Step: Celebration of the Sacraments of Initiation*
The celebration of the sacraments of initiation is usually integrated into the Easter vigil. In this celebration the elect are initiated through baptism, confirmation, and the eucharist.[6]

Through this process of initiation the unbaptized person hears the mystery of Christ proclaimed, consciously and freely seeks the living God, and enters the way of faith and conversion as the Holy Spirit opens his or her heart.[7]

THE RCIA AS A MODEL OF CHURCH

What would it mean to have the RCIA be a model of parish life? It means simply that the process used for the initiation of new members would be a normative style of church. One of the essential elements of the pre-catechumenal phase is that of evangelization and outreach. In Chapter 14 we addressed the issue of evangelization and small communities, so suffice it to say here that the task of all Christians is evangelization. As evangelists, all parishioners are asked to welcome others.

The second phase of the RCIA is catechetical formation. It is the lifelong task of the Christian to learn. The parish community is about the task of formation and seeks to create for all parishioners an environment where conversion and formation can happen.

> Through this catechetical formation, the parish seeks to create an environment where the stories and lives of individuals enter into dialogue with the story and life of the Church. There are many structures, organizations and movements which can be part of the pastoral formation of Christians: parish catechetical programs, Cursillo, Marriage Encounter, Legion of Mary, Charismatic Renewal, Catholic schools, youth ministry, sacramental programs, etc. To the degree that these various activities are integrated within the total parish mission, the parish is well on its way in the experience of a catechumenal model. The Liturgy of the Word and the celebration of the sacraments will assume greater significance as the formation experience deepens.[8]

Phase three of the RCIA focuses on spiritual growth, conversion, and reconciliation. Part of the mission of the parish is to assist all parishioners in their spiritual growth and development. This mission presupposes that by virtue of baptism all Christians are called to ongoing growth in holiness. Avery Dulles summarizes the call that each has to be a disciple, to grow spiritually:

> Discipleship suggests a response to the call of Jesus that is both personal and demanding. The call comes individually to each Christian, who is invited to imitate Jesus in a unique way, corresponding to a personal grace and a particular call from the Holy Spirit. While discipleship can be realized at many levels, it continually urges us to go beyond where we now are. To embark on the road to discipleship is to dispose oneself for a share in the cross (cf. Jn 16:20). To be a

Christian according to the New Testament, is not simply to believe with one's mind; it is to become a doer of the word, a wayfarer with Jesus.[9]

The parish is the primary place that this growth in discipleship can happen.

The last phase of the RCIA leads the neophyte to mission and ministry, which is the primary effort of all members of the church. As a model of church, the catechumenate is understood "primarily in terms of its formational process, helping people to mature in their faith commitment by developing their gifts and ministries. The beneficiaries would be the Christian community itself and the larger secular society which is affected by the witness and service of the Church."[10] Again all Christians are called to service, witness, and mission.

The catechumenal model of church understands that all Christians are on a journey, a spiritual journey, sharing, praying, reaching out, transforming, evangelizing.

THE RELATIONSHIP OF SMALL CHRISTIAN COMMUNITIES AND THE RCIA

The relationship between the RCIA and small Christian communities is readily evident. No RCIA effort can be totally effective if the parish itself is not striving to become a more faith-filled, evangelizing community. Small Christian communities are an effective means of creating such a parish. Small Christian communities and the RCIA are a natural "fit." The catechumenal group itself is invited to become a small Christian community, and experience has shown that when it is implemented in parishes it is an ideal model of small Christian community.

Charlie and Peggy Lockwood, catechumenate coordinators in Presentation Parish in Upper Saddle River, New Jersey, reflect upon the RCIA and small Christian communities:

In September of 1978, our pastor invited us along with ten other parishioners to study the catechumenate in the hope of launching this conversion process one year later. We discovered the power of the Spirit of God at work in this process, evangelizing and forming everyone involved, not only the inquirers and candidates. Our study team evolved into a nurturing, faith-sharing small group, and we naturally have the small group model in all our RCIA outreaches.

Now, we feel the call to evolve even more toward the integration of the RCIA and the growing small community ministry that we are blessed with in our parish. Through this, inquirers and catechumens benefit from more active concern and nurturing, not only from the catechumenate team and their individual sponsors, but from so many others in the parish.

The sequential periods of the RCIA suggest that conversion happens in a prescribed developmental way with a beginning, middle and end. We feel from experience that this is somewhat artificial because evangelization, catechesis, conversion, discernment and service happen continually throughout the process of our lives, and they happen in all different orders. Thus to have a particular RCIA experience grounded in an ongoing small community environment frees the individual person to have conversion be an integral part of daily life with its differing rhythms.

The small community is a natural sponsor of the RCIA and of all who are involved. The RCIA and small communities not only need one another, they are part of the same Spirit.

Not every parish has yet implemented the total catechumenal process, but initiating small Christian communities will provide a big boost to its ongoing development. Once the RCIA team has been developed, they too are called to become a community of faith. They welcome, initiate, instruct, and provide spiritual formation experiences.

The following schema is offered to show how small Christian communities and the RCIA might be integrated. The RCIA can only be truly implemented within the context of a faith-sharing community. A movement in that direction is based upon the following conditions:

1. The parish has implemented or is moving toward the implementation of the RCIA in the fullest sense.
2. The RCIA team or catechumenal team is growing as a small Christian community itself.
3. A process of educating the parish about the RCIA and small Christian communities has been undertaken.
4. Small Christian communities are already operative or the parish is looking to foster their development.

When these conditions are present the integration of small communities and the RCIA can occur in the following manner:

The Inquiry or Pre-Catechumenate Period

The small Christian community itself is in an ongoing process of evangelization. Community members are called to reach out to people they know who are searching for something more in their lives and to welcome these people into their sharing. A living room in the home of one of the members of the small community may be a more attractive place for newcomers to be welcomed than a large church hall. If the small Christian community is indeed an evangelizing community, hospitality and welcoming of these newcomers will be a key component of the community's awareness and practice. Community members will share their stories of faith with those potentially interested and introduce the newcomer into the parish life and the process of the catechumenate.

In the case where an unbaptized or uncatechized adult comes to the parish on his/her own or through parishioners (who are not members of a small Christian community), it is ideal to have that person become a member of a small Christian community as a part of the initiation process. The community which would be most appropriate for the inquirer is discerned by the parish staff members, the inquirer, and the small community which will potentially receive the inquirer.

The small Christian community plays a very important role in the Rite of Acceptance which takes place as the inquirer becomes ready to make a declaration of intent to proceed further. The small Christian community is responding to its call to evangelize and the inquirer is given a loving community with which to share and from which to learn.

In some instances where there are no small communities in existence, the parish could organize a group of those parishioners who are interested in initiation ministry and then move forward with the establishment of small groups at large. In this situation a small Christian community would be formed composed of "inquirers," their sponsors, and a group leader. Using the elements of a small Christian community they move toward the Rite of Acceptance.

The Catechumenate Period

Following the inquiry period, small Christian communities provide an opportunity for catechumens (and those seeking reception into full communion with the Catholic Church)[11] to be "one with" the faithful in experiences of word, worship, service, and community.

In the Rite of Christian Initiation of Adults the period of the catechumenate is described as a time that "catechumens learn to turn more readily to God in prayer, to bear witness to the faith, in all things to keep their hopes set on Christ, to follow supernatural inspiration in the deeds, and to practice love of neighbor, even at the cost of self-renunciation."[12] This, however, is not only the call of catechumens, but the call of the entire parish community.

The catechumenal community itself meets at various times, and the primary gathering point for the catechumens (and candidates) occurs when they are dismissed from the assembly at the conclusion of the liturgy of the word. While the catechumens (the candidates), their sponsors, and appropriate catechists form the catechumenal community, the intention of the RCIA is not to create a separate ongoing community. Instead, catechumens (and candidates) are encouraged along with their sponsors to be involved in other small Christian communities and/or ministry groups of the parish. Participation in these small communities can provide opportunities for supplementary catechesis. In many cases, the most appropriate small communities for catechumens are the ones in which they began their early contact with the parish. That community may be the most appropriate community to offer continuing support since its members know and love the catechumen.

Period of Purification and Enlightenment

During the period of purification and enlightenment small communities provide the occasion for the faithful and the elect to witness their faithfulness to Christ and to share their conversion stories.

During Lent the entire parish community is focusing on the great Lenten stories of transformation. The whole parish is on a journey. For the catechumen this may be a "first time" journey; for others it is a renewal of their baptismal journey into faith and deeper transformation. While the elect continue to meet together, they can also join with their small Christian community who would also be focusing on appropriate Lenten themes. Thus the catechumen and the small Christian community are sharing this Lenten journey.

During this time the faithful and the elect (and/or the candidates) are together and can share appropriate retreats, group meditations, and reflections. Again the most natural small community for catechumens could be the community with which they began. That community would be helpful in being a part of the reflection on the scrutinies to help the catechumen better appreciate them. (Scrutinies are special rites in which the community prays that the elect will be enlightened and purified and that any evil influences within their hearts will be removed by the grace of God.) The small Christian community also has the opportunity to provide the catechumen a retreat experience in the small group itself.

Period of Mystagogy or Post-Baptismal Catechesis

The entire parish now celebrates the Easter mysteries. Just as the entire parish focused on the paschal mysteries in Lent, so the parish continues to look at what this transformation means for their call to mission in the world. It is an important time for parishioners to live out in all areas of their lives the values of the gospel.

Once the elect (and/or the candidates) become neophytes and share full membership in the universal church, the small Christian community continues to play a significant role in their faith journey. During the Easter season the neophytes together with the other members of their small Christian communities unfold the mysteries of our faith by "meditating on the gospel, sharing in the eucharist, and doing the works of charity."[13] This is to prepare themselves for entering anew the evangelizing ministry of the church celebrated on Pentecost.

In the year following the neophyte's initiation the small Christian communities are instrumental in nurturing the faith of these newcomers and in helping them discern appropriate ministries both within and beyond their particular parish.

It is so easy for a new person to have a sense of being lost in the midst of a large parish. Many priests in the past may have wondered, "Whatever happened to those to whom I gave instructions?" When the neophyte is a member of an already existing community of faith, there will be no need to wonder about what happened to the person.

MODEL FOR INTEGRATING SMALL CHRISTIAN COMMUNITIES
AND THE RCIA

Father Thomas Caroluzza of Holy Spirit Parish in Virginia Beach, Virginia who has worked for a number of years with the catechumenal process suggests three models that have been tried and proven successful.[14] He acknowledges that, to begin with, there is the assumption that there are small communities in the parish or that at least the parish wishes to establish such communities.

The three models look something like this:

(1) The small Christian communities of the parish learn how to listen to each other, care for and support one another. They must reach out in their homes, their neighborhoods, where they work and recreate, inviting interested people to join them for prayer, faith sharing, ministry, or whatever is of concern that gathered them in the beginning. In essence, the small communities are about the process of evangelization in their everyday lives, with family, friends, co-workers, even strangers.

When someone indicates an interest, the members of the community into which the person is brought help the inquirer raise questions and concerns. The community members need to be open to the newcomer/inquirer even as far as setting the agenda. In essence, this small community is doing the pre-catechumenate, that is, they are opening up the spirit of the community to the inquirer, the first proclamation of the living God.

When the small community discerns the inquirer's readiness to enter the catechumenate, they, as a community, would present that candidate to the parish catechumenal team and offer sponsorship. In this particular model, the small community does not have to participate in the catechumenate itself. In most cases, one of the members of the small community would be the sponsor for the catechumen and have a greater role in his or her faith development.

That particular sponsor would share with all the members of the small community the progress of the catechumen. The community would continue to offer support from afar as well as more intimate friendship and informal contact with the catechumen.

During Lent the candidate would return to the small community where prayer, fasting and the works of charity could be practiced with the small community. All members of the small community who have come to know the candidate will want to give testimony at the Parish Rite of Sending and to be actively involved in the Lenten rites and the Easter vigil.

During the Easter season, the small community would help discern the gifts of the neophyte and how those gifts could be exercised in the parish and the world. The tender faith of the neophyte continues to be nurtured and nourished in the small community in the months and years ahead.

In this model there is little need for follow-up programs for new members. The new Catholic is nurtured and supported by friends known intimately over many months. When ten, twenty, or fifty small communities are exercising their responsibility for evangelization in this way, there will be not only larger numbers of inquirers and catechumens each year, but greater numbers of the parishioners directly involved in the process and the rites.

(2) A second model that has been tried and proven successful is to have some parish communities focus specifically on pre-catechumenate and evangelization while others focus on catechesis and still others on the content of the Lenten and Easter seasons. In this model the sponsor takes the inquirers and the catechumens to various communities at different times for different reasons. After the Easter season the neophyte chooses one of those communities with whom to continue to share and grow.

The advantage to this second model is the greater number of parishioners the candidates come to know over the many months of their journey. The disadvantage is that this experience is less intimate and therefore less bonding takes place between the candidates and the members. Those who have used this model feel that this kind of bonding will take place when the neophyte chooses a stable community after Easter.

(3) A third model that has been tried is having the small community provide supplementary and individualized catechesis. In this model the catechetical needs of each catechumen are the primary concern. Various communities develop a specialized area of catechesis in order to help the catechumens learn about the Catholic faith. The parish designs a plan to ensure that all areas of catechesis are provided.

The catechumenate group meets each Sunday after dismissal. The special needs of this group are supplemented by a small community that takes a particular formational focus. Each sponsor assumes responsibility for bringing the catechumen to those communities for one or more sessions. In other words, the catechumenate community itself would be the primary community, but catechumens would have the opportunity to meet many parishioners and become "formed" in a community model by visiting different communities. After Easter the neophyte would be encouraged to become a regular member of one of the already existing small communities.[15]

SUMMARY

Obviously there are many more possibilities, and great creativity can be utilized to implement the RCIA in a parish which is structured as a community of small communities or where there is some focus on the development of small communities. Small communities provide both the environment and the opportunity for formation that is essential to the RCIA. Just as we are all called to evangelization, we are all called to implement the RCIA process in our local parishes.

In a survey of four hundred and ten parishes conducted by Tom Warren of the Institute for Christian Ministry, the lack of a sense of responsibility for the catechumenate on the part of the people in the pews was the most frequently mentioned problem of the catechumenate. When there is a parish-wide lack of understanding and participation in the RCIA, the rites could seem to the average parishioner to be unauthentic, and may sometimes smack of formality, empty ritual, and play-acting. Family members, the sponsor, and the catechumenal teams can give testimony at the Rite of Election, but many parishioners are so distanced themselves from any level of relationship with the catechumens that they can do little more than watch the catechumenal team and sponsors.[16]

"In light of what is said in *Christian Initiation,* General Introduction (no. 7), the people of God, as represented by the local Church, should understand and show by their concern that the initiation of adults is the responsibility of all the baptized."[17] While it is true that the RCIA speaks of delegating some members of the community to fulfill certain roles in the process of initiation, the rite is also clear that delegation does not mean that others abdicate their roles.

A small community structure for the catechumenate, besides providing a solution to many of the concerns expressed above, helps meet other challenges as well: sponsorship, follow-up, working with varying backgrounds of inquirers and catechumens, just to name a few. In the small communities model of the catechumenate, the catechumenal team benefits from working with small Christian communities and is assisted in exercising the functions, roles, and responsibilities in the process of initiation.

In the past few years, an understanding of the importance of meeting the needs of alienated and returning Catholics has also emerged from the experience of the catechumenate. This process of reconciliation is known as the "Re-Membering Church." Like the RCIA, the Re-Membering Church is brought together as a small faith sharing group.

All that has been said previously about initiating new members into the church can be underlined when we speak of returning Catholics. If a person who has been alienated is coming back to deepen his or her faith what better place to begin than in a small community where intimacy is possible and questions and concerns can be dealt with. Any one of the three models discussed above could be utilized equally as well with returning Catholics.

Since all small communities are responsible for the work of evangelization, having a new or returning Catholic not only will enrich the community, but will offer the newcomer support and love in a faith sharing environment.

"See how these Christians love one another." What greater invitation will there be than to see that truth in action?

CHAPTER 16

The Domestic Church and Small Christian Communities

The family is the domestic church! What powerful implications that statement has for us as church. In this chapter we will look at the family today, how it models community, and the relationship between the family as domestic church and small communities. We will specifically examine how families and small Christian communities complement one another and suggest ideas for developing family-centered small communities.

The reality of the family holds great importance. "The family is the basic cell of society. It is the cradle of life and love, the place in which the individual is born and grows."[1] According to Vatican II, the family will fulfill this mission to be that first and vital cell of society "if it shows itself to be the domestic sanctuary of the church through the mutual affection of its members and the common prayer they offer to God . . ." (AA 11).

In many ways the family, the domestic church, holds the keys to a deeper understanding of what it means to be church today. We spoke earlier about moving toward a more relational style of church where sharing stories of our own faith with others is essential. Each day the story of today's faith-filled experiences can be shared. Families share meals; families celebrate joys; families heal one another's hurts; families learn forgiveness first-hand; families are there when someone dies. Every day the sacred is revealed in the ordinary. God is at work among us, continuing our creation through the intimate relationship of family.

Small Christian communities are not unlike the family. They too provide an atmosphere where stories can be shared and the stuff of life addressed. The intimacy and bonding in a small Christian community is in some ways like that which is experienced in the family.

Small Christian communities have a great deal to offer families and, in turn, families are the model and support for the small community. Those who participate in small communities are strengthened to bring communal values, and the spiritual growth gained from the community, more concretely into their family environments. Likewise, all discussion about the development of small communities ought to be done with a family perspective. Small communities need to be cognizant of the family roles and responsibilities of its members and build on those family support systems.

FAMILY PERSPECTIVE

First of all, let us look at what we mean by "a family perspective." Family perspective is viewing all individuals in the context of their family relationships and their other social relationships. It is using family relationships as a criterion to assess the impact of the church's and society's policies, programs, ministries, and services.

The family is a system, and when one member is changed (perhaps through a small community) the whole family system changes. Steve Preister, noted for his work on family perspective, writes: "Any change in a family, or in a family member, or in a family's environment, affects the life and functioning of the family and each of its members. Therefore, the issues that are present in the life of a family must be part of the agenda of those who are working with any member of a family."[2]

Each person has some idea what it means to be family. We hear of the "family of man" which today we would call the "family of humankind." The use of the term "family" in this sense is generic and we understand it to include all people who have ever been created. But each of us has been born into one particular family. Most of us know that family well, but some have been separated from that family early in life and were raised by a different family or even by an institution. Whatever the personal experience, we all have some perception of what family is supposed to be.

Family provides not only a home, but a place of socialization where one learns about faith, where one is taught ideas and skills, where one is loved and nurtured. Family members learn from one another. They learn to love and care. They learn about conflict, dialogue, and forgiveness. They learn to share.

Families teach profound yet simple things to children. "Don't fight with your brothers and sisters." "Sit up straight." "Share with your sister." "Don't throw sand." "Play fair." "Be quiet for a while."

"Go to your room until you can settle down." Children learn profound lessons: sharing, loving, honesty, crying when you're hurt, praying, helping. Families teach and children learn unproductive lessons as well: "Mom and Dad love you more when you're good!" "You're stupid!" "Do as I say, not as I do!"

The unconditional love, forgiveness, belonging, and recognition of the sacred in the ordinary events of daily life are the components of family spirituality. This spirituality is lived out in the system of relationships between members of the family.

Thus it is not surprising that ever since the beginning of humankind there has been particular interest in the family as the primary unit of formation and education for each human being. Many of us have been conditioned to think of the ideal family as two parents with children, an adequate home, and all the necessities of life. However, sometimes there is much pain because the often-held images of a close-knit, nurturing family are not realized by many. When families dissolve or are not intact, everyone suffers. We know this particularly today when divorce rates are higher than ever and the make-up of families has changed. Today we have "the many faces of family."

Small Christian communities can and do support and offer those communal values of nurturing and caring when the nuclear family is not intact. They can give a sense of belonging and bonding to people who, for whatever reason, do not have the spiritual and psychological support of other family members.

We can better understand the power of the small community to support family life when we look at one of the fastest growing spiritual support groups today: Adult Children of Alcoholics. Using the twelve steps of Alcoholics Anonymous as a spiritual program of recovery and the traditions of unity and service as a basis, large numbers of adults are gathering weekly, sometimes daily, to share, receive support, and learn new ways of living a more spiritual life. Through the small groups, adult children of alcoholics learn that, while their parents did the best they could, and there is no benefit to blaming parents, new healthier behaviors and feelings are needed in order to be in right relationship with God and other people.

Small communities, however, are not only for those who have had serious struggles in their family. Small Christian communities provide families which are intact a place to evaluate their commitment to family and receive support for the everyday challenges of family life.

Even intact families are changing. Only seven percent of the nation's families live in the so-called traditional arrangement: a working father, a stay-at-home mother, and one or more children. Forty-eight percent of mothers with infants under one year of age work outside the home at least part-time. The previous generation clearly defined the roles of wife and husband, mother and father. Today each family must define these roles and responsibilities for itself. While this can be seen as an opportunity, it is also a serious source of stress for many families.[3]

Two or three generations ago it would have been the "norm" to have families living in the same town or neighborhood for many years. Families supported one another in many of their daily and crisis needs because they were "just next door." This is not true today. In fact, it has been estimated that between 1970 and 1980 just over fifty percent of Americans changed their residences.

With that kind of mobility, many do not have the kind of built-in community and family support system that once was possible. How many Americans today still live a local phone call away from parents, brothers and sisters, aunts and uncles? How many of those who have moved in the past few years do not even know the names of their neighbors? A society that used to have many family and neighbor support systems just does not have as many such systems today.

Does all this mean that family life and values are no longer possible? Obviously the answer is no. Quite the contrary, the family perspective is more resilient and adaptable now than ever. However, with the "many faces of family" and the growing change in the nuclear family, small Christian communities not only enhance family life, but offer increased support to strong as well as struggling families.

PARISH: A FAMILY OF FAMILIES, A COMMUNITY OF COMMUNITIES

The church has over the past years had very positive movements to support family life: Christian Family Movement (CFM), Marriage Encounter, Cursillo, all based very much on a communal model of church.

Pope John Paul II in his address to the members of the Hispanic community in San Antonio, Texas in 1987 spoke of the importance of the family in parish life today. He spoke of the parish's task of building up a living community and called every parish "a family of families." He states: "The vitality of a parish greatly depends on the spiritual vigor, commitment and involvement of its families. The family in fact is the basic unity of society and of the church. It is 'the domestic church.' Families are those living cells which come together to form the very substance of parish life."[4]

Each person has inherent value as a child of God. When two people marry they become a family. As children are born they extend that nuclear family. Many families coming together in a parish create this beautiful image of a family of families. As families come together they become communities. The parish is, at its best, a family of families, a community of communities.

The question is: How do we enable the development of that spiritual vigor, commitment, and involvement of families? Much of what has been said previously about the benefits of small communities applies here. Small communities can provide families with spiritual growth experiences and opportunities. Communities provide an environment where families can come together or individuals can come separately, not to detract from the importance of the family, but to build the family.

Small Christian communities provide a place where Christian tradition and values can be better grasped and strengthened. If small communities commit themselves to strengthening their families, these values can be brought back to the domestic church renewed and revitalized.

In fact, many action responses of the small community directly relate to family life. Let us take, for example, the struggles of parents with teenagers. The small community provides a safe place for parents to look at how they are relating to their teens. They also provide support for parents in the hard decisions that they must make in fostering Christian values in their children. The small community has the capacity to assist single parents in action responses that enhance their relationship with their children. For example, community members could support a single parent's need for relaxation through providing babysitting assistance to a parent who is overwhelmed at times with all the responsibilities of being a single parent.

Action responses can relate very directly to family life in such areas as family affirmation, support, and reconciliation. Through sharing in a small community a member may decide to return home to reconcile with a child or a spouse.

If, in fact, parents are sharing what it means to be a parent in today's society and are receiving support from a small faith-filled group of people, they will be better parents. If couples share their faith in this larger arena, they will grow in intimacy with one another and God.

The entire decade of the 1980s was named by the church as "the decade of the family." A synod was held on the family and the resultant *Apostolic Exhortation on the Family* contains instruction on the dignity and holiness of the vocation of marriage and family. No clearer message could be given on the family than that it is an "intimate community of life and love" (GS 48).

This apostolic exhortation contains clear instruction on the importance of the family perspective:

> The church, which is at the same time a saved and a saving community, has to be considered here under two aspects: as universal and particular. The second aspect is expressed and actuated in the diocesan community, which is pastorally divided up into lesser communities of which the parish is of special importance.
>
> Communion with the universal church does not hinder, but rather guarantees and promotes the substance and originality of the various particular churches. These latter remain the more immediate and more effective subjects of operation for putting the pastoral care of the family into practice. In this sense every local church and, in more particular terms, every parochial community must become more vividly aware of the grace and responsibility that it receives from the Lord in order that it may promote the pastoral care of the family. No plan or organized pastoral work at any level must ever fail to take into consideration the pastoral area of the family.[5]

As an institution, ideally the family is a small Christian community. The synod went on to emphasize four general tasks for the family:

1. forming a community of persons;
2. serving life;
3. participating in the development of society;
4. sharing in the life and mission of the church.

We will look at each of these tasks in relation to small communities. As the family addresses these tasks, it becomes evident that the values underlying the life of the Christian family are foundational to small Christian communities. Love is the principle and power of both. Using the four tasks outlined by the synod, we will look at how small communities and family can complement one another.

Forming a Community of Persons

For both the family and small Christian community, love, the kind of unconditional love given to us by God is paramount. According to Pope John Paul II's apostolic exhortation *Familiaris Consortio:* "The family, which is founded and given life by love, is a community of persons: of husband and wife, of parents and children, of relatives. Its first task is to live with fidelity and the reality of communion in a constant effort to develop an authentic community of persons."[6]

The family of today desperately needs external as well as internal supports to develop that love. A small Christian community is a marvelous vehicle to offer that support. Loving is not confined to family or small community but is all-embracing. If I want to love unconditionally, I will love in all aspects of my life. At any given time I may need more support from family or my small community, or I may feel more connected with one or the other, but love, if it is real, is unconditional in all aspects of life.

Bonding and fidelity are key elements of forming a community of persons. Human relationships, whether with family or small community, can only be in right order through the power of God's spirit. The two arenas of family and community provide a particular invitation to deep communion with others.

There are different degrees of bonding and communion, but the values remain the same for families as well as communities. In the family the communion between husband and wife is characterized by unity as well as indissolubility. While fidelity is different for small communities, commitment to the community and its growth is obviously of great importance.

Sharing, support, challenge and mutual correction, important values in community, are also key to family life. While a family may be related through blood, there is no guarantee they are not just a group of people living together unless there is conscious sharing and support, just as is necessary in small Christian communities.

Honest sharing in a small community should, in fact, enhance family members in their ability to share faith within their homes. Family members who share honestly and support other family members will find it natural to do the same in their small community. There is a great richness in the relationship between small communities and family when people reflect on and share their journeys and thus come to recognize the sacred in the ordinary events of life.

Serving Life

For families, one of the primary means of serving life is through giving birth and parenting. No other earthly experience provides such a concrete expression of God's great gift of creation. Parents not only create life; they also model and encourage virtue and provide education for their children. Pope John Paul II teaches: "The task of giving education is rooted in the primary vocation of married couples to participate in God's creative activity: By begetting in love and for love a new person who has within himself or herself the vocation for growth and development, parents by that very fact take the task of helping that person effectively to live a fully human life."[7]

Education is begun in infancy, progresses in childhood, and matures in adulthood. Education is not over when one graduates from school or when one leaves home. In many ways, education about various aspects of life just begins. Catechesis, spiritual formation, ongoing learning—these mature in adulthood. In small Christian communities catechesis is of essence in order to help adults appreciate and grow in faith in order to serve life more fully. The process of learning is ongoing; the process of giving and serving life happens when structures facilitate adult growth.

A recent, growing phenomenon in the area of catechesis is family-centered catechesis. Families come together in communities of faith.

> The community of faith is the context; interactions between generations are the means of education. In learning about living, the multigenerational approach allows for more facets to be considered: the older generation is one of history and tradition, the middle-aged generation is one of the present, dealing with "the here and now," the younger generation is one of vision and hope. Together they form a kaleidoscope of religious experiences which seem to be the best way to share catechesis in a time of rapid social change amidst pluralistic values in a technological society.[8]

This kind of catechesis can also be helpful to small communities. Effective catechesis must lead to a lived faith that serves the world.

Participating in the Development of Society

No small group is truly a Christian community unless there is significant outreach into the development of society. Both the family and the small Christian community are one tiny cell of a much larger society. Yet as is true with all living organisms, each tiny cell plays a significant role in the life of the whole. If one cell is healthy, it adds to the health of the whole; if one cell is diseased, the entire organism suffers.

Thus the first order of business for both families and small communities is being in right relationship within. The second and equally important order of business is participating in the transformation of society. "The family is . . . the place of origin and the most effective means for humanizing and personalizing society: It makes an original contribution in depth in building up the world, by making possible a life that is, properly speaking, human, in particular by guarding and transmitting virtues and 'values.' "[9]

Families humanize; small Christian communities humanize; families personalize society; small communities personalize society. Again the values and tasks of families and communities are so similar. The deeper the bonding and support in families and communities, the greater the probability that there will be the awareness that we are a world community, bonded together by God's love. What a wonderful partnership to have small communities available to support families and family life and values available to support the growth of this pastoral direction.

Sharing in the Life and Mission of the Church

Our understanding of social responsibility is deepened in small communities which in turn can help families understand their mission. The element of mission in small communities complements the family's task of sharing time, talents, and goods with the larger community.

Among the fundamental tasks of the Christian family is being a sign of the reign of God in history by participating in the life and mission of the church. Both family and small community are called to the ministry of evangelization. It is only to the extent that members of communities or families accept the gospel of Jesus and live it out in the ordinary events of their lives that they become evangelizers.

The family, like the church, ought to be a place where the gospel is transmitted and from which the gospel radiates. In a family which is conscious of this mission, all the members evangelize and are evangelized. The parents not only communicate the gospel to their children, but from their children they can themselves receive the same gospel as deeply lived by them. And such a family becomes the evangelizer of many other families and of the neighborhood of which it forms part.[10]

Evangelization happens in the marketplace. It happens in work settings; it happens in home settings. Small communities assist families in evangelization efforts through sharing and support. Families provide an important atmosphere for evangelization. All experiences in each person's life are the "places" for evangelization.

FAMILY/SMALL CHRISTIAN COMMUNITY MODELS

As we have shown above, there are numerous ways that families and small Christian communities share similar values and are supportive of one another. Let us now turn to some concrete ways that small Christian communities can meet the needs of families.

In the first model, the small Christian community meets regularly for prayer, faith sharing, support, learning and outreach with only the adults attending these gatherings. Spouses are encouraged to be a part of the same community, but in some situations that may not be possible.

While children do not attend the regular gatherings, they are very much a part of the life of the community as parents share their daily joys, struggles, and experiences. Children are included in many other planned activities, such as Christmas parties, Advent gatherings, Lenten experiences, camping trips, summer outings, helping at a soup kitchen, etc.

Core communities and small Christian community members need to have a clear understanding of the community members' preferences. In some cultures it would be inconceivable to have gatherings without children present for everything. In other situations, participants may feel it is easier to share without small children who need a great deal of attention. Some communities would want to include teenagers; others may wish to encourage teens to gather in peer groups.

Small communities plan activities to be done by families at home, such as the preparation and prayers for the Advent wreath, or gathering canned food for the needy. Small communities facilitate prayer experiences for families to utilize in their homes. Small communities allow the richness of family experience to be shared. They can help members learn to recognize the sacredness of their everyday family lives by reflecting on their vocation as mother, father, son, daughter, etc.

A second means of meeting the needs of families is through creating family small communities. In this model entire families gather regularly for prayer, sharing, support, learning, and mission.

During the meetings, the families may break up into various age groups with someone designated to be the group leader for the children. The theme and the reflection would be the same, but children would share and learn in a simpler form. The experiences for children are filled with more activities, perhaps songs and some sharing time. The entire family regathers for the closing prayer and social time. Time might also be given for family sharing or at least directions for continuing the experience at home as a family.

Adults in these small communities may share the role of working with the children. Some communities may ask just one person to take that primary responsibility.

The important point is to recognize the needs of all community members. In our diverse world today, we have many single and elderly persons who do not have children. We have families with small children and families with grown children. Families and small communities will grow with great diversity.

CALLED TO BE DOMESTIC CHURCH

Some of the focus of this chapter has been on the development of small Christian communities as a support to the domestic church. The family has been already identified as the domestic church. In many ways the family is the ideal model for communities and, in turn, communities can strengthen families to live in loving, supportive relationships with other family members.

Small communities can help the family by providing an environment for sharing and support in dealing with difficult family problems. They provide an environment for adults and children to share and bond with other adults and children in a spiritual atmosphere. They touch into the heart of family life values of love, bonding, service, participation in the world, and evangelization in our world today. Small communities strengthen parents and children for their journeys in life.

We go back to the gospel again for a final reflection in this chapter on the family. Jesus spent thirty years of formation in his family, with a loving and faith-filled mother and father. He learned so many of the communal values we have addressed. Jesus went on to share those values with twelve special apostles. He created a small Christian community. Jesus shared what he learned in his family with his community, and is it not likely that he also shared with his family what he had learned in community?

CHAPTER 17

Concrete Approaches to Prayer

Prayer is not primarily doing something; it is being with someone you love. We are a people who place much emphasis on accomplishments. We are uncomfortable just sitting around, reflecting, observing, taking time to go over our commitments, our promises, our worries. For many of us, to do is to be worthwhile, to make a mark in life. To take time apart from seeking success in order to be with ourselves, with others, and with God in quiet attention and exchange seems irrelevant. However, the consequence of always rushing in order to perform is emptiness and boredom. We wonder why our life seems so unconnected! Prayer is a way of being with God. Connections are made through scripture, through adoration and gratitude, through prayer for help. Connections are made when we take a long, loving look at the wonderful gifts God has given us—friendships, a marriage, children, nature, even in brokenness that seeks healing from our God. Prayer means lifting up our minds and hearts to God who is with us always.

> Prayer is basically giving yourself to God. The only way to pray well is to give yourself to God often—sometimes while you're on the run, at other times when you settle down to really communicate with the Lord. In learning how to pray, try to remember two things. First, prayer is not so much what you *do*, as what you do *not* do. You have to stop running in order to open yourself to God's Presence. . . . At prayer time try to relax your mind and body to some extent. Sit still. Control your body and offer this little discipline as your way of giving yourself to God.[1]

Prayer is a constant invitation from God and a willingness on our part to seek and make contact with God. Jesus is the very word of God. He is the good news who communicates the love, mercy, and forgiveness of a loving God. We respond to that love by allowing God to live a life of goodness through us.

PRAYER FORMS

Prayer is an essential component of small Christian communities. Small communities themselves need to be praying communities. Shared prayer in the small community gatherings requires preparation and time. Besides the communal prayer, it is also important that individuals grow in their own appreciation for and experience of prayer in their daily lives. Therefore, in this chapter we will be looking briefly at various prayer forms that small communities and individuals in small communities may be using or may wish to utilize in their spiritual life. Specifically, we will examine spontaneous prayer, official prayers of the church, shared prayer in small community settings, and personal prayer. While we can suggest different prayer forms, an important thing to remember is that the ultimate path to prayer is a desire for and openness to a close intimate relationship with God so we can respond to God's action in our lives.

Spontaneous Prayer

Spontaneous prayer is a way of letting God know what is going on for me at this particular moment—what I am afraid of, what I am grateful for, what I need. This type of prayer requires honesty and open-mindedness. It requires an open heart, asking for knowledge of God's will and the strength to conform to that will. Spontaneous prayer can happen in a small community setting, in the quiet of one's heart, in a liturgical setting, or anyplace people attuned to God's presence find themselves.

Spontaneous prayer, speaking from one's heart, may be a difficult form of prayer for some, but a comfort level can be achieved if people understand that praying from one's heart is like speaking with a loving friend. All of us have much to say about our lives, our needs, how we feel, what has happened to us. Speaking with God is essentially telling God about our lives—our fears, disappointments, joys, and dreams. It is not that God doesn't already know all of this, it is rather that we need to communicate about our lives.

Sometimes we wait and listen as we would with any loving friend. Sometimes we are just grateful as we would be with a friend who just listened to us. Sometimes we may be overcome with joy and awe at the magnificence of God. We each need to speak with God as a "best friend," as one who understands.

Spontaneous prayer includes the recognition of the depth of God's love which is given freely and unconditionally. Acceptance of that love is not possible unless we also accept God's will in our lives. Many situations which we pray about are beyond our control. For example, parents may be praying desperately for the return of their runaway teenager. In essence, the parents have no power to control when the child will return. Prayer, however, can help. Prayer helps people with their legitimate worry to gain a sense of calm and hope, and to receive the inspiration of the Spirit helping them to respond in a particular situation. While their worry may not be resolved as they would have wished, a new perspective, a fresh start, a renewed sense of what is important can readily flow from a praying heart. God is with us through the power of the Holy Spirit in the ordinary and the everyday events of our lives.

We can call upon God to help us in any given situation. Likewise, we can turn to God as a loving friend in times of great joy and tell our friend how grateful we are for the depth of love. We can praise God whenever we become aware of great beauty, a sunset, the singing of birds, the love of a friend, etc. Sometimes we just want to sing songs of praise and thanks.

Spontaneous prayer in a small community or in a liturgical setting invites us to speak aloud our needs, our thanks, our praise. Spontaneous prayer alone, with family, or with one or two friends can happen at any moment; in fact, it can happen almost all the time. We are told by St. Paul to pray always! What a great gift to know we can have contact with God at any moment of our lives.

Prayers of the Church

The church has provided us with many helpful ways to pray. For our purposes here we will focus on two primary forms: the eucharistic liturgy and the Liturgy of the Hours. First, let us look at the power of prayer in the eucharistic liturgy.

The Eucharist is a place of deep prayer.

Of all the possible forms of communal prayer the most esteemed, is liturgical prayer, especially that which occurs at the Eucharist. The Eucharist itself is the greatest prayer. In it we join our own prayer to that of the Eucharist's chief priest, Christ himself. There is a most intimate connection between our prayer which occurs outside the

Eucharistic liturgy and our participation in the Eucharistic sacrifice or offering.
   The Eucharist structures our prayer life. It instructs us concerning what should characterize the basic framework of our Christian lives, including the life of prayer. The liturgy is constantly teaching us that we go to the Father, in Christ, by the Holy Spirit. . . . The liturgy, by its communal, ecclesial setting, also instructs us that we are to live the spiritual life as members of the Christian community, the Church. The communal dimension of Christian existence, so vividly portrayed by the liturgical celebration, is to be operative at all other times also.[2]

Another great gift of the church is the Liturgy of the Hours. For centuries this has been the official prayer of the church used primarily by clergy and religious. Today many lay persons have found praying the Liturgy of the Hours to be an essential part of their day. Some parishes have the practice of using the Liturgy of the Hours for their morning prayer with parishioners and staff together.
   The Liturgy of the Hours is a way of praying developed by the church which is celebrated at different periods throughout the day. The format for the major hours contains psalms, canticles, readings, prayers, and a song. As the official prayer of the church, it is a marvelous prayer to share with others, but it can also be said alone. The Liturgy of the Hours attunes us to various seasons and feasts throughout the year. We are enabled to resonate more with the whole church's call to Advent expectation, to Lenten penance, to resurrection hope. The saints enable us to see courage, commitment, conviction in so many diverse situations in human history. What great power and unity to think of so many praying the same prayers at one time in the church!

Shared Prayer in Small Communities

An essential ingredient for small community gatherings is shared prayer. All community members will want to help create a quiet, peaceful, prayer environment. The atmosphere throughout the faith sharing needs to be prayerful and appealing to the whole person—head, heart, all the senses. The use of symbols and ritual can enrich our prayer experience.
   Silence, too, is important—as important, in fact, as the spoken word. It is a great asset for any community to be comfortable with

silence. Generally, prior to the beginning of prayer, the community is invited by the leader to become mindful of God's presence. In developing prayer experiences for the community, the following elements are suggested:

1. Greeting: Acknowledging God's abiding presence within each one of us, God's promise to be with us. (An opening prayer or song may be used to help remind us of God's presence.)

(Leader) God, you are with us, in our midst and in our hearts. In the stillness and silence of this moment, help us simply to enjoy your company, to be with you, meet you, and welcome you.

(or)

An appropriate quieting song

2. Readings: A psalm as well as another scripture reading would be appropriate. (Keep in mind that more does not always mean better; sometimes the simpler, the better.)

For variety, try praying the psalms in different ways. Have half the group read the first stanza, the other half read the next. Or have one person read the first stanza and all read the next. You could also have two people read and all respond with the antiphon. Sometimes you may wish to sing the psalms. There are many psalms that have been set to music or perhaps someone from the small community has the gift of singing or playing an instrument to accompany the psalm.

3. Response: The response can vary in form. At times it may be good to have silence; at other times there could be another reading, sharing, etc. Since it is a response, give people the opportunity to reflect for a few minutes. The response should be structured in such a way as to allow all to participate.

4. Spontaneous Prayer:	It is good to include time for people to share personally—their needs, their praise, their thanks, whatever the Spirit is moving them to pray about.
	Let people know initially that after the response or reading they should feel free to share prayer spontaneously. Obviously no one should feel as though he or she has to speak; everyone is sharing by his or her very presence. Shared silence can also be a sacred time.
	The community will also wish to allow the Spirit to pray within a person at other times as well. For example, someone might be moved to pray immediately after the song. It is important not to rush prayer.
5. Closing:	The time of prayer can be brought to closure in a variety of ways. One service might conclude the sign of peace, another a blessing using holy water, a song of praise or thanksgiving.

Like personal prayer, shared prayer is based upon a relationship. Thus in developing prayer experiences for the community, listening and sharing, appreciation and honesty are key elements.

Small community leaders may wish to develop their own prayer experiences or ask other members to take turns. It is also important to note that there are many prepared prayer experiences available through publications that can be utilized as is or adapted to individual circumstances. When looking for planned prayer experiences, it is helpful to make sure that certain components are a part of the prayer: silence, a time for listening, a time for speaking to God, an appropriate prayer response. Two good resources for prayer include *Praying Alone and Together* (Art Baranowski, St. Anthony Messenger Press) and *Forgiveness: A Guide to Prayer* (Jacqueline Bergan and S. Marie Schwan, St. Mary's Press).

Personal or Solitary Prayer

Personal or solitary prayer is essential to one's life of faith. Yet the term "solitary" can be misleading.

It suggests being alone by yourself in an isolated place. When we think about solitaries, our mind easily evokes images of monks or hermits who live in remote places secluded from the noise of the busy world. . . . On occasion this isolation is necessary to develop this solitude of heart, but it would be sad if we considered this essential aspect of the spiritual life as a privilege of monks and hermits. It seems more important than ever to stress that solitude is one of the human capacities that can exist, be maintained and developed in the center of a big city, in the middle of a large crowd and in the context of a very active and productive life. A man or woman who has developed this solitude of heart is no longer pulled apart by the most divergent stimuli of the surrounding world but is able to perceive and understand this world from a quiet inner center.[3]

All who are serious about the spiritual journey need to establish daily prayer as a regular part of their lives. It is suggested that all small community participants set aside at least twenty minutes each day for prayer. In some ways time has little meaning in prayer, yet it is essential to give some structure to our day in order to give adequate time to God.

In their book, *Lord Jesus, Teach Me to Pray*, Sister Lucy Rooney and Father Robert Faricy describe the conditions necessary for prayer: fidelity and openness.

Fidelity is spending time with the Lord regularly. I put time and effort into anything that is important to me. No relationship of love endures and grows unless time is spent together. But the Lord is not a time-keeper. It is not the time itself that matters, but the fidelity to the time spent with him.

One cannot be fickle in friendship. That is what the Lord offers me. He said, "I no longer speak of you as slaves—instead, I call you friends" (John 15:15). The Lord is always present with me. I need to turn to him, to be faithful in meeting him each day. The first step to that is putting in time. Then I am saying to him: "You are important to me. My relationship to you is the most important thing in my life (and is the foundation of all my other relationships). I might have to miss a meal to come to our meeting—but being with you means more to me than eating or sleeping. I want to put nothing in your place, nor ahead of you in my heart."

So I come faithfully to meet the Lord. What do I do then? I am open, attentive to him—just being there, looking in love, knowing in my heart what his attitude to me is.[4]

In many ways personal prayer is taking a long, loving look at our God. It is perhaps more being than doing. In prayer I open myself up to God's love. I forget all my needs, my wants, my fears, and rest quietly in God's care.

In looking at personal prayer now, we will briefly describe six different prayer forms: Meditation and Meditative Reading, Contemplation, Centering Prayer, Healing Prayer, Journaling, and Devotions. We each have our own personality needs and preferences; one or two of these may seem more appropriate at certain times in our lives than others. Prayer practices are keys, nothing more, but they open the door to the room which is a relationship with God.

1. Meditation and Meditative Reading

In meditation and meditative reading the style of prayer is reflective, imaginative, relation-centered. Frequently the scriptures are used since we can most easily hear God speaking in scripture. In meditation we can welcome Jesus into our lives and open ourselves to him. If we meditate on Jesus we learn who he is for us and what he wants to reveal to us.

Father M. Basil Pennington, O.C.S.O., well noted for his teaching and reflections on prayer, suggests a simple process for meditative reading:

- Take the Sacred Scriptures with reverence and call upon the Holy Spirit.
- For five minutes (or longer if so drawn) listen to the Lord speaking to you through the text, and respond to him.
- At the end of the time, choose a word or phrase (perhaps one will have been "given" to you) to take with you, and thank the Lord for being with you and speaking to you.

Following is a more detailed form for meditative reading:

- Ask God for the willingness to hear the words of Scripture in your heart.
- In a quiet place read the Scripture passage.
- Image the scene as described in the Scripture passage (i.e., Matthew 4:18–22—Jesus calls four fishermen). What does this scene look like. Four simple fishermen are going about their daily work tasks. Suddenly this man, Jesus, comes up to them and says: "Come with me and I will teach you to catch people." They follow at once. What do I imag-

ine these men to be like? What do I imagine Jesus to be like? Who was this man who was so attractive that they would follow immediately? Reflect upon what this says to me in my life. How do I experience Jesus' call as I am going about my daily tasks? How might my feelings and fears be similar to those of the fishermen? How do I respond? Do I really believe Jesus asks me to follow him? In what way?

Pray for the power of the Spirit to know God's will and the grace to do God's will in my daily tasks.

Lastly, a word of thanks to God for God's wondrous works in us.[5]

In meditation and meditative reading, then, we read over the passage slowly, stay with the words and images that especially catch our attention, stay aware of the feelings and images that are awakened and read the passage lovingly, being grateful to our God for loving us.

2. Contemplation

Contemplation is a gift whereby we are drawn into God's presence. The contemplative person is one who is sensitive and open to God's presence, one who lives in the awareness of God.

> In Catholic tradition contemplation is a form of prayer which is God's gift following upon faithful commitment to the Christian vocation. St. Teresa of Avila, a doctor of the Church and a teacher in the ways of prayer, noted that active prayer, our efforts, can lead to consolations and to a sense of peace. Contemplative prayer results in spiritual delights . . . which are passively received. Contemplative prayer is marked by a profound sense of God's loving presence coupled with the desire to give our love away to our brothers and sisters.[6]

Thomas Merton wrote a great deal about contemplative prayer. Shortly before his death Merton shared these reflections:

> In prayer we discover what we already have. You start where you are, you deepen what you already have, and you realize that you are already there. We already have everything, but we don't know it and we don't experience it. Everything has been given to us in Christ. All we need is to experience what we already possess.
>
> The whole thing boils down to giving ourselves in prayer a chance to realize that we have what we seek. We don't have to rush after it. It is there all the time, and if we give it time, it will make itself known to us.[7]

Merton goes on to talk about the importance of taking the presence of the Holy Spirit in prayer seriously. He says the purpose of contemplative prayer is to bring the presence of the Spirit in our lives into our awareness:

> . . . to bring our hearts into harmony with his voice, so that we allow the Holy Spirit to speak and to pray within us, and to lend him our voices and our affections that we may become, as far as possible, conscious of his prayer in our hearts.
> For it is the Holy Spirit "who teaches us to pray, and who, though we do not always know how to pray as we ought, prays in us, and cries to the Father in us."[8]

In contemplation God wants to love us and asks that we come to know and love God in return. Contemplative prayer is characterized by a simple awareness of God's presence within us and around us in the ordinary and the everyday. This gift intensifies our desire to respond to the Lord through the service and love of others.

3. Centering Prayer

Centering prayer is so-called because it focuses on the presence of God at the center of our very being, our spirit. We move toward the center of our very being. Some start with an exercise to bring about relaxation. Breathing is one such exercise. Taking some deep breaths in order to get in touch with our inner spirit is one concrete way to begin centering prayer.

> Centering prayer is a very simple, pure form of prayer, frequently without words; it is an opening of our hearts to the Spirit dwelling within us. In centering prayer, we spiral down into the deepest center of ourselves. It is the point of stillness within us where we most experience being created by a loving God who is breathing us into life. To enter into centering prayer requires a recognition of our dependency on God and a surrender to His Spirit of love.[9]

How does one go about centering prayer? First, set aside about twenty minutes of time. Then settle yourself down in a quiet manner. Choose a comfortable position for yourself, usually sitting. It is best to keep the back straight. Then close your eyes. Once you have settled, turn your attention to God who is present within you.

One way of becoming more attentive to God who is within is to repeat a particular word or phrase that fosters concentration, such as:

"My Lord and my God," "Jesus, Lord, have mercy," "Come, Lord Jesus." It could be a word or even a phrase from the psalms, etc.

Whenever, during the time of prayer, you become aware of other things, simply use the word or phrase which gently helps you to return to the divine presence. Sometimes it will be important to use the word often; other times, you may not need to use it at all. It is simply a time when God can do with you as God likes. All your attention is on God.

End your prayer very gently. Praying the Our Father slowly and reflectively is a good way to close. Let each phrase come forth with all its meaning.

Fathers M. Basil Pennington and Thomas Keating have developed many materials and workshops on centering prayer which are extremely helpful to anyone who would like to make a commitment to centering prayer.

Father Pennington summarizes the steps of centering prayer in a simple manner:

- Sit relaxed and quiet.
- Be in faith and love to God who dwells in the center of your being.
- Take up a love word and let it be gently present, supporting your being to God in faith-filled love.
- Whenever you become aware of anything else, simply, gently return to God with the use of your prayer.
- Let the Our Father (or some other prayer) pray itself.[10]

Centering prayer allows us to go deeply into the place within where we can rest in God. In many ways centering prayer is learning self-surrender. It is letting go into a loving reality.

In centering prayer one does not reflect upon images. One is not so much concerned with pleasant thoughts or reflections and more concerned about movements of love and thanksgiving, praise and adoration welling up within one's heart. As Father Thomas Keating expresses it:

This awareness tells you that the core of your being is eternal and indestructible and that you as a person are loved by God. Take everything that happens during the periods of centering prayer peacefully and gratefully, without putting a judgement on anything. Even if you should have an overwhelming experience of God, this is not the time to think about it. Let the thoughts come and go.

Don't judge centering prayer on the basis of how many thoughts come or how much peace you enjoy. The only way to judge this prayer is by its long-range fruits: whether in daily life you enjoy greater peace, humility and charity. Having come to deep interior silence, you begin to relate to others beyond the superficial aspects of social status, race, nationality, religion, and personal characteristics.

To know God in this way is to perceive a new dimension to all reality. The ripe fruit of contemplative prayer is to bring back into the humdrum routines of daily life not just the thought of God, but the spontaneous awareness of (God's) abiding Presence. . . . In this prayer we confront the most fundamental human question: "Who are you, (God)?"—and wait for the answer.[11]

4. Healing Prayer

Matthew and Dennis Linn have done a great deal of work and reflection on prayer to heal life's hurts. They too offer helpful and healing workshops and classes for anyone who may wish to become more familiar with inner healing. We will look briefly at this process of inner healing which includes spiritual and emotional healing.

All of us carry within ourselves painful memories. Some are conscious, and others are not. Perhaps we do not recall exact circumstances, but we do know that a particular situation or type of personality usually causes us pain. Spiritual healing means being open to and receiving the forgiveness of our sins, thus coming to an inner wholeness. Emotional healing means the healing of hurtful feelings. Many of those painful feelings may go back to early childhood or even before. The healing of these memories may alleviate much of the spiritual and emotional pain.

Rooney and Faricy suggest some prayers for the healing of memories. Here is one example:

Prayer for Healing of Memories from Childhood

I cannot remember anything about my birth, Lord, but I know I suffered, that it was difficult for me. All that light, the noise, the strangers, the cold hostile world. Heal these buried memories. Let me hear your reassuring voice calling me to life, calling me by name. Take that little child I was in your hands, hold me up to your cheek and tightly to you so that I can hear the beating of your heart. Comfort and console me, give me the love that you desire so that I may be filled with your love.

I can see you, Lord, at home where I used to sleep and eat and play. Everything is bathed in your presence. You are looking at the child that I was. Moments of solitude, of sadness, of misunderstanding and of fear. . . . Heal me, Lord, from all the hurts inflicted on me during the first few years of my life.

Even if I have him no longer, I remember my father as I saw him then. I thank and praise you for his goodness, for everything he did and underwent for me. But he was not perfect. I want to forgive him now, in your presence, for the times he humiliated me and made me feel unwanted or inadequate, for the times he caused me suffering because of his absence, his misunderstanding and severity, or by ill-treating my mother or my brothers and sisters.

In my imagination, I move toward him and hug him, saying 'I forgive you!' . . . Unite us, Lord, in your Spirit of love and forgiveness. Heal our relationship.

Help me, Lord, to remember in you all the unhappy moments of my childhood. I offer you everything you want to heal. When I was little it was difficult and often painful for me to socialize with other children. But you, Lord, loved me just the same . . . and now you want to heal those hurts and remove all those things which are rooted in my painful memories and constitute an obstacle between you and me, and between myself and others.

Heal me, Lord Jesus, and I shall be healed![12]

Matthew and Dennis Linn and Sheila Fabricant Linn also offer numerous resources for the healing of memories.[13] These, or similar prayers which speak to other particular hurts in our lives, can help heal our hurts.

5. *Journaling*

Journaling, or keeping a diary, is a very useful tool for spiritual growth. It is simply meditative writing when we sit down with a pen in hand and write our thoughts, feelings, hopes and dreams to our God. In many ways journal writing is like writing a love letter. We recall memories, we clarify confusions in ourselves; we may discover suppressed emotions, hopes, or dreams.

Ira Progoff[14] has developed many helpful tools for good journaling. Again there are extremely helpful workshops and workbooks available to help in the beginning process.

Journaling can take various forms. Some will journal in the form of a letter addressed to God; others will write out a dialogue with a person, perhaps Jesus, another person, or even an event. It may be helpful to journal a response to a question, taking a line from scripture, such as Jesus' question to Peter, "Do you love me?" Sometimes it is best in journaling just to allow Jesus or another person in the scriptures to speak through the writing. Whatever the focus, journaling can provide a beautiful prayer experience.

6. Devotions

One of the forms of prayer with which many people in the church are familiar is the prayer of devotion. Devotional prayer is largely associated with forms of prayer that come to us from the lives of saints or from other ecclesial sources (e.g. novenas). Devotional prayer is a form of vocal or recited prayer which has enjoyed a long tradition in the church.

Devotion "consists of emotions and affections which are common and appropriate responses to commitment to Jesus Christ and belief in his gospel within the church. Some components of Christian devotion are admiration at God's wonderful works, a feeling of familiarity with Jesus, abiding sorrow for sin, a sense of security because of God's providential care, the consequent habit of frequently praying about important events in one's life, and joy in companionship with other believers in the church. Devotion links Christian belief and Christian action."[15]

Devotions can also be utilized in ongoing spiritual growth and in coming to know God better. Not everyone is attracted to the same devotions but the church has endorsed a variety of devotions throughout history. Probably the most widely used has been the rosary. The rosary connects us to Christ through the various mysteries—joyful, sorrowful, glorious. The rosary continues to be a beautiful prayer to God with special attention given to Mary, the mother and first disciple of Jesus.

We can learn a great deal about prayer and can deepen our relationship with God by looking at Mary. Mary is the model of how we as human beings are called to respond to God. She teaches us how to say "yes" to the mysterious ways of our God, not always knowing the outcome, yet trusting in God's wisdom and goodness.

Mary was a simple woman, living a very ordinary life. With the angel Gabriel's call, God invited Mary into a relationship far beyond what she could have imagined. Her relationship with God grew within a busy life. Mary had many daily responsibilities, yet maintained an attitude of openness to God's presence. "Mary kept all these things, reflecting on them in her heart" (Lk 2:19). Like Mary, we too find much to reflect upon in the ordinary moments of our lives. Through reflection those ordinary moments become very extraordinary.

Devotions often repeat the central mysteries of the Christian faith. Novenas, prayers to the Sacred Heart, the Angelus, the Morning Offering, the Memorare are all examples of beautiful and affirming prayers which keep our focus on the power of the divine in our lives and on our complete dependence on God.

Summary

These reflections on prayer and its various concrete expressions are by no means exhaustive. Many books are available on the subject of prayer. Our tradition is rich and varied. Committed Christians know and experience the importance of being prayerful. Prayer to God transforms our own consciousness; we tend to grow more and more in terms of our discipleship of Jesus Christ. We sense the needs of our world and respond in gospel images of concern and action. Prayer binds together the love of God and the love of neighbor.

It is only appropriate that we close this chapter with a "faith story" of prayer. It is the letter of a layman included in John T. Catoir's book, *Enjoy the Lord.*

I love to pray and I pray at any time, in any place, in any way. My day starts off with the reciting of formal prayers of the Church. Through these, I've come to know about many great Christians—not from the sense of history but because of their feeling and their love of God and His people. The Memorare was the most meaningful. . . . Many others followed. More than once I have suddenly realized that a part of my life has been transformed by one of these prayers, and just as suddenly, that that prayer no longer seems special to me and another suddenly speaks to my heart. I've come to recognize this as a way Jesus is leading and teaching me. . . .

As time has gone on, I've been led into many different prayers and ways of praying. I've sat in silence just staring at the cross and Jesus until I thought my heart would break. I've sung for joy—shouted Alleluia! And then at times . . . I've found myself wording my own prayer to our God in ways that at times have astounded me. I've knelt, sat, laid down, stood up, squatted; but it never seems to matter, Jesus always listens. Sometimes, it's with my arms . . . extended to heaven, yearning to reach and hold my God.

The Rosary still holds a special place of prayer for me and has acted most often as a spring prayer for a variety of other forms of prayer during and after completing it, which at times has taken me an hour or more to do. My car has become an especially good place to pray and traffic and gas lines don't seem nearly as long.

At times, I've just sat or stood in awe looking out at (God's) beautiful world. . . . I guess this is the best prayer—letting (God) speak to me. That, and the constant repeating of the name 'Jesus' all through the day. What a beautiful and powerful name it is.

All in all, the most exciting thing about my prayer is its infinite variety and excitement as the Spirit leads me from and through one form to another.[16]

CHAPTER 18

Concrete Approaches to Mission

Throughout the book we have spoken about five elements which are essential in moving people from being a group to being a community. One of these essential elements is *mission* or *outreach*. As church we are all called to be missionary, to continue the mission of Jesus in our world, to assure the growth of the reign of God. Mission "places emphasis on overcoming the limitations of sinfulness in society in order to bring about a transformation that will lead to the realization of the (reign of God)."[1] In an effort to fully live this mission, each of us is called to specific action or outreach.

Outreach is defined as the act of reaching out or the extending of services or activities beyond current or usual limits. Small communities are not meant to be turned in upon themselves, but to reach out, to act upon the values of Jesus. In this chapter we will be looking at some concrete approaches to the action of reaching out, often reaching out beyond what we might consider our normal limits. Thus we will be talking about living the mission of Jesus in everyday life.

RENEW has learned that the most difficult element to realize in a faith community is the action response or the outreach. It is a challenge for us as Catholic Christians to concretize our spirituality in our everyday relationships, particularly our relationship with the wider society. Not that many have not grown in this area, but translating the gospel into ordinary life is a continuing struggle for all Christians alive today.

Why is it difficult to get people involved in concrete actions? Perhaps many people equate action, mission, or outreach with involvement in particular activities that they would find difficult or questionable. While some Christians are called to be involved in picket lines or marches, others may address the same problem through political actions such as writing their congressional representative. Still others may find their greatest challenge in their family and work relationships.

People react to the call to outreach in a variety of ways. They may be afraid. They may be tired. How often have we heard the statement: "I'm already too busy." "The kids have so many things going on, I can't keep up with everything I have to do now."

Gregory Pierce reflects on the difficulties of motivating any religious congregation to action:

> How many congregations have a "social action" or "justice and peace" committee made up of an assistant pastor or rabbi and six laypeople who are involved in everything from migrant farmworkers to nuclear disarmament? Despite countless sermons and leaflets, this committee has difficulty producing more than a yawn or a paternalistic pat on the back from the rest.
>
> There are three very good reasons for this. First, people tend to have a healthy respect for existing institutions and leaders. For this reason, they are not about to make fools of themselves or those institutions by grabbing a picket sign and protesting every issue. . . . Second, people do not like to waste their time on unattainable goals. If they don't think that they can win or at least make a difference, then they don't tend to get involved. . . . Third, people usually have a clear sense of their own self-interest. If something doesn't affect them pretty directly, they feel that they should leave it alone and let those whom it does affect deal with it.[2]

The three reasons cited by Pierce explain well why people may have difficulty becoming involved in social action. While we are not necessarily suggesting that everyone join a picket line, we do want to look at the three difficulties he proposes.

We, as Christians, are challenged to grow beyond these three roadblocks to action. In regard to the first reason, the church and its leaders tell us that we have to critique our institutions, their structures and systems and condemn what is not conducive to human life. "(The) social order requires constant improvement. It must be founded on truth, built on justice, and animated by love; in freedom it should grow every day toward a more humane balance. An improvement in attitudes and widespread changes in society will have to take place if these objectives are to be gained" (GS 26). Attitudes change and positive values are supported in small communities. A small Christian community may be the only place a person can honestly look at changes needed in the social order. Here a person can share doubts and be supported in taking concrete actions in unjust situations.

In regard to the second reason for the difficulty in motivating congregations to action, people have to feel they can make a difference.

If the goal is unattainable, people feel overwhelmed. Thus it is impor-tant in our social involvement that we set attainable goals and means by which we can have clear successes. In small communities people help one another discern a concrete action they can achieve. The focus is on concrete and measurable actions, steps that are attainable.

Regarding the third reason, when something is suggested as an action response to the gospel or a ministry or mission, unless it touches people's lives directly there is not a great response. In small communi-ties people are moved to act when they can see the connection between that action and their everyday lives—neighborhood, family, job, politi-cal life, the environment, etc.

An action step, or concretely living out the mission of Jesus, is something each Christian is challenged to do in every aspect of life. Too often people think of an action step as an extra thing to do. One gentleman in a small Christian community chose as his action to help monthly in the local soup kitchen. He came from a wealthy back-ground and found a great deal of satisfaction in helping the poor. While that action was good, he had not as yet begun to think through how he could more clearly live out the mission of Jesus in the decisions in which he was involved as an executive of a major U.S. company. As vice president of public relations for a utilities company, he had re-sponsibility for the "public image" of that corporation. Gradually, through his sharing in his small community and their mutual reflection on the bishops' economic pastoral *Justice for All,* he began to see that responding to the needs of the poor by not shutting off people's gas in the winter would be the Christian response and would also help with the company's self-image. By working out a plan in the company, he was able to bring about more flexibility in providing heating fuel to the poor.

This man's action response, his living out the mission of Jesus, was becoming very much a part of his daily life.

OUTREACH IS NOT AN OPTION

Outreach or action is not an option for the committed Christian. It is a mandate, issued to us from the life of Jesus and communicated to us through the scriptures and documents of the church. One of the clearest directives of Vatican II is the call addressed to all of us to scrutinize the signs of the times and interpret them in the light of the gospel (GS 4). Vatican II challenged all of us with the call for people of faith to make life more human. "Christ is now at work in the hearts of (people) through the energy of his Spirit. He arouses not only a desire for the age to come, but, by that very fact, he animates, purifies, and strengthens those noble longings too by which the human family strives to make its life more human and to render the whole earth submissive to this goal" (GS 38).

We are all called by virtue of baptism to make life more human, more caring, more just. We are called by our church to respond not just intellectually or in theory to transforming the earth, but through concrete action. We share in the mission of Jesus to proclaim the good news to the poor, liberty to captives, sight to the blind. We all share in the life and activity of the church which is missionary by its very nature (AG 2). As baptized Christians, we share in the priestly, prophetic, and kingly mission of Jesus. Mission is not an option; it is a response to our baptismal call.

Small Christian communities are not truly Christian communities if they are only sharing, prayer, study or support groups. They are communities if they recognize that they are empowered by the Holy Spirit to proclaim and to live the good news of Jesus. Through the power of the Holy Spirit, Christians are continually in the process of conversion; the Spirit changes hearts and behaviors. We need only look to Jesus to see action and outreach that was completely generated by a total love for God. While love is a feeling and a desire, it is also an action.

The most valuable materials the small communities can use are those which lead people to action. Usually these materials will follow the time-honored process: observe, judge, act. In other words: What is happening in my own life and the world in which I live? What does Jesus or my Christian tradition tell me about how I am to respond? What will I do differently to respond with Christian values to the various situations in my life? How can my action be specific?

Faithfulness to living Christian values in contemporary society requires vigilance, courage, and conviction, and yet more than ever we are called to act with Christian values in all areas of our lives. The small Christian community is an invaluable resource in supporting individuals in such fidelity. As communities help each person grow in knowing the call of Jesus in their personal lives, they need also help individuals grow in living out the values of Jesus.

Where we have a value, we believe it should show up in aspects of our living, in our behavior. We may do some reading about things we value. We may form friendships or join organizations that nour-

ish our values. We may spend money on values. In short, for a value
to be present, life itself must be affected. Nothing can be a value that
does not, in fact, give direction to actual living. The person who
talks about something but never does anything about it is acting
from something other than a value.[3]

In the small community gatherings it is essential to reflect on
action responses and outreach efforts. During each meeting, there
should be some initial time to listen to each person's outreach commitment from the previous meeting—what it was, how it was implemented in life, what further areas of outreach are needed. Likewise, in
each meeting there needs to be time to have each person or the entire
community decide on an area of outreach.

Very simply, the purpose of outreach is to help persons grow in
their ability to respond to the call to love one another and to live out
the Christian life in a concrete manner. In this way they will be fulfilling the mission of Jesus which enlightens the world with the saving
action of God. What persons have received as gift, they must give
as gift!

THE "HOW" OF OUTREACH

No two small communities will respond in exactly the same manner in the area of outreach. Some may focus more on individual outreach; others may do more outreach together as a community. For
example, an individual in the community may make a concrete decision to do something differently in work-related areas. That will be an
individual response. On the other hand, an entire small community
may wish to begin working on a serious concern they may have about
people who are hurting in their parish or world hunger or
homelessness.

The outreach or action may be affected by the type of community.
Action is essential for the seasonal small groups that meet. It may be a
temptation to omit that part of the sharing because it is the most
difficult, but small group leaders need to give special attention to this
aspect of the group meeting. If the community is primarily ministerial,
then the action may focus on that particular ministry. For example,
with a community of teachers in a school, the outreach may focus
primarily on relating to students or other teachers. However, one of the
areas of growth for ministerial communities may be to have ministers

also look at responding to and living the mission of Jesus in other areas of their lives. If the group is a small Christian community, then the action response needs to be ongoing and stronger in all aspects of life.

The important thing to recognize is that actions and outreach flow from the very stuff of life. One woman who was in a small community had a six month old child. In her small group was a single mother who struggled to be patient with her two small children. Through sharing, the first mother became aware of the need to assist the other woman with child care which could reduce stress and lower the possibility of abuse of a child. Her action response was to take the two children one afternoon a week to give the single mother some time for herself.

In another situation a man was struggling with a fellow employee at his place of business. Because of some negative history, competition over the job and just some general dislike for the other person, there was a constant strain in their work relationship. For his action response, he decided that Jesus' words to "love one another" were much more powerful than his dislike for a certain employee. His first concrete attempt to live out his faith in this situation was to greet the man each morning with a friendly hello. He also decided to pray daily for this gentleman. He was able to share that after a few months his dislike for the other fellow had lessened and from his perspective God had intervened.

In another example, a woman who had been working for many years in a professional capacity became aware of the needs of the homeless whom she saw every day. She became involved in efforts to develop low income housing and reduce crime in her neighborhood.

Sometimes the stuff of life is not as obvious. Direct service can be more obvious than an action for systemic change. For example, it is easier to gather clothes for the poor than to work for adequate housing for the poor or even address the economic realities which keep people poor in our society.

Small communities can help people begin to see structural injustices with new eyes, and to take concrete action steps to change systems. In small communities the sharing and interchange not only help people accept gospel/church values, but also produce prudent, sensible, and realistic action responses. The small community gives people the courage to act, and it builds in accountability. Each time the small community meets there is an accountability time for participants to share their success or failure with outreach. With support and commitment to living out the mission of Jesus in all aspects of their daily lives, small community members will continue to grow together as disciples of Jesus.

The point is that there is a serious need for all Christians to choose just actions on every level of life. Each time someone chooses to respond with Christian values—faith, hope, and love—the world becomes a better place. Each time a choice for Christian action is not made, we lose the opportunity for the message of Jesus to be more real. Christian mission then flows from our ability to observe a situation realistically, judge it in light of gospel values and act in accordance with that judgment.

Outreach has to do with changing behavior and a concrete action. For example, if I say "I want to be your friend" but never call, write, or make any effort to get to know you, my words are empty. If I say to myself and to others "I would like to become more prayerful" but do not allot any time in my daily schedule for prayer, then I will not grow in that area.

Outreach needs to be specific and measurable. Little will happen if a small community says, "For our action we will become more aware of the poor." Instead, the community would need to set some specific and measurable goals to become more aware of the poor. For example: "This week we will volunteer at the local soup kitchen on Wednesday night." Or, "This week we will write to our congressional representative about the need for low income housing."

Whether it be a seasonal small group, a ministerial community, or a small Christian community, it is helpful to move beyond the community itself at times and collaborate with others in outreach. The parish social concerns community or a local interfaith council may be helpful to small communities in networking. Learning what other churches or community groups are doing in a particular area of need may be of great benefit. For example, many city and church groups work cooperatively in meeting the needs of the poor and homeless in their area. In fact, in many small towns, it is essential to collaborate with other congregations in meeting needs in order to be effective and not duplicate efforts.

AREAS OF MISSION

In many ways when we use the term mission, we could substitute other words like justice or evangelization. To reach out in justice is to be doing the mission of Jesus. Evangelizing is promising the good news of peace and justice, "to bring glad tidings to the poor . . . proclaim liberty to captives and recovery of sight to the blind, to let the oppressed go free, and to proclaim a year acceptable to the Lord" (Lk

4:18–19). Outreach, action, justice, is living the beatitudes: "Blessed are the poor in spirit; blessed are they who mourn; blessed are the meek; blessed are they who hunger and thirst for righteousness; blessed are the merciful; blessed are the clean of heart; blessed are the peacemakers; blessed are they who are persecuted for the sake of righteousness" (Mt 5:3–10).

Through its social encyclicals and explication of its social mission, the church has indicated the kind of actions that are incumbent on a Christian. Pope John XXIII outlines clearly the standard for basic human existence to which all human beings are entitled:

> Every person has the right to life, to bodily integrity, and to the means which are necessary and suitable for the proper development of life; these are primarily food, clothing, shelter, rest, medical care, and finally the necessary social services. . . . A human being also has the right to security in cases of sickness, inability to work, widowhood, old age, unemployment, or in any other case in which he is deprived of the means of subsistence through no fault of his own. . . . Every human being has the right to respect for his person, to his good reputation; the right to freedom in searching for truth and in expressing and communicating his opinions, and in pursuit of art . . . to share in the benefits of culture . . . to a basic education and to technical and professional training in keeping with the stage of educational development in the country to which he belongs to honor God . . . to choose freely the state of life which he prefers . . . to establish a family . . . to work . . . to private property, even of productive goods . . . the right of assembly and association . . . to freedom of movement and of residence . . . and when there are just reasons for it, the right to emigrate to other countries and take up residence there . . . to take an active part in public affairs and to contribute one's part to the common good of the citizens . . . to a juridical protection of his rights.[4]

These basic rights, other social teachings of the church, and the scriptures are standards by which we can judge our action and outreach.

While we said earlier that self-interest was an important ingredient to motivate people to action, it is also important to note that the small community leader can help the community grow in its awareness in many areas of need. The leader might encourage members to become aware of parish, city, and global concerns by working closely with the social concerns community of the parish. The social concerns community itself is an excellent vehicle for providing information and resources on parish needs, local, and global concerns.

How are we as committed Christians to act to address the needs of our world today? There are a number of approaches needed. Catholic Charities, a significant social movement in the United States Catholic Church, articulated three goals for itself and all Christians in its 1972 self-study: to be of service when there is a direct need, to work collaboratively with others toward a just social order, and to convene people to discern ways to accomplish the Christian works of charity and justice.[5]

Wherever someone is hurting, action is needed. It may be some very obvious hurt like a hungry homeless person or someone with a serious illness, or a not so obvious hurt like the tears of a child who got in a fight with a friend, or the pain of a broken relationship. Responding to someone who is hurt may be comforting a husband when he comes home from a disappointing day at the office or a friend in emotional pain. Many of our action responses we do as Christians are not things we do, but rather are a normal response to God's children who are hurting. There are numerous organizations that can also offer ideas and opportunities—food pantries, Hospice, clothing centers, Catholic Charities, nursing homes, to name just a few.

A second area of action, and perhaps a more difficult one, is critiquing systems and structures and working to change them when they are unjust and oppressive. Individuals and small communities together can begin to look at what actions they can take to begin to transform unjust systems. Writing letters to or visiting legislators, being informed on political issues, organizing local groups for change, becoming involved in community organizations, changing spending patterns, working with national and international groups (e.g. Pax Christi, Bread for the World, Network) can be very important outreach actions. Learning and implementing different models of parenting through such resources as Kathleen and James McGinnis' resources *Parenting for Peace and Justice* and *Helping Families Care* can be a powerful action step.

The last area of outreach that was articulated by Catholic Charities is that of convening or networking. There are many ways a small community could convene or network around a social concern or need in the parish or broader society. Pat and Jerry Mische, in their work in creating a more human world order, suggest the following ideas:

> The key to developing a world-order readiness is to relate the need for world-order institutions to people's particular concerns and preoccupations. Each of us *hurts* in a number of profoundly personal ways. Our hurt may be that we are ill-housed, or malnourished, or

suffer from inadequate health care. We may be elderly, considered a nonproductive burden in a society. Our hurt may lie in fear of walking the streets alone. Or it may be the alienation of living in a dehumanized society without meaning. It may be the fear of facing a future that seems closed—or a future-shock world with no chance regulators. Our concern may be the inexorable deterioration of the local environment and of the earth's fragile life-support system. We may be women, frustrated because we are locked out of decision-making positions, or our concern may lie in the realization that nuclear proliferation makes a nuclear confrontation more likely each year.

It is relating the need for world order to each person's personal and specific sense of powerlessness that is the basis for mobilizing people. Consciousness raising begins with specifics. It articulates the linkages between a person's or group's particular area of powerlessness.[6]

People need other people for support. An important action step may be to meet and join efforts with others who have similar concerns. The Misches suggest four types of networks which are "natural groups" for convening on many different levels:

1. Issue networks.
2. Religious networks.
3. Educational networks.
4. Professional networks.[7]

Within the small community itself, there may be the opportunity for action in creating networks of support, but when that is not possible because of different interests, schedules, etc., individuals within the small community can continue to glean support from their community in order to network with other groups.

Perhaps the important point here is that it is not always necessary to participate in more actions, but rather that the daily networks and connections we already have can be strengthened and nurtured with Christian values. If all Catholics lived out their faith today, we would have very different parishes, towns, cities, and countries. We would see significant change in the world, since so many Catholics hold key positions in the political, economic, and social arena.

SUMMARY

The call of the gospel is clear; the message of Jesus is challenging. We are to bring the good news to the poor, liberty to captives, sight to the blind. We are called to be evangelizers. But we know from our experience that those things do not just happen. In order to translate knowledge of the gospels into practice, each person needs support, help, and discernment. Each time a small community gathers, each participant is encouraged and supported in outreach. Only through the loving interaction of disciples of Jesus committed to living out the gospel in everyday life will there be a true transformation of the earth.

CHAPTER 19

Paths to Implementation

How, then, does a parish go about beginning this process of implementing the vision of their parish as a community of small communities? Much of the material in this book is a reflection of over thirteen years of experience with RENEW in the United States, Canada, and many other parts of the world. Thus this chapter will take a look at two paths of implementation: dioceses and parishes which have implemented the RENEW process, and those which have not.

DIOCESES/PARISHES THAT HAVE DONE RENEW

RENEW itself is a comprehensive three year spiritual growth process for parishes. In most cases entire dioceses have adopted this spiritual development process. Over ninety dioceses in the United States have utilized RENEW as a primary tool of spiritual formation. Countless other parishes, in dioceses which have not chosen RENEW as a diocesan effort, have also joined in the journey.

Bishop Stanley J. Ott of the Baton Rouge diocese has written about his enthusiasm for RENEW.

> In 1983 Pope John Paul II named me the new diocesan bishop of Baton Rouge. Shortly after my installation, I began to reflect on ways to promote evangelization and renewal in the parishes. At that time I started the RENEW process, and over the next three years I experienced changes with my clergy and faithful beyond our expectations. Originally, we had dreamed that ten thousand of the faithful would gather together in small groups to pray, to read Scripture, and to share their journey of faith. To our surprise more than twenty thousand Catholics participated in five, six-week sessions over a two-and-a-half year period.[1]

RENEW has been a very effective vehicle in helping people get to know Jesus in a more personal way, and to develop a deeper love for prayer and the scriptures. It has enabled people to become more comfortable in talking about Jesus and to grow in their appreciation and response to the poor and oppressed. RENEW has also been effective in helping people grow in their commitment to the sacraments. Much of the above happened through the small groups that are an integral part of the RENEW process.

While the spiritual growth efforts in RENEW were not entirely focused on the small group faith sharing, every parish and diocese, without exception, reported that the small groups were a very effective means of spiritual growth. Statistics gathered and stories told confirm this. It is, in fact, the interest, growth, and enthusiasm of the RENEW small groups which have helped many to come to the vision of the parish as a community of small Christian communities. Whenever a parish has finished the five seasons of RENEW, invariably the question is asked, "How can we keep our groups going?"

The question we ask, however, is not just how to keep those RENEW groups going, but how to make small communities become a normative part of parish life. Built into the RENEW process itself, there is the opportunity to begin to ask these questions before the actual end of RENEW. In fact, in working with dioceses, the International RENEW Service Team initiates a "Day of Listening and Planning" after the first year of RENEW in order to help the diocesan and parish leadership begin the process of reflecting on the power of small faith sharing groups. People speak often about how conversion has happened in their RENEW groups.

Following the "Day of Listening and Planning" and midway in the three year process, the bishop is encouraged to begin the task of planning for small community development beyond RENEW.

Throughout the three years of RENEW, the diocesan staff is encouraged to look at this pastoral direction and see how small community development may be incorporated into their ministry efforts.

Six months prior to the end of RENEW, diocesan and parish leadership are encouraged to reflect on how this pastoral direction could contribute ongoing vitality to their parish life. They are asked to begin to plan the process of implementation. Parish leadership is encouraged to begin the process of establishing a core community. They reflect on how to begin communicating this direction with their parish. (See Chapter 12.)

In order to help with the implementation parish staffs need to look at the use of their time in current ministry and begin to discern how some changes in the use of their time could be made. While it may require only changing about five to fifteen percent of their time schedule in order to work with the development of small communities, it could be helpful for staffs to decide on some concrete ways they can begin the implementation.

Depending upon the structure of the parish, the parish pastoral council can and should be helpful in bringing this pastoral direction to reality in the parish. (See Chapter 11.) The core community or a representative of the core community meets regularly with the parish pastoral council and they work collaboratively.

The next step in implementation might be to initiate a parish process for listening and planning shortly after RENEW so that the entire parish can gain ownership of the vision. Ideally this would happen during the Easter season, since in the liturgy between Easter and Pentecost we hear about how the early church developed numerous Christian communities. This could be an especially grace-filled moment in the parish, as parishioners listen with "new ears" to the Acts of the Apostles and reconnect with the early church.

RENEW small group participants who wish to continue their small groups will probably be greatly interested in this process, but special invitations and encouragement should also be given to all other parishioners to attend.

As the parish is gaining ownership, the core community needs to be preparing itself prayerfully for its ongoing tasks. (See Chapter 9.) At the same time preparation can begin for the small community leaders. (See *Called To Lead* for a sound preparation.)

The parish as a community of small communities is a natural follow-up to RENEW. In many ways RENEW is like a laboratory experience. Through people's experience they can look at what happened in RENEW and structure the positive results into an ongoing style of parish life.

Continuing the RENEW small groups and helping them grow into committed small Christian communities, initiating seasonal groups, and helping ministerial committees blossom into communities can happen with clear planning and the power of the Holy Spirit. RENEW provides a fertile environment for planting the seeds of community. With careful nurturing, leadership, and prayer these seeds will produce healthy, holy communities.

DIOCESES/PARISHES WHICH HAVE NOT
IMPLEMENTED RENEW

Dioceses and parishes which have not engaged in the RENEW process may choose to do so because of the broad-based experience it will provide in working toward this pastoral direction. Some parishes which wish to move toward a small community vision of parish life have utilized other spiritual renewal models. If these models have given parishioners an experience of the value of a small group based renewal effort, the parish again may have a natural entrance into this pastoral direction. Other parishes may want to initiate seasonal small groups at various times during the year. Autumn, Advent, Lent and the Easter season are all appropriate times. The point is that people need the experience and become readied to move toward small communities when they have had the opportunity to be a part of a small group conversion process. It is difficult to have a parish gain ownership if parishioners have not had the experience of the ways small groups can help them grow spiritually.

If a parish has had some "conversion experiences" through small groups, and wishes to initiate this pastoral direction, it is suggested they begin by setting up a core community. That core community, along with the pastoral staff and parish pastoral council, would be responsible for some of the tasks described in Chapter 9. The core community would initiate seasonal groups, help ministerial groups grow into communities and nurture already existing small Christian communities. They would be involved in helping the parish gain ownership through a parish process of listening and planning and a parish pastoral council reflection process. They would provide resources and assist with the development of small community leaders. The companion volume to this book *Called To Lead* will assist core communities a great deal in developing strong leadership for the small communities.

Parishes may also find it of great benefit to enter into an alliance with other parishes. By building an alliance of parishes or through collaboration with neighboring parishes, they would receive a great deal of ongoing support, encouragement, and knowledge.

A helpful resource person for building an alliance with other parishes is Father Art Baranowski, author of *Creating Small Faith Communities, A Plan for Restructuring the Parish and Renewing Catholic Life*,[2] who developed small Christian communities in his parish. Baranowski provides workshops to form parishes which wish to restructure their parishes into an alliance with each other. A small planning team, including the pastor, from five or more area parishes meet for a two day workshop. During this time, each parish team slowly and methodically devises its own step-by-step plan for restructuring. This planning team continues to work together back in the parish.

After the workshops, the planning teams of five or six parishes meet together regularly. This cooperative effort has the following purposes:

- to share practical wisdom from their ongoing experience;
- to keep each other accountable in working toward the vision of small communities and not to slip back into the activity-centered parish approach;
- to help the next pastor sent to any parish in that alliance.

The pastoral plan Baranowski shares grew out of thirteen years of experience in a very ordinary parish with a very ordinary staff. (In other words, parishes do not need to have extensively trained staff in order to begin the implementation.) His workshop has been given for parishes in numerous dioceses. Hundreds of parishes are restructuring, succeeding at it and helping each other.

SUMMARY

The following is a summary of the steps for implementation of the pastoral direction:

1. Establish a core community.
2. Help the diocese/parish gain ownership of the pastoral direction through articulating it as a diocesan/parish vision.
3. Keep prayer as a priority (staff, parish pastoral council, core community, entire parish).
4. Hold a parish process for listening and planning.
5. Speak about the pastoral direction from the pulpit.
6. Begin leadership development of small community leaders.
7. Coordinate all activities relating to community development (e.g. seasonal groups, ministerial committees growing into communities, small Christian communities).
8. Continue to pastor the groups, communities, leaders, staff.
9. Keep clear lines of communication open with all concerned.
10. Work with other parishes and national and international small community efforts.

Each parish has its own history, its own composition, its own concerns. However, following some of these simple steps will help and greatly support an individual parish. In the next chapter we look at the importance of the diocese in providing some assistance in this process of implementation.

CHAPTER 20

A Diocesan Approach

A convinced and strongly supportive diocesan leadership is a powerful asset in the implementation of the vision of the church as a community of many small communities. A diocese wishing to implement this vision would do well to develop a pastoral direction highlighting the importance of small Christian communities.

If diocesan pastoral leadership has experienced the impact of small faith sharing groups in people's lives, and they wish this to continue, they will recognize that realistically parishes need help in furthering this development.

How might the diocese help in bringing this vision to fruition? Let us suggest a few ways.

ROLE OF DIOCESAN PASTORAL LEADERSHIP

1. Help with Accepting the Vision

If the pastoral direction of small communities is truly to take root in a comprehensive manner, it has to have a wider base and more authoritative sanctioning than is found in an individual priest or parish. In order to foster the acceptance of the vision, some dioceses have established an office of small Christian communities or have designated a person who will concentrate on this. In other dioceses, the entire diocesan staff has reached a common understanding and commitment to this pastoral direction and is utilizing this pastoral direction in all areas of ministry. Currently more than forty dioceses in the United States have designated a person or team working with the development of small communities in the parish.

2. Providing Leadership Development

Providing leadership development is an important resource service a diocese can provide for parishes. Many times parish leadership will not feel themselves sufficiently qualified to provide all the leadership development necessary. The diocese can be most helpful in providing this resource to their parishes.

Ideally, diocesan personnel will be assisting in the training of the parish core communities. (Refer to Resource D in *Resources* for a program for developing core community leaders.) They will also be of great service in the development of small community leaders. (Sessions for leadership development for small community leaders are available in the companion volume of this work, *Called To Lead.*)

3. Providing Reflective/Growth Opportunities

Diocesan staff members serve a most helpful purpose when they are ready and available to offer nights/days of reflection for small communities and for leadership groups. Many parishes hunger for these spiritual growth opportunities.

4. Providing Help with the Development of Materials

A diocesan office can be extremely helpful in assisting parishes research small community materials that will be most beneficial for small community use. There is a great need to do good researching of faith sharing materials on the market. Perhaps the diocesan office can even assist with the development of such materials.

5. Encouraging All Diocesan Offices and Agencies To Become Part of the Fabric of This Pastoral Direction

When all diocesan offices and agencies collaborate and work in a unified fashion toward a common vision, it is not only helpful to parishes but also a wonderful model of church unity. At times parishes feel there is an overabundance of directives and ideas coming from diocesan offices. While diocesan offices may provide good opportunities, parish staffs sometimes feel overwhelmed by various workshops and programs. With a clear statement of what it means to be church and a pastoral direction to which all offices and agencies will be accountable, parishes will have a greater opportunity to focus their efforts and initiate an invitation for diocesan assistance based upon their particular needs.

6. Networking with Other Dioceses

Networking with other dioceses in fostering the vision of the parish as a community of small communities can be a real benefit. Through networking, diocesan leaders can continue to articulate the vision, resource and support one another. Diocesan leaders could participate in the North American Forum for Small Christian Communities, an organization composed of diocesan staff representatives from over forty dioceses in the United States and Canada who gather annually to share their experience and expertise in mutually building this style of church.

A DIOCESAN OFFICE FOR SMALL CHRISTIAN COMMUNITIES

One of RENEW's greatest learnings is the importance of a diocese working together for the spiritual development not only of individual people, but of all parishes and the entire diocese. In RENEW the diocese adopts a vision of spiritual growth for all its people. It agrees that for three years the primary emphasis will be helping people learn and witness to the power of the word of God in their lives, helping parishes become more vibrant faith communities, and assisting parishioners in their ability to act justly. Following RENEW or any clearly defined spiritual growth effort, it is extremely helpful if the diocese sets forward a clear pastoral direction in order to continue to focus and foster this spiritual growth.

A diocese committed to developing small Christian communities as an ongoing style of parish life embraces its present and future with enthusiasm and hope. But this cannot be done blindly. A tremendous amount of commitment and creative planning is required. It is essential that certain questions be addressed: Who will assume responsibility for bringing form to the vision? How will it happen? Who will nurture it? That which is everyone's responsibility is easily in danger of becoming no one's responsibility. What may become one more added responsibility to an already unrealistic list of responsibilities for an office will probably never be addressed. RENEW's experience confirms that unless a person is specifically named to direct the efforts of small Christian communities, the task will likely go unattended.

The creation of a diocesan office for small Christian community development speaks clearly to the kind of commitment the diocese gives to such a vision. However, due to financial constraints, it may be necessary to assign these responsibilities to an already existing office. Let us look at how a Small Christian Communities Department or another office assuming the responsibilities could operate.

The staff for small communities serves parishes throughout the diocese in a number of ways: first, by visiting parish staffs and leaders in order to better understand the current pastoral life of the parish; second, by helping the parish to articulate a pastoral direction of small communities as an ongoing part of parish life; third, by assisting parishes in developing a step-by-step realistic plan to serve their individual needs.

The specific goals and objectives of a diocesan small community office flow from the conviction that a diocese serves its people most faithfully when it not only responds to their expressed needs, but also offers the visionary gift of leadership to discern a way of moving together toward the "not yet" where the reign of God will be more fully realized.

Ideally the diocese will articulate its own pastoral direction. Many dioceses have articulated mission statements. This pastoral direction could be incorporated within the diocesan mission statement or the pastoral direction could be written separately and seen as a means of living out the mission statement.

PLAN FOR DEVELOPING A SMALL CHRISTIAN COMMUNITIES OFFICE

(In order to be as concrete as possible, we would like to include a plan of action which could be developed by a diocesan Small Christian Communities Department. While not every diocese may wish to develop a separate office, the following outline can provide a good model for looking at the responsibilities of those implementing this pastoral direction. This is a comprehensive plan which could be adjusted depending on the size and resources of the diocese.)

This particular plan outlines eight components of responsibilities for a Small Christian Communities Department. (This plan could also be a model for offices already in existence in the diocese who would assume responsibility for small Christian community development.) The model outlines the kind of tasks involved and offers some concrete goals and objectives.

1. **Articulate a Vision of Church after the RENEW Process** *(or if the diocese has not implemented RENEW, at an appropriate time following a synod or some spiritual growth opportunities.)*

A. Develop a process for formulating a pastoral direction—evaluating one's experience. (See Parish Process for Listening and Planning, Resource F, for ideas.)

1. Discern those components of RENEW (or related spiritual activity) that had the greatest impact on parish community life.
2. What would you like to see endure and grow?
3. Explain the need for small communities from a theological, sociological, and pastoral perspective.

B. Develop a process for the diocese to gain ownership of this pastoral direction.

2. **Articulate Approaches for Organizing the Office of Small Christian Communities** *(or the diocesan office which will assume responsibilities for small community development)*

A. *Purpose of the Department*

The Small Christian Communities Department (or office assuming responsibility) exists to bring about the acceptance and support of small communities as an ongoing way of parish life.

The department consists of one or more full-time persons who will assume responsibility for parish visitations and ongoing support, preparing materials for use by small Christian communities, surfacing needs, recruiting writers and editors for publication of materials, and working with diocesan offices and agencies.

B. *Goals and Objectives of Staff*

To support the attitudes and behavior of parish staff in implementing this pastoral direction.

Rationale: The department members accept and affirm their primary role as change agents both promoting and providing for a new way of being church (envisioning the parish as a community of communities) among parish staffs.

Objectives:

(a) to phone and visit each parish staff person to discuss this pastoral direction;
(b) to assist parish staffs in assessing the needs of their parish in relation to the small Christian community vision;
(c) to establish ongoing contact with parish staffs and encouragement for them;
(d) to develop a plan of action with staff;
(e) to encourage staff persons to recognize and develop a core community for small community development;
(f) to encourage staff prayer and faith-sharing on a regular basis;
(g) to develop clusters of parish staffs who gather to share witness stories and provide support systems among parish staffs;
(h) to strengthen skills and resources of parish staffs through workshops and ongoing education about the pastoral direction;
(i) to encourage parish staff members to join a small community to experience its possibilities and witness its credibility;
(j) to promote the visitation of small communities by parish staff members.

3. To Have the Small Christian Communities Department Model a Faith-Sharing Community

Rationale: The Small Christian Communities Department accepts its call to model to local parishes and the entire diocese a style of community that is rich and life-giving.

Objectives:

(a) to be God-centered as individuals and as a community of faith; to express this faith ecclesially in a liturgical and sacramental way;

(b) to share one another's life events, faith stories and ministerial experiences;
(c) to support one another through caring, listening, encouraging;
(d) to be personally committed to one another through daily prayer for and with one another as an ecclesial priority;
(e) to continue ongoing education through sound catechesis, reading, workshops and shared learning experiences with other staff members;
(f) to ensure outreach as vital to Christian ministry by providing for ongoing development and sharing of ministerial gifts with others;
(g) to come together as community on a regular, weekly basis with importance given to prayer and faith sharing;
(h) to celebrate life together with days of prayer/fun/relaxation;
(i) to be loyal to one another;
(j) to have a clear understanding of each staff member's role within the group;
(k) to devise both individual and communal evaluation tools for the members of the department;
(l) to assist one another in the process of ongoing conversion to Jesus Christ.

4. To Enable Parish-Based Small Christian Communities

Rationale: Recognizing and rejoicing in the rightful place of the laity in the renewal of church, the department looks to the commitment and strength of small communities as the hope and creative energy for parish life in the future.

Objectives:

(a) to visit parish staffs;
(b) to visit small groups and small communities within the parish;
(c) to provide training for small Christian community leaders and group members on a regional and parish basis;
(d) to assist parishes in establishing "core communities" as the means of promoting the small community model;
(e) to work with parish pastoral councils and assemblies;
(f) to provide materials for small communities;
(g) to develop and broker good ideas among parish small communities;

(h) to nurture the development of small Christian communities among various cultural and ethnic groups;

(i) to encourage small communities to celebrate together as a united larger parish community;

(j) to work with parish staff in surfacing small community leadership;

(k) to maintain ongoing contact with the ministerial development center or similar diocesan structures;

(l) to encourage and enable parish existing committees to become more communal in their style;

(m) to establish a mailing list of small Christian community contacts;

(n) to offer to facilitate parish assemblies or processes for listening and planning as opportunities to reflect on this pastoral direction.

5. To Foster Ownership of the Small Christian Communities Pastoral Plan as an Ongoing Way of Parish Life Among Diocesan Agencies, Organizations and Their Personnel

Rationale: The Small Christian Communities Department understands that the diocesan pastoral direction will only be realized to the extent that all diocesan organizations and agencies demonstrate commitment to it through implementing the small Christian communities concept in their plans and programs.

Objectives:

(a) to develop an ongoing relationship with other diocesan agencies by meeting with them regularly;

(b) to work with the diocesan pastoral structures in implementing the pastoral direction through parish, deanery, vicariate, and diocesan pastoral councils;

(c) to provide a process for commitment to the small community pastoral direction;

(d) to offer direct assistance to offices and agencies helping them to develop their own initiatives and connections with the pastoral plan (e.g. the Religious Education Office may design sacramental programs with small community components for parents and children);

(e) to assist other agencies in designing new materials that are small Christian community related and using existing materials to serve their needs;

(f) to support initiatives taken by other diocesan offices to further the pastoral direction;

(g) to maintain a priority commitment to ongoing communication with the bishop/vicars/directors of diocesan offices, etc.;

(h) to cooperate with responsible offices integrating the pastoral direction with the RCIA.

6. To Develop Materials for Small Christian Communities

Rationale: The Small Christian Communities Department realizes the need for the development of materials consistent with the components for and growth of small Christian communities.

Objectives:

(a) to develop materials consistent with the needs of the people;

(b) to ensure that the materials being utilized provide a balanced approach to the Christian vocation, e.g. ecclesial, sacramental, ministerial, etc.;

(c) to maintain continuous dialogue and experiences with small communities to meet their needs effectively;

(d) to connect with needs of special groups, i.e. youth, family life, etc.;

(e) to develop an expanding library relating to small communities;

(f) to contact prospective writers who could develop materials;

(g) to edit materials received from writers;

(h) to provide writers with a clear outline of content, style, questions/answers, prayer and action desired in their manuscripts;

(i) to pilot materials with small communities;

(j) to evaluate materials through feedback of parish staffs and small communities;

(k) to maintain an ongoing list of priority materials.

7. To Share the Pastoral Direction and Experiences of the Small Christian Communities Department with Other Dioceses

Rationale: The small Christian communities staff ideally will keep in close contact with other diocesan staffs to promote and support this pastoral direction.

Objectives:

(a) to provide opportunities for ongoing communication with other dioceses;
(b) to share information on available materials.

8. Evaluation

Rationale: Evaluation is an essential tool for learning. Regular evaluations will be helpful to diocesan and parish personnel in monitoring how the pastoral direction is being implemented.

(As stated earlier, the above plan is one suggestion of how a diocese may outline responsibilities for implementing this vision. Each diocese will want to consider components like those listed above in developing an appropriate plan for itself.)

QUALITIES OF DIOCESAN STAFF

While a specific job description for the staff of a diocesan Small Christian Communities Office can be gleaned from the above goals and objectives, we would now like to suggest qualities to look for in selecting staff for a Small Christian Communities Department or selecting already existing diocesan staff who would assume responsibility for the development of small communities.

1. Highly Relational

The Office of Small Communities exists to be of service to people. The gift of relating well with a wide spectrum of persons, individuals and groups, lay, religious and priests, is critical to the development of small Christian communities as a pastoral direction for parish life.

2. Initiating

The diocesan coordinator of small communities needs to be an initiator—one who can assess the present reality of a given parish and respond to the felt needs of staff and people with concrete and creative ways of initiating small communities as an ongoing means of promoting vibrant parish life.

3. Visionary

One entrusted with the ministry of small Christian community development must be in touch with the present, aware of the past, and alert to the future in order to shape the future church in faithful continuity with its gospel roots. The diocesan staff person will ideally have some theological expertise and be committed to the growth of the church.

4. Persevering

Moving toward the "not yet" requires a high degree of patience. Flexibility, light-heartedness, and untiring commitment contribute to a spirit that will not give in to discouragement. The quality of perseverance in people who are in the role of nurturing small communities is important since much of their contribution may not be known until sometime in the future. Perseverance will enable a person to continue in the significant work of developing small Christian communities.

5. Motivational

An important quality for a diocesan staff member is the ability to inspire and motivate others in developing small communities. Often this quality is best nurtured through the staff member's own small Christian community experience.

6. Organized

In addition to intuitive, relational gifts, the coordinator and staff of a Small Christian Communities Department need to be well organized. The pastoral direction has many tasks and the ongoing task is to clarify, concretize, and strategize realistic goals and objectives and then measure the outcomes so that movement is observable.

IMPORTANCE OF A DIOCESAN APPROACH

In closing, then, let us reiterate the importance of a diocesan approach. A diocese without a dream, a vision, a pastoral direction can become cold and business-like. The diocese "constitutes a particular church in which the one, holy, catholic, and apostolic Church of Christ is truly present and operative" (CD 11). This local church needs a clear pastoral direction in order to carry on the mission of Jesus.

It is appropriate, then, that we conclude the last chapter of the work stressing the importance of a diocesan approach. Every vision or pastoral direction needs to be nurtured. The vision of the church as a community of small communities is not new. It was so much a part of how Jesus related to his disciples and how the early church developed. But for many of us in our twentieth century experience of church, it is a new experience. Diocesan leadership is in a unique position to provide spiritual and structural support for developing the parish as a community of many small communities and thus be an expression of the reign of God today.

Epilogue

We have tried to cover this topic of small Christian communities from various pastoral aspects, to be as complete as possible. There is always "the more."

As we go to press, we are heartened by the words of John Paul II in his encyclical on missionary activity, *Redemptoris Missio* (December 7, 1990).

> A rapidly growing phenomenon in the young churches . . . is that of "ecclesial basic communities". . . . These communities decentralize and organize the parish community, to which they always remain united. They take root in less privileged and rural areas, and become a leaven of Christian life, of care for the poor and neglected, and of commitment to the transformation of society. Within them, the individual Christian experiences community and therefore senses that he or she is playing an active role and is encouraged to share in the commn task. Thus, these communities become a means of evangelization and of the initial proclamation of the Gospel and a source of new ministries. At the same time, by being imbued with Christ's love, they also show how divisions, tribalism and racism can be overcome (51).

We offer this work as one effort to share the benefits of small Christian communities and to foster their development in the parish.

Through this work we enter into dialogue with all others who are in small Christian communities or who desire to foster and develop them for the renewal of our church and world.

We realize that ultimately community is a gift. It is not human effort that will build small Christian communities. It is the Spirit of God working in and through all of us who will set hearts aflame and bring us into communion with one another, with all creation, and with God.

The love of Christ impels us!

Abbreviations

Documents of Vatican II are abbreviated according to the two first words of the Latin text.

AA   *Apostolicam actuositatem:* Decree on the Apostolate of the Laity.

AG   *Ad gentes:* Decree on the Church's Missionary Activity.

CD   *Christus Dominus:* Decree on the Bishops' Pastoral Office in the Church.

DV   *Dei Verbum:* Dogmatic Constitution on Divine Revelation.

GS   *Gaudium et spes:* Pastoral Constitution on the Church in the Modern World.

LG   *Lumen gentium:* Dogmatic Constitution on the Church.

OT   *Optatam totius:* Decree on Priestly Formation.

PO   *Presbyterorum ordinis:* Decree on the Ministry and Life of Priests.

SC   *Sacrosanctum concilium:* Constitution on the Sacred Liturgy.

Notes

Introduction

1. James A. Coriden, Thomas J. Green, and Donald E. Heintschel, eds., *The Code of Canon Law: A Text and Commentary* (Mahwah: Paulist Press, 1985) 122.

2. Vatican Secretariat for Promoting Christian Unity, *Sects or New Religious Movements in the World: Pastoral Challenges,* United States Catholic Conference, May 3, 1986, 13.

3. Joseph Cardinal Bernardin, "Evangelizing the Active Catholic," in *Pentecost '87 Supplement, A National Satellite Celebration of Catholic Evangelization,* Saturday, June 6, 1987 (Washington, DC: Paulist National Catholic Evangelization Association) 17.

Chapter 1

1. Various contemporary scholars have named the times in which we live the post-modern era. Among them is Joe Holland. See "The New Debate Over Faith and Culture" in *American and Catholic: The New Debate* (South Orange: Pillar Books, 1988) 1–14.

2. Max Delespesse, *The Church Community, Leaven and Lifestyle* (Ottawa: The Catholic Centre of Saint Paul University, 1968) 16.

3. Raymond F. Collins, "Small Groups: An Experience of Church," *Louvain Studies,* 13 (1988) 116.

4. Delespesse, 18.

5. Collins, 117–18.

6. Albert J. Nevins, M.M., *The Maryknoll Catholic Dictionary* (New York: Grosset & Dunlop, 1965) 260–61.

7. Robert C. Broderick, *The Catholic Encyclopedia* (New York: Thomas Nelson, Inc., 1976) 249.

8. *New Catholic Encyclopedia* (New York: McGraw-Hill, 1976) Vol. XIII, 409.

9. David C. Leege, ed., "Parish Organizations: People's Needs, Parish Services, and Leadership," in *Notre Dame Study of Catholic Parish Life* (Notre Dame: University of Notre Dame, July 1986) #8.

10. Nevins, 610.

11. Nevins, 126.

12. Chuck Mathey, *Successful CFM Leadership* (Ames: Christian Family Movement, 1988) 1.

13. Thomas Aquinas, *Summa Theologica,* II, II, Question 47, Article 8.

14. Bernard J. Lee and Michael A. Cowan, *Dangerous Memories: House Churches and Our American Story* (Kansas City: Sheed & Ward, 1986) 37–45.

15. In addition, the Congregation for the Doctrine of the Faith has issued two documents on liberation theology: "Instruction on Certain Aspects of the Theology of Liberation," in *Origins* (September 13, 1984) 193–204 and "Instruction on Christian Freedom and Liberation," in *Origins* (April 17, 1986) 713–28. In the first document there is a concern about the formation of base communities without sufficient catechetical and theological preparation. Since catechetical and theological preparation is essential for small Christian community development, we have particularly emphasized this preparation in the leadership development sessions in our companion volume. The second document touches upon the reality of small groups in diverse ways.

16. Joseph Healey, "Comparing 'Basic and Small' Christian Communities," in *AMECEA Documentation Service* (Nairobi), 284, May 8, 1984, in "Communities," *Ministries and Communities* (Leuven, Belgium: Pro Mundi Vita, 1984) #3, 2.

17. Joseph H. Fichter, "Parochial Realities in America," in *A Sociologist Looks at Religion* (Wilmington: Michael Glazier, Inc., 1988) 205.

18. Collins, 115.

19. Bernard Lonergan, "Dimensions of Meaning," *Collected Works of Bernard Lonergan,* eds. Frederick E. Crowe and Robert M. Doran (Toronto: University of Toronto Press, 1988) 235.

20. Vatican Secretariat for Promoting Christian Unity, ibid. 12.

21. Ibid. 12–13.

22. John Naisbitt, *Megatrends, Ten New Directions Transforming Our Lives* (New York: Warner Book, Inc., 1982) 156. An article in *Newsweek* magazine (February 5, 1990) supports these statistics. Cf. "Unite and Conquer," 50–55.

23. George Gallup, Jr., "Evangelizing the Unchurched American," in *Pentecost '87 Supplement, A National Satellite Celebration of Catholic Evangelization,* Saturday, June 6, 1987 (Washington, DC: Paulist National Catholic Evangelization Association) 4.

24. RENEW evaluations from bishops, pastors, and diocesan staff support this testimony. In addition many other sources could be listed. To name a few: the testimony of leaders from nineteen dioceses gathered at the National Forum for Small Christian Communities, October 24–27, 1988, in Cleveland, Ohio; Rev. Arthur Baranowski's book *Creating Small Faith Communities,* published by St. Anthony Messenger Press; numerous articles, e.g. "Illinois Hispanics put on clinic for the Church" by Robert Johnson, *National Catholic Reporter,* Vol. 25, No. 4 (November 11, 1988).

25. Fichter, 205.

Chapter 2

1. Wilfred Ward, *The Life of John Henry Cardinal Newman,* 2 (New York: Longmans, Green, 1912) 147.

2. Peter Coughlan, *The Hour of the Laity: Their Expanding Role* (Philadelphia: E.J. Dwyer, 1989) 33.

3. John Paul II, "Los Angeles Meeting of the Pope and U.S. Bishops," *Origins* 17 (October 1, 1987) 257.

4. Sandra M. Schneiders, I.H.M., *New Wineskins: Re-Imagining Religious Life Today* (New York: Paulist Press, 1986) 238.

5. National Conference of Catholic Bishops, "Called and Gifted: Reflections of the American Bishops, Commemorating the Fifteenth Anniversary of the Issuance of the Decree on the Apostolate of the Laity," *Origins* 10 (1980) 369–373.

6. National Conference of Catholic Bishops, "The Hispanic Presence: Challenge and Commitment, A Pastoral Letter on Hispanic Ministry," United States Catholic Conference December 12, 1983, 27.

7. Vatican Secretariat for Promoting Christian Unity, ibid. 13.

8. Avery Dulles, S.J., *The Reshaping of Catholicism: Current Challenges in the Theology of Church* (San Francisco: Harper & Row, 1988) 23.

9. Ibid. 31.

10. Vatican Secretariat for Promoting Christian Unity, ibid. 10.

11. John Paul II, *On Social Concern* (Sollicitudo Rei Socialis), Encyclical Letter, December 30, 1987, United States Catholic Conference, 72–73.

12. Synod of Bishops, *Justice in the World* (Washington, DC: United States Catholic Conference Publications Office, 1972) 34.

13. Philip J. Murnion, "Parish Renewal: State(ments) of the Question," *America* (April 24, 1982) 317.

14. Avery Dulles, S.J., *A Church to Believe In: Discipleship and the Dynamics of Freedom* (New York: Crossroad, 1986) 17.

Chapter 3

1. German Catechetical Association, comp, *CREDO, A Catholic Catechism* (London: Geoffrey Chapman, 1984) 29.

2. Coughlan, 37.

3. Thomas M. Gannon and George W. Traub, *The Desert and the City: An Interpretation of the History of Christian Spirituality* (Chicago: Loyola University Press, 1969) 10.

4. Joe Holland, "Beyond a Privatized Spirituality," *New Catholic World* 231 (July/August 1988) 176.

5. Ibid. Holland cites testimony from Bishop Paul Cordes, a Vatican official at the Pontifical Council on the Laity, Dolores Leckey of the Office of the Bishops' Committee on the Laity, and Reverend Robert Kinast, author of one

of the official reports from the consultations of the laity in preparation for the
October 1987 Synod.

6. Catholic News Service, Wire Report, November 11, 1988.

7. John Paul II, "Christifideles Laici: Apostolic Exhortation on the Vocation and the Mission of the Lay Faithful in the Church and in the World,"
Origins 18, no. 35 (February 9, 1989) #29.

8. Donal Dorr, *Spirituality and Justice* (Maryknoll: Orbis Books, 1984)
16.

9. Lee, 10.

10. Thomas Berry, *The Dream of the Earth* (San Francisco: Sierra Club
Books, 1988) 120.

11. John Paul II, *On Social Concern,* pp. 72–73.

Chapter 4

1. Synod of Bishops, "Message to the People of God," *Origins* 19 (November 12, 1987) #10.

2. John Paul II, "Apostolic Exhortation on the Laity," ibid. #29.

3. Bernardin, 17.

4. National Conference of Catholic Bishops, *The Parish, A People, A Mission, A Structure: A Statement of the Committee on the Parish.* November 1980
(Washington, DC: United States Catholic Conference, 1981) 3.

5. Bernardin, 16.

6. Subsequent chapters will draw out and explore these implications in
greater detail.

7. National Conference of Catholic Bishops, *The Parish: A People . . .* 11.

8. Ibid. 17.

Chapter 7

1. Staff to the Committee on the Parish, National Conference of Catholic
Bishops, *Parish Life in the United States, Final Report to the Bishops of the
United States by the Parish Project* (Washington, DC: United States Catholic
Conference, November 1982) 63.

Chapter 8

1. Henri J.M. Nouwen, *Behold the Beauty of the Lord, Praying with Icons*
(Notre Dame: Ave Maria Press, 1987) 65.

2. John F. McDermott, "A Personal Reflection," Church of the Presentation, Upper Saddle River, N.J.

3. Dorr, 8–18.

4. Alfred McBride, *A Short Course on the Bible* (New York: The Bruce Publishing Co., 1968) 11.

5. Staff to the Committee on the Parish, *Parish Life,* 61.

Chapter 10

1. United States Catholic Conference, "Bishops' Committee on Priestly Life and Ministry, Reflections on the Morale of Priests" (1988) 18.

2. Ibid.

3. John Paul II, "Apostolic Exhortation on the Laity," #61.

4. Ibid. #18.

5. James and Evelyn Whitehead, *The Emerging Laity* (New York: Doubleday and Co., 1986) 108–14.

6. Robert E. Lauder, *The Priest as Person: A Philosophy of Priestly Existence* (Whitinsville: Affirmation Books, 1981) 97–98.

7. National Conference of Catholic Bishops, *The Parish, A People . . .* ibid.

Chapter 11

1. Permission given by Father Michael Hammer and Paul to use Paul's story.

2. Mary Benet McKinney, *Sharing Wisdom: A Process for Group Decision Making* (Allen: Tabor Publishing, 1987) 155. A complete section on "Communal Discernment in the Tradition" is given, 155–162, which may prove helpful to core community members.

Chapter 12

1. Thomas Sweetser, and Carol Wisniewski Holden, *Leadership in a Successful Parish* (San Francisco: Harper & Row, 1987) 15–20.

2. Ibid. 16.

3. Ibid. 17–18.

4. Synod of Bishops, "The Final Report of the 1985 Extraordinary Synod of Bishops," *Origins* 15 (December 19, 1985), #6.

5. Ibid.

Chapter 13

1. Pope John Paul II, "Apostolic Exhortation on the Laity," #14.

2. Ibid. #22.

3. Ibid. #19.

4. Henri Nouwen, *Reaching Out* (Garden City: Doubleday & Co., 1975) 51.

Chapter 14

1. Paul VI, *On Evangelization in the Modern World* (Washington, DC: United States Catholic Conference, 1976) #2.
2. The Catholic Bishops of Texas, "Mission: Texas: A Pastoral Letter on Evangelization" (March 1989) 3.
3. Paul VI, *On Evangelization in the Modern World,* #18.
4. Ibid. #58.
5. Ibid. #10.
6. Ibid. #24.
7. John Paul II, "Apostolic Exhortation on the Laity," #34.
8. Dr. Dean R. Hoge, *Converts, Dropouts, Returnees: A Study of Religious Change among Catholics* (Washington, DC: United States Catholic Conference, 1981).
9. Ibid.
10. Dr. Dean R. Hoge, *The Proceedings of a Symposium on Renewal in Catholic Evangelization* (Gainesville: Koch Foundation, 1986) 68.
11. *Origins* 14, 465.
12. The Catholic Bishops of Texas, "Mission: Texas: A Pastoral Letter on Evangelization," 10.
13. Father Patrick Brennan, *The Evangelizing Parish* (Valencia: Tabor Publishing, 1987) 72.
14. The Catholic Bishops of Texas, "Mission: Texas: A Pastoral Letter on Evangelization."
15. Pope Paul VI, *On Evangelization in the Modern World,* #18.
16. Archbishop Dennis Hurley, "Address to the International RENEW Convocation," 1989.

Chapter 15

1. Thomas P. Ivory, *Conversion and Community: A Catechumenal Model for Total Parish Formation* (Mahwah: Paulist Press, 1988) 5.
2. International Commission on English in the Liturgy and Bishops' Committee on Liturgy, *Rite of Christian Initiation of Adults: Study Edition* (Chicago: Liturgy Training Publications, 1988) #10.
3. Ibid. #19.
4. Ibid. #21, 22, 26.
5. Ibid. #37, 39.
6. Ibid. 14.
7. Ibid. #1.
8. Thomas P. Ivory, 13.
9. Avery Dulles, *A Church to Believe In,* 10–11.

10. Thomas P. Ivory, 15.

11. Although the RCIA is intended primarily for unbaptized adults, it envisions including uncatechized baptized adults (either in the Catholic Church or in other Christian communities) in an adapted process. To reflect this inclusive vision of the document both categories of people are used in this section. The references to baptized adults will be placed in parentheses to indicate our understanding that an adapted process can be used with these people.

12. International Commission on English in the Liturgy and Bishops' Committee on Liturgy, *Rite of Christian Initiation of Adults: Study Edition*, #75.

13. Ibid. #37.

14. Thomas Caroluzza, *Parish Catechumenate: Pastors, Presiders and Preachers* (Chicago: Liturgy Training Publications, 1988).

15. Thomas Caroluzza, "Catechumenate in Small Groups," International Office of RENEW Training Manual, 1985.

16. Ibid.

17. International Commission on English in the Liturgy and Bishops' Committee on Liturgy, *Rite of Christian Initiation of Adults: Study Edition*, #41.

Chapter 16

1. John Paul II, "Apostolic Exhortation on the Laity," #40.

2. United States Catholic Conference, *A Family Perspective in Church and Society* (Washington, DC: United States Catholic Conference Publishing, 1988) 8.

3. The National Center for Family Studies at the Catholic University of America, "Contemporary American Families: Facts and Fables" (Washington, DC, 1985).

4. John Paul II, "Address to the Hispanic Community in San Antonio, Texas," 1987.

5. John Paul II, *Apostolic Exhortation on the Family* (Washington, DC: United States Catholic Conference Publishing, 1981) #70.

6. Ibid. #18.

7. John Paul II, *Apostolic Exhortation on the Family*, #36.

8. United States Catholic Conference, *Family Centered Catechesis* (Washington, DC: United States Catholic Conference Publishing, 1979) 13.

9. John Paul II, *Apostolic Exhortation on the Family*, #43.

10. Paul VI, *On Evangelization in the Modern World*, #71.

Chapter 17

1. John T. Catoir, *Enjoy the Lord: A Path to Contemplation* (Staten Island: Alba House, 1988) 6.

2. Edward Carter, S.J., *Prayer Perspectives* (Staten Island: Alba House, 1987) 85–86.

3. Henri J.M. Nouwen, *Reaching Out* (Garden City: Doubleday & Co., 1975) 25.

4. Lucy Rooney, S.N.D. and Robert Faricy, S.J., *Lord Jesus, Teach Me To Pray* (Garden City: Doubleday & Co., 1988) 5.

5. M. Basil Pennington, OCSO, "Finding Peace at the Center," Pamphlet from Food for the Poor, Pompano Beach, 2.

6. John Welch, O. Carm., *Spiritual Pilgrims* (Mahwah: Paulist Press, 1982) 19.

7. David Steindl-Rast, "Recollections of Thomas Merton's Last Days in the West," *Monastic Studies* 7 (1969), 2–3.

8. Thomas Merton, *Spiritual Direction and Meditation* (Collegeville: Liturgical Press, 1960) 78–79.

9. Jacqueline Bergan and Sr. Marie Schwan, *Forgiveness: A Guide to Prayer* (Winona: St. Mary's Press, 1985) 4.

10. M. Basil Pennington, "Finding Peace at the Center."

11. Thomas Keating, *Open Mind, Open Heart* (Amity: Amity House, 1986) 114–15.

12. Lucy Rooney, S.N.D. and Robert Faricy, S.J., 33–35.

13. Matthew Linn, Dennis Linn and Sheila Fabricant, *Prayer Course for Healing Life's Hurts* (Mahwah: Paulist Press, 1983).

14. Intensive Journal Program, 80 E 11th St., Room 305, New York, NY 10003, (212) 673–5880.

15. Joseph Komonchak, Mary Collins, Dermot Lane, eds., *The New Dictionary of Theology* (Wilmington: Michael Glazier, 1989) 283.

16. Catoir, 54–55.

Chapter 18

1. James Ferguson, C.S.C., "The Demise of Mission," International Papers in Pastoral Ministry (University of Notre Dame: February 1990) 3.

2. Gregory F. Pierce, *Activism That Makes Sense: Congregations and Community Organizations* (Mahwah: Paulist Press, 1984) 24–25.

3. Louis Raths, Merrill Harmin, and Sidney Simon, *Values and Teaching,* 2nd ed. (Columbus: Charles E. Merrill Publishing Company, 1966) 28.

4. John XXIII, "Pacem In Terris," David O'Brien and Thomas Shannon, eds., *Renewing the Earth* (Garden City: Doubleday and Company, 1977) 126–30.

5. "Toward a Renewed Catholic Charities Movement" (Washington, DC: National Conference of Catholic Charities, 1972).

6. Gerald and Patricia Mische, *Toward a Human World Order* (Mahwah: Paulist Press, 1977) 280–81.

7. Ibid. 288.

Chapter 19

1. Bishop Stanley J. Ott, "Bringing the Christian Message to Modern Men and Women" in *Catholic Evangelization* (January/February 1988) 22.

2. Art Baranowski, *Creating Small Faith Communities, A Plan for Restructuring the Parish and Renewing Catholic Life* (Cincinnati: St. Anthony Messenger, 1988).

Bibliography

Baranowski, Arthur. *Creating Small Faith Communities, A Plan for Restructuring the Parish and Renewing Catholic Life.* Cincinnati: St. Anthony Messenger Press, 1988.

Bergan, Jacqueline and Schwan, Sr. Marie. *Forgiveness: A Guide to Prayer.* Winona: St. Mary's Press, 1985.

Bernardin, Joseph Cardinal. "Evangelizing the Active Catholic." *Pentecost '87 Supplement, A National Satellite Celebration of Catholic Evangelization.* Saturday, June 6, 1987, Washington, DC: Paulist National Catholic Evangelization Association.

Berry, Thomas. *The Dream of the Earth.* San Francisco: Sierra Club Books, 1988.

Brennan, Patrick. *The Evangelizing Parish.* Valencia: Tabor Publishing, 1987.

Caroluzza, Thomas. "Catechumenate in Small Groups." International Office of RENEW Training Manual, 1985, 77–85.

Caroluzza, Thomas. *Parish Catechumenate: Pastors, Presiders and Preachers.* Chicago: Liturgy Training Publications, 1988.

Carter, Edward, S.J. *Prayer Perspectives.* Staten Island: Alba House, 1987.

Catholic Bishops of Texas. "Mission: Texas: A Pastoral Letter on Evangelization." March 1989.

Catoir, John T. *Enjoy the Lord: A Path to Contemplation.* Staten Island: Alba House, 1988.

Collins, Raymond F. "Small Groups: An Experience of Church." *Louvain Studies* 13, 1988.

Coriden, James A., Green, Thomas J., Heintschel, Donald E., eds. *The Code of Canon Law: A Text and Commentary,* Mahwah: Paulist Press, 1985.

Coughlan, Peter. *The Hour of the Laity: Their Expanding Role.* Philadelphia: E.J. Dwyer, 1989.

Delespesse, Max. *The Church Community, Leaven and Lifestyle.* Ottawa: The Catholic Center of Saint Paul University, 1968.

Dorr, Donal. *Spirituality and Justice.* Maryknoll: Orbis Books, 1984.

Dulles, Avery, S.J. *A Church to Believe In: Discipleship and the Dynamics of Freedom.* New York: Crossroad, 1986.

Dulles, Avery, S.J. *The Reshaping of Catholicism: Current Challenges in the Theology of Church.* San Francisco: Harper & Row, 1988.

Ferguson, James, C.S.C. "The Demise of Mission." International Papers in Pastoral Ministry. Notre Dame: University of Notre Dame. February 1990.

Fichter, Joseph H. "Parochial Realities in America," in *A Sociologist Looks at Religion.* Wilmington: Michael Glazier, Inc., 1988.

Gallup, George Jr. "Evangelizing the Unchurched American." *Pentecost 87 Supplement,* A National Satellite Celebration of Catholic Evangelization, Saturday, June 6, 1987. Washington, DC: Paulist National Catholic Evangelization Association.

Gannon, Thomas M. and Traub, George W. *The Desert and the City: An Interpretation of the History of Christian Spirituality.* Chicago: Loyola University Press, 1969.

German Catechetical Association. comp. *CREDO: A Catholic Catechism.* London: Geoffrey Chapman, 1984.

Healey, Joseph. "Comparing 'Basic and Small' Christian Communities." *AMECEA Documentation Service* (Nairobi) 284, May 8, 1984. In "Communities," *Ministries and Communities,* Leuven, Belgium: Pro Mundi Vita, 1984, #3.

Hoge, Dr. Dean R. *Converts, Dropouts, Returnees: A Study of Religious Change Among Catholics.* Washington, DC: United States Catholic Conference, 1981.

Hoge, Dr. Dean R. *The Proceedings of a Symposium on Renewal in Catholic Evangelization.* Gainesville: Koch Foundation. 1986.

Holland, Joe. "Beyond a Privatized Spirituality." *New Catholic World* 231, July/August 1988.

Hurley, Archbishop Dennis. "Address to the International RENEW Convocation." Raleigh, June 1989.

International Commission on English in the Liturgy and Bishops' Committee on Liturgy. *Rite of Christian Initiation of Adults: Study Edition.* Chicago: Liturgy Training Publications, 1988.

Ivory, Thomas P. *Conversion and Community: A Catechumenal Model for Total Parish Formation.* Mahwah: Paulist Press, 1988.

John Paul II. "Address to the Hispanic Community in San Antonio, Texas," 1987.

John Paul II. "Apostolic Exhortation on the Family." Washington, DC: United States Catholic Conference, 1981.

John Paul II. "Christifideles Laici: Apostolic Exhortation on the Vocation and the Mission of the Lay Faithful in the Church and in the World." *Origins* 18, February 9, 1989, 561–95.

John Paul II. "Los Angeles Meeting of the Pope and U.S. Bishops." *Origins* 17, October 1, 1987, 253–76.

John Paul II. *On Social Concern,* Sollicitudo Rei Socialis. Encyclical Letter, December 30, 1987, Washington, DC: United States Catholic Conference.

John XXIII. "Pacem in Terris." David O'Brien and Thomas Shannon, eds., *Renewing the Earth.* Garden City: Doubleday and Company, 1977, 117–70.

Keating, Thomas. *Open Mind, Open Heart.* Amity: Amity House, 1986.

Komonchak, Joseph, Collins, Mary, Lane, Dermot, eds., *The New Dictionary of Theology.* Wilmington: Michael Glazier, 1989.

Lauder, Robert E. *The Priest as Person: A Philosophy of Priestly Existence.* Whitinsville: Affirmation Books, 1981.

Lee, Bernard J. and Cowan, Michael A. *Dangerous Memories: House Churches and Our American Story.* Kansas City: Sheed & Ward, 1986.

Leege, David C., ed. "Parish Organizations: People's Needs, Parish Services, and Leadership." *Notre Dame Study of Catholic Parish Life.* Notre Dame: University of Notre Dame, July 1986.

Linn, Matthew, Linn, Dennis, Fabricant, Sheila. *Prayer Course for Healing Life's Hurts.* Mahwah: Paulist Press, 1983.

Lonergan, Bernard. "Dimensions of Meaning." *Collected Works of Bernard Lonergan.* Frederick E. Crowe and Robert M. Doran, eds. Toronto: University of Toronto Press, 1988.

Mathey, Chuck. *Successful CFM Leadership.* Ames: Christian Family Movement, 1988.

McKinney, Mary Benet. *Sharing Wisdom: A Process for Group Decision Making.* Allen: Tabor Publishing, 1987.

Merton, Thomas. *Spiritual Direction and Meditation.* Collegeville: Liturgical Press, 1960.

Mische, Gerald and Patricia. *Toward a Human World Order.* Mahwah: Paulist Press, 1977.

Murnion, Philip J. "Parish Renewal: State(ments) of the Question." *America,* April 24, 1982, 314–17.

Naisbitt, John. *Megatrends: Ten New Directions Transforming Our Lives.* New York: Warner Book, Inc., 1982.

National Center for Family Studies at the Catholic University of

America. "Contemporary American Families: Facts and Fables." Washington, DC: 1985.

National Conference of Catholic Bishops. "Called and Gifted: Reflections of the American Bishops. Commemorating the Fifteenth Anniversary of the Issuance of the Decree on the Apostolate of the Laity." *Origins* 10, 1980.

National Conference of Catholic Bishops. "The Hispanic Presence: Challenge and Commitment, A Pastoral Letter on Hispanic Ministry." United States Catholic Conference, December 12, 1983.

National Conference of Catholic Bishops. *The Parish, A People, A Mission, A Structure: A Statement of the Committee on the Parish.* November 1980. Washington, DC: United States Catholic Conference, 1981.

National Conference of Catholic Charities. "Toward a Renewed Catholic Charities Movement," Washington, DC: 1972.

Nouwen, Henri J.M. *Behold the Beauty of the Lord. Praying With Icons.* Notre Dame: Ave Maria Press, 1987.

Nouwen, Henri J.M. *Reaching Out.* Garden City: Doubleday & Co., 1975.

Ott, Bishop Stanley J. "Bringing the Christian Message to Modern Men and Women." *Catholic Evangelization,* January/February 1988, 22–25.

Paul VI. *On Evangelization in the Modern World.* Washington, DC: United States Catholic Conference, 1976.

Pennington, M. Basil, O.C.S.O. "Finding Peace at the Center." Pamphlet from Food for the Poor, Pompano Beach, Florida.

Pierce, Gregory F. *Activism That Makes Sense: Congregations and Community Organizations.* Mahwah: Paulist Press, 1984.

Raths, Louis, Harmin, Merrill, and Simon, Sidney. *Values and Teaching.* 2nd ed. Columbus: Charles E. Merrill Publishing Company, 1966.

Rooney, Lucy, S.N.D. and Faricy, Robert, S.J. *Lord Jesus, Teach Me To Pray.* Garden City: Doubleday & Co., 1988.

Schneiders, Sandra M., I.H.M. *New Wineskins: Re-Imagining Religious Life Today.* New York: Paulist Press, 1986.

Staff to the Committee on the Parish, National Conference of Catholic Bishops. *Parish Life in the United States, Final Report to the Bishops of the United States by the Parish Project.* Washington, DC: United States Catholic Conference, November 1982.

Steindl-Rast, David. "Recollections of Thomas Merton's Last Days in the West." *Monastic Studies* 7, 1969.

Sweetser, Thomas, and Holden, Carol Wisniewski. *Leadership in a Successful Parish.* San Francisco: Harper & Row, 1987.

Synod of Bishops. *Justice in the World.* Washington, DC: United States Catholic Conference, 1972.

Synod of Bishops. "Message to the People of God." *Origins* 19, November 12, 1987, 385–99.

Synod of Bishops. "The Final Report of the 1985 Extraordinary Synod of Bishops." *Origins* 15, December 19, 1985, 441–56.

United States Catholic Conference. *A Family Perspective in Church and Society.* Washington, DC: United States Catholic Conference, 1988.

United States Catholic Conference. "Bishops' Committee on Priestly Life and Ministry. Reflections on the Morale of Priests," 1988.

United States Catholic Conference. *Family Centered Catechesis.* Washington, DC: United States Catholic Conference, 1979.

Vatican Secretariat for Promoting Christian Unity. *Sects or New Religious Movements in the World: Pastoral Challenges.* United States Catholic Conference, May 3, 1986.

Welch, John, O. Carm. *Spiritual Pilgrims.* Mahwah: Paulist Press, 1982.

Whitehead, James and Evelyn. *The Emerging Laity.* New York: Doubleday and Co., 1986.

Index

Enjoy the Lord, 231, 270
episcopal households, 7
eucharistic ministers, 94
evaluation form, 112
evangelization, 176–190, 264,
   265, 269, 270, 272
Evangelization 2000, 176
Evangelizing Parish, The, 187,
   269
evening of reflection, 78, 88, 110,
   163, 172
examen, 109

faith, v, viii, ix, x, 2, 3, 6, 10, 13,
   17–20, 23–26, 30, 33, 34,
   38–42, 45, 48–58, 60, 62–
   65, 67, 264, 265, 272
family, viii, 9, 11, 16, 24, 34, 35,
   38, 44, 48, 53, 56, 65, 265,
   270
family life, 18, 19, 58
family of families, 208, 209
family perspective, 206, 208, 210
Faricy, Robert, 223, 228, 271
Fichter, Joseph H., 10, 13, 265
folk group, 94
follow-up celebration, 70, 71, 78,
   112
forgiveness, 271
fundamentalist communities, 12,
   133

Gallup, George, 13
Gannon, Thomas, 33, 266
Green, Dawn, v, 45
guidelines for small community
   members, 133, 139, 140
guidelines for staff, 138, 139
guilds, 8

Hammer, Fr. Mike, 145, 268
healing, 34, 228

Helping Families Care, 241
historical overview, 6–10
Holden, Carol Wisniewski, 151,
   268
holiness, 29, 30, 33, 34, 38, 65
Holland, Joe, 35, 264, 266
Holy Name Societies, ix
Holy Spirit, 4, 16–18, 20, 31, 32,
   84
homebound, 91, 94, 95, 174, 150
homeless, 12, 89–91, 147, 189,
   237–239, 241
hospital visitation, 131
hospitality, 52
house churches, 6

Illig, Alvin, 185
individualsim, viii, 16
inquiry period, 192, 193, 198
Institute for Christian Ministry,
   203
International RENEW Service
   Team, 245
invitation, 31, 49
Ivory, Thomas, 269, 270

Jesus, 1, 6, 9, 11, 15, 16, 21, 22,
   24, 25, 29–34, 38–42, 46,
   52, 57, 63–65
John Paul II, 17, 22, 36, 43, 47,
   51, 267–270
John XXIII, 271
journaling, 224, 229, 230
justice, x, xi, 14, 21–24, 26, 27,
   32, 39, 45, 46, 57, 267
Justice in the World, 22

Keating, Thomas, 271

laity, 9, 15, 35, 36, 47, 48, 59,
   263, 266, 267, 273, 276; role
   of, 15, 157